REPRINTS OF ECONOMIC CLASSICS

Communism in Central Europe
In the Time of the Reformation

COMMUNISM

In Central Europe
In The Time of the Reformation

By

Karl Kautsky

[1897]

REPRINTS OF ECONOMIC CLASSICS

AUGUSTUS M. KELLEY · PUBLISHERS
NEW YORK · 1966

LIBRARY OF CONGRESS CATALOGUE CARD NUMBER

66 - 22631

PRINTED IN THE UNITED STATES OF AMERICA
by SENTRY PRESS, NEW YORK, N. Y. 10019

*COMMUNISM IN CENTRAL EUROPE IN THE
TIME OF THE REFORMATION*

Communism in Central Europe in the Time of the Reformation

By

Karl Kautsky

EDITOR OF *DIE NEUE ZEIT*, AUTHOR OF "THE
GROWTH OF POPULATION AND SOCIAL
PROGRESS," "FROM PLATO TO
THE ANABAPTISTS,"
ETC.

Translated by J. L. and E. G. Mulliken

LONDON
T. FISHER UNWIN
1897

CONTENTS

CHAPTER I

CHAPTER II

CHAPTER III

CHAPTER IV

CHAPTER V

CHAPTER I

I. *The Papacy the Centre of the Attacks of Heretical Communism.*

NOTHING can be more erroneous than the widespread idea that communism is antagonistic to the existence of man—antagonistic indeed to human nature itself. This is not the case. Communism dates from the childhood of the race, and has been the social foundation of almost all nations, even to the present day.

The history of communism bristles with far greater difficulties than those encountered by the historian of other phases of national growth. But, obscure as the subject is, owing to the lack of trustworthy sources of enlightenment, we believe that such knowledge as we possess will be sufficient to enable us to give some insight into its character and tendencies. As some assistance to our scanty information, we propose to glance over all the better-known evidences we can gather of the progress of communism during the period of the Reformation, and to consider its political effects, even though so little is known of the course of its inner development that all statements with regard to it must rest on conjecture alone.

The great difficulties which confront us in our efforts to gain a more intimate knowledge of the growth of communism lie in the purely oral character of the teaching, and the secrecy with which heretical sects were forced to carry out their propaganda and organisation. Our information is derived, not from the literature of the communists themselves, but solely from that of their opponents. Their mysticism constitutes another difficulty, and there is yet a greater arising from the want of distinct outward differences between the various heretical sects. Their persecutors took no pains to form an unprejudiced estimate of them, or to give an unbiassed statement of their doctrines, or even to make any distinction between them. The designations by which single sects were known were chiefly nicknames invented by their opponents and indicating the most opposite tendencies. In the present day, it would be an exaggeration to assert that all "Nihilists" must necessarily be socialists, and even more untrue to declare that no socialists exist among the Nihilists. Similarly, it cannot be said that the Waldenses, Beghards, Lollards, &c., were wholly and entirely communists. Nevertheless, we must not jump to the conclusion that these sects had never shown any communistic tendencies, for that would be to "empty the bath of water *and* child." Such tendencies are clearly enough evidenced, exhibiting no accidental, but rather a perfectly normal character—a character which repeatedly shows itself during the Middle Ages in all places where traces of communism became noticeable.

The most salient feature of the communism of the twelfth century is that antagonism to the Papal power, which lent to the movement an ever-increasing heretical character. It was almost imperative for those who had the interest of the poor at heart to rebel against the Papal Church, standing as it did in the front rank of the propertied classes of the Middle Ages. It was the wealthiest and the greatest among the exploiters, and held sway over the whole social life of the times, intellectually as well as economically.

Its dominance might be compared to that of *La Haute Finance*, or the Stock Exchange in the present century. In these days great banking institutions control social and political life, and in the Middle Ages the Papal hierarchy was, in a similar way, the mightiest of all the ruling powers, and, like the Stock Exchanges, decided the fate of Ministries —nay, even of Kings—founding and overturning kingdoms. The jurisdiction of the Papal power was quite as much disputed, however, as is that of *La Haute Finance* at the present time. Both have, in common, the faculty of exciting the enmity of all other ranks of society—not only of the exploited classes, but also of the exploiters. Both are compelled to relinquish much of their spoils to the greatest of all exploiters, and both view the treasures of the latter with eager, covetous eye. Nothing is more erroneous than the opinion that the obedience shown to the Papal power during the second half of the Middle Ages was either hearty or stupid. It was neither. It might rather be designated as a sullen submission, always resentful, and rebellious whenever chance offered. But so long as the foundations of a new order of society and government were non-existent, the Papacy was quite as impregnable as *La Haute Finance* has hitherto proved itself to be. Every conflict—nay, every far-reaching social catastrophe, every war, every pestilence, every famine, every rebellion, served then, as in the present day, only to increase the opulence of the spoiler of spoilers.

This condition of affairs was, on the whole, favourable to the propagation of communistic ideas, but highly unfavourable to the development of the special class-conflict carried on by the poor. To illustrate the comparison with *La Haute Finance* still further, we might say that the circumstances were similar to those existing during the ascendency of the French bourgeoisie (1830 to 1848). At that time, owing to its monetary power, and to a miserable electoral law, in conjunction with the political insignificance of the working classes, *La Haute Finance* held an almost unlimited sway by means of Parliament and King. It roused the opposition not only of farmers and wage-earners, but also that of the industrial capitalists and shopkeepers. The struggle against the common enemy united these classes, and to a great extent effaced the antagonism between them. It was, therefore, difficult for the proletariat to acquire a special class-feeling, and, in consequence, it usually remained under the leadership of the petty townsmen, or, rather, of the bourgeoisie. Another result was the lulling of the distrust felt by the bourgeoisie for the proletariat. They were formerly disposed to forget that their riches depended on the poverty of the latter, and, their pity being roused for the poor and outcast, they felt encouraged to make efforts for the abolition of poverty.   Many of them even coquetted with socialism, the most widely-read authors of that time being socialists, among whom we need mention only Eugène Sue and Georges Sand.

Then followed the revolution of 1848.   The kingdom of *La Haute Finance* was overthrown and deprived of its political privileges.   Political power fell into the hands of industrial capitalists, petty bourgeois, small farmers, and labourers.   The common enemy had scarcely been overcome, however, before the special interests and antagonisms of these classes became more or less prominent, or, at any rate, were brought vividly to their own consciousness.   The most manifest and bitter opposition was that between the bourgeoisie and the proletariat.   The revolution had shown the latter its power, and had, moreover, proved that socialism, far from being the dream of visionary literati which some imagined it to be, had, in fact, taken a strong hold of the most revolutionary class, and, ceasing to be a plaything, threatened to become a deadly weapon.

Thenceforward the bourgeoisie resisted with all its energy not only each independent movement of the working class, but also everything that seemed to savour of socialism.   In fact, their excited imagination pictured as a proof of socialism many a deed which was simply the expression of the most harmless philanthropy.   Socialism was, in consequence, boy-cotted in bourgeois society, and its partisans were forced to decide between two alternatives.   If they chose to remain loyal to their opinions, they were excluded from association with their compeers, and their names never more mentioned ; if they wished to avoid such a fate, they were obliged, once for all, to renounce any ideas that so much as savoured of socialism.   From that moment socialism in a political and literary sense was dead; dead, *i.e.*, until the aspiring class had grown sufficiently strong to compel respect by its own might.

Similar, but naturally much more protracted, was the development of socialism in the Middle Ages, in which the Reformation played the *rôle* taken by the representatives of labour in the year 1848. But, slow as this growth was, it can be distinctly traced in Germany during the fifteenth and in the first part of the sixteenth centuries, when circumstances were, in many respects, much more favourable to communistic tendencies throughout society than in the former half of our own century.

II. *The Antagonism between Rich and Poor in the Middle Ages.*

The distinctions between rich and poor, though more openly and aggressively displayed, were not nearly so great during the Middle Ages and Reformation period as they have become in the present capitalised state of society. Then, as now, these distinctions were chiefly found in towns ; but, whereas modern towns count their millions of inhabitants, and the districts of the poor lie far removed from those of the wealthy, in the times of which we are treating a population of from 10,000 to 20,000 constituted a large city, and men were drawn more closely together. Moreover, life was carried on to a far greater extent in public—work as well as pleasure—and the joys and sorrows of one class remained no secret to the others. Political life and festal life went on chiefly in open places—in the markets and squares, in churches and halls. The market-places were the scenes of trade, but, when possible, the work of the handicrafts was pursued in the streets, or, at least, with open doors.

One feature of those times, however, stands out in marked contrast to our own. In these days the chief object which the capitalist sets before himself is the accumulation of wealth. Your modern capitalist can never have enough money. His great desire is to employ his whole income in amassing capital, expanding his business, undertaking fresh enterprises, or ruining his competitors. After acquiring his first million he strives for a second, for he fears being outstripped by some rival, and wishes to secure his possessions. The capitalist never employs his whole income for his personal consumption unless, indeed, he is a fool or a spendthrift, or unless his income is insufficient for his wants.

Moreover, the wealthiest millionaire can lead the simplest of lives without diminishing the respect in which he is held. Whatever luxury he may permit himself, he keeps out of sight of the general public—in ball-rooms, *chambres-séparées*, in hunting-boxes, card-rooms, &c. Consequently, the millionaire is indistinguishable from the mass of his fellow-citizens when he is in the street.

A very different state of things existed under the system of natural production and petty manufacture. The incomes of the rich and powerful, whether in natural products or money, could not be invested in shares or government bonds. The only use to which they could put their revenues was that of consumption, or—so far as they consisted in money—in the accumulation of valuable and imperishable things—precious metals and precious stones. The larger the incomes of temporal and spiritual princes and nobles, of patricians and merchants, the greater their luxury. Being by no means able to expend their wealth on themselves, they employed it in keeping up large establishments of servants, in the purchase of fine horses and dogs, in clothing themselves and their dependents in sumptuous apparel, in building lordly palaces and furnishing them as magnificently as possible. The craving for amassing treasure contributed only to the increase of luxury. The haughty lord of the Middle Ages did not, like the timorous Hindoo, bury his treasure in the ground ; nor did he deem it necessary to shield it from the sight of thieves and tax-collectors, as do our modern capitalists. His wealth was the sign and source of his power, and he displayed it proudly and ostentatiously in the sight of all men ; his garments, his equipages, his houses, glittering with gold and silver, with precious stones and pearls. That was indeed a golden age ; and a golden age for art as well.

The misery of those times, however, made itself quite as conspicuous as the widespread opulence. The proletariat was only in the first stage of development ; though it was powerful enough to spur deep-thinking and sensitive men to meditate upon the ways and means by which want could be banished from the world, it was not sufficiently strong to count as a danger to state and society.

Thus the primitive Christian doctrine which had found its chief supporters among a tatterdemalian proletariat, now fell on fertile soil ; the doctrine that poverty is no crime, but rather a providential, God-given condition, demanding earnest consideration. According to the teaching of the gospel the poor man was a representative of Christ who had said : " Inasmuch as ye have done it unto one of the least of these my brethren, ye have done it unto Me " (Matt. xxv. 40). In practice the proletarian did not benefit to any great extent by this precept, for " the representative of Christ " was sometimes treated in a most unchristian manner. But society was still far from possessing those contrivances of the modern police system which are intended to sweep all social as well as other rubbish from the path of the rich, not for the purpose of preventing misery, but merely to hide it out of sight. During the Middle Ages the poor were not shut up in almshouses, workhouses, reformatories, and the like. Begging was an acknowledged right ; every church service, and especially every church festival, united the greatest splendour and the most abject want under the same roof—the roof of the Church.

At that time, as at the present, society could be defined by the Platonic description, " the two nations." In the decline of the Middle Ages however, the " two nations " of the rich and the poor still remained, at least, two neighbourly ones, understanding and knowing each other. In these latter days they have become such complete strangers, that when the " nation " of the wealthy desires to learn something about that of the proletarians a special expedition is required, as if it were a question of exploring the interior of Africa.

In the Middle Ages the rich had no need to study the proletariat in order to understand it. Unveiled misery met the observer everywhere, in glaring contrast with wanton and excessive luxury. It is not surprising, therefore, that this contrast, besides arousing the anger of the lower classes, should have excited the nobler spirits of the higher ranks against it and in favour of tendencies towards the re-establishment of equality.

III. *The Influence of Christian Tradition.*

The transmission by tradition of ideas originating in earlier conditions of society has an important influence on the march of events. It often retards the progress of new social tendencies, by increasing the difficulty of arriving at an apprehension of their true nature and requirements. At the close of the Middle Ages, on the contrary, it favoured their development.

After the violent disturbances which took place during the general migrations of nations and the barbarism that followed it, and from the time of the Crusades, the peoples of occidental Christendom began to rise to a scale of civilisation which, in spite of its peculiar characteristics, accorded in many respects with the highest point attained by Attic and Roman society just before the decline. Literature, that treasury of thought bequeathed by this society to succeeding generations, harmonised fully with the needs of the newly rising classes at the close of the Middle Ages.

The revival of ancient literature and learning fostered to an extraordinary degree the self-consciousness and self-knowledge of these classes, and in consequence became a powerful motive force in social progress. Under such circumstances tradition, usually conservative in its influence, became a revolutionary factor.

It was natural that each class should appropriate to itself from the treasury of tradition whatever best accorded with its condition. Burgesses and princes appealed to the Roman law, because it appeared to them well adapted to the needs of simple production, trade, and the despotic power of the State. They rejoiced in pagan literature—a literature of the pleasures of life and even of wantonness.

Neither the Roman law nor classic literature could please the proletariat and its sympathisers ; they found what they were seeking in another product of Roman society—the *Gospels.* The traditional communism of primitive Christianity was well suited to their own necessities. As the foundations of a higher order of communistic production were not yet laid, theirs could only be an equalising communism ; which meant the division and distribution of the rich man's superfluity among the poor who were destitute of the necessaries of life.

The communistic doctrines of the *Gospels* and *Acts of the Apostles* did not create the analogous tendencies of the Middle Ages, but they favoured the growth and dissemination of the latter quite as much as the Roman law aided the development of absolutism and the bourgeoisie.

Hence the Christian and religious basis of the communistic tendencies. Conflicts were inevitable with the Church, the richest among the rich, which had indeed for a long time denounced the demands of the prevailing communism as a devilish heresy, and had sought by all kinds of sophistries to distort and obscure the communistic purport of primitive Christian writings.

If, however, the effort to establish a communistic order of society necessarily conduced to heresy, so, on the other hand, the struggle with the Church favoured the growth of communistic ideas. The time had not yet come when men could harbour the thought of dispensing with the Church. It is true that during the declining period of the Middle Ages there existed in the towns a culture far above that represented by the hierarchy. The newly rising classes—the princes with their courtiers, the merchants, the Roman jurists —were at that time far from being Christian-minded, and were, indeed, still less so the nearer to Rome they resided. The metropolis of Christendom was itself the headquarters of unbelief. Any new form of government or secular bureaucracy which could step into the place of the spiritual organisation had scarcely begun to be fashioned, and the Church as a supreme governing power remained indispensable for the ruling, *i.e.*, for the unbelieving classes. The task of the revolutionary portions of society was not to destroy the Church, but to conquer it, and, by its means, to govern the community and advance their own interests, just as, in the present day, it is the work of the proletarians to conquer the state and make it subservient to their own ends.

The increase of unbelief among the upper classes led them to concern themselves more than hitherto about the orthodoxy of the lower orders, and to use every means in their power to withhold from the latter every form of culture which could raise their views above the horizon of the Christian doctrines; no very difficult task certainly, for the social condition of the peasants, handicraftsmen, and proletarians was such that it was impossible for them to attain to a higher culture.

Nevertheless, the Papal Church gained very little by this circumstance; for it did not prevent the development of great popular movements against the money-making hierarchy. Its only effect was to enable the participants in these movements to appeal with greater weight to religious arguments in confirmation of the reasonableness of their efforts.

The literary productions of primitive Christianity offered an arsenal full of weapons to all those who, on any grounds whatsoever, might wish to confiscate the wealth of the Church; for it was fairly evident from these writings that Jesus and His disciples were poor, and that they required voluntary poverty in their followers; but the wealth of the Church belonged not to the priesthood, but to the community.

The return to primitive Christianity, the restoration of "the pure Word of God" which the Papal Church had falsified and interpreted in a sense opposed to the true one —these were the objects striven for by all parties and classes who were enemies to the papacy. It must be confessed that each of these parties construed the "pure Word of God" differently and in a manner consonant with its own interests. Only on one point were they unanimous—the despoliation of the Church. It is true that the various Protestant parties diverged from each other widely with regard to the question whether that "pure Word" demanded the reorganisation of the Church government or the introduction of the community of goods. As, however, according to the evidence of tradition, democratic organisation and community of goods had existed in primitive Christianity, any one who reverenced that form of Christianity must have had very large interests in the opposite state of things to enable him to find anything in the "pure Word of God" upholding different views. Hence every candid member of the propertied classes who took part in a heretical movement, and was in a position to raise himself mentally above the interests and prejudices of his particular faction, could with comparative ease be won over to democratic communism. This was especially the case so long as the Papal government was regarded by the wealthy classes opposing it as an overpowerful enemy, while at the same time communism seemed to be the harmless toy of eccentric idealists. Their partisanship of the communistic doctrine would, however, cease when they were confronted with the necessity of uniting all antagonistic elements in one phalanx. At first heretical communism showed itself to be dangerous only to the accumulation of wealth by the papacy, and hence easily acquired the tolerance of the upper classes, where these were heretically minded.

Taking all these circumstances into consideration, it is comprehensible that, at the period when heretical movements had as their object the overthrow of the Papal power, communistic tendencies were able to acquire a force and vogue out of all proportion to the strength, extent, and self-consciousness of the proletariat.

But directly they made any attempt to assail the whole existing order of society, instead of uniting their efforts with those of the wealthy classes against the papacy only, the collapse of heretical communistic movements was, as a rule, sudden and inevitable, apparently leaving no trace behind it.

The class-character of these movements from the twelfth and thirteenth centuries to the era of the Reformation was much more effectually concealed by the veil of religion, under whose guise they first made their appearance, than was the case with the other popular agitations of that period. This resulted from the circumstances already enumerated, viz., the lack of class-feeling among the poor, a proportionately greater interest in communistic strivings among the wealthy (merchants, nobles, and particularly the ecclesiastics), and the powerful literary influence of the communistic records of primitive Christianity.

Nevertheless, the spirit of the proletariat had already impressed itself upon communistic movements. The proletariat of the Middle Ages differed from the proletariat of Rome in the days of her degeneration, and also from that of modern times. Moreover, the communism which it upheld differed from that of primitive Christianity and from that of the nineteenth century. It constituted a transitional stage between the two.

IV. *Communism in Articles of Consumption.*

Modern communism or collectivism is built upon the economic revolution which capitalism has brought about by doing away with production on a small scale. In the Middle Ages petty production still prevailed. In every industrial establishment division of labour (except that between husband and wife) had scarcely developed, and even in general affairs was in its infancy. The greater part of the population belonged to the peasantry, who nearly all supplied their own needs. In such a primitive stage society demands private, not a collective, property in the means of production. Modern socialism wishes to make the nationalisation of the means of production the basis of society, widely differing in this respect from the communism of the Middle Ages and from that of the Reformation period. In so far as the latter was not satisfied with simply denying the right to private property, and inscribing on its banner the equality of the " beggar's wallet " and universal poverty, and in so far as it attained to the formation of a social programme and organisation, it founded these on a communism of the consumers, not of the producers ; on communal housekeeping, not on communal labour. Whenever we find co-operative production among communistic sects of the Middle Ages, it is the effect, not the cause of housekeeping in common.

A good insight into the nature of this communism is offered to us in the description of the origin of the Beghard Houses in Bruges, given by a certain Damhouder, in the thirteenth century. " Thirty years ago," he relates, " thirteen weavers lived here ; unmarried laymen, who earnestly endeavoured to lead a life of piety and brotherhood. They hired from the Abbot Eckhuten a large and comfortable building with a piece of ground near the town wall, for a yearly rental of six pounds groschen (*libris grossorum*), and a certain amount of wax and pepper. It was not long before they began to carry on their trade, conducting their household in common, and paying its expenses out of the proceeds of the common labour (*ex communibus laboribus simul convivere coeperunt*). They lived under no strict rule, nor were they bound by any vows, but all wore a brown costume, and formed themselves into a pious community of Christian freedom and brotherhood."[1] They bore the name of "Weaving Friars." Not until 1450 did the Beghards of Bruges give up their looms and join the Franciscan monks, and then only to protect themselves from persecution.

The organisation of the society, termed the "Fraternity of Life in Common," is also characteristic. It was founded by Gerhard Groot van Deventer in the Netherlands in the fourteenth century. The members of the "Fraternity," though closely bound together, formed a free society. No vow for life was required on admission, and the Friars were not strict concerning the rules as were the monks. The ordinary disposition of the Fraternity was as follows. About twenty Friars lived together in one house, having money and food in common. The novice had a year's probation, during which he underwent very severe treatment. He was expected to relinquish his private property for the common use. Florentius (a friend and pupil of Gerhard) says in his address : "Woe to him who, living in the community, sought his own interests, or said that anything was his." The duties of the Friars were equally divided. The various handicrafts necessary for the whole community were carried on by special persons. Among the laws of the Fraternity at Wesel, we find the regulations for the Friars as clothiers, barbers, bakers, cooks, gardeners, and cellarers, as well as teachers, secretaries, bookbinders, librarians, and readers. In spite of this division of labour, however, a certain interchange of duties was expected. The clerical and learned Friars undertook, as far as possible, every handicraft (the charge of the kitchen they were all obliged to take in turn), and the serving-men shared in all the work which was the province of the clergy ; so that,

---

[1] See Mosheim, *De Beghardis et Beguinabu commentarius*, p. 177. Leipzig, 1790.

in mutual assistance, the entire community always resembled a family of co-workers. Certain hours daily were fixed for writing, of which a specified number were devoted to the benefit of the poor." [1]

This community bore the character of a monastic institution, and we shall yet see that even the Anabaptists of the sixteenth century could not completely avoid following in the same steps. In two essential points only did they differ from the monastery : first, in having no binding, life-long vow, and in remaining a free society out of which it was possible to withdraw ; and, secondly, in their independence of all ecclesiastical control. In fact, they usually became directly hostile to the Papacy, and we find that their animosity increases as we approach the end of the Middle Ages.

It is obvious, however, that public communistic association inimical to the Papacy could be formed only in those places where people were successful in overthrowing the Papal domination. In localities in which the communists first declared war against the Pope, we can find no such associations.

The earliest public organisation of heretical, revolutionary communism is met with in the country which was the first to throw off the Papal yoke and to carry out victoriously a reformation of the Church, viz., in Bohemia. But we shall see that even this organisation was based upon the community in articles of consumption.

This heretical communism presents the greatest contrast to that of the monks, in that the latter were the most determined defenders of the Papacy, with which they stood or fell. Moreover the monks, having long ceased to be workers, had become exploiters, their communism consisting merely in the common consumption of booty. But the economic basis of heretical communism is the same as that of the monastery, viz., a community of the household ; and this gave rise to a series of features common to both monastic and heretical communism, much as these were opposed in other points.

[1] Ullman, *Reformatoren vor der Reformation*, vol. ii. pp. 79–102. Hamburg, 1842.

The monk and the communist were in agreement in one point only—in their aversion to marriage.

This is a subject which merits closer examination.

V. *Aversion to Marriage.*

Communism in the means of *production*, after which the modern social democrat strives, is quite compatible with separate family life. Not so, however, common property in the articles of *consumption*. The private household—the private family—has always a tendency to demand a recognition of private property. Where the right to private property has been abolished and separate family life has been permitted, communism of this particular kind has proved to be untenable.

Communism in articles of consumption, therefore, leads to a certain hostility to separate family life, and necessarily also to a certain dislike to individual marriage. This is particularly the case where the community is living in the midst of a society in which the right of inheritance has already been established. The practice of individual marriage inevitably prepared the way for a reversion to private family life, for the separate interests of a man and wife were in natural opposition to the general interests of the communistic circle.

This hostility was, indeed, necessary so long as the production of the community was too limited for communism to be founded on the practice of holding property in common, and its aim continued to be, as at first, not a universal co-operative association, but an all-embracing family.

This is no mere speculative conclusion. We find this aversion to family life and marriage in Plato, in the Essenes, in the cloister, and also in some communistic societies in the United States.

These examples not only prove that aversion to marriage is necessarily connected with this primitive communism, but also that the feeling can be expressed in very different ways; by the demand for celibacy on the one hand, and by the common possession of women on the other. The latter was required alike by Plato and by the Perfectionists of Oneida. Dislike to marriage by no means implies hostility to women. On the contrary, the emancipation of woman from separate households always has the tendency to raise her position in the community. This can be seen in Plato's description of communism, and is still exemplified in the American communistic colonies.

The general bias of mediæval communism on the marriage question is easily understood, as well as its uncertainty on the point. The consequences of its tenets drove its partisans to require either complete continence, or the possession of women in common; but their whole environment, their petty citizenship and small peasant households made separate families and separate marriages necessary. It is in the opinions held concerning the relation of the sexes that custom is an all-powerful factor; it is here, too, that new ideas have continually to encounter the greatest difficulties, for, in the sexual sphere, the extraordinary always appears to be disgusting and repulsive.

Mediæval communists held very diverse opinions on marriage : one marked characteristic, however, distinguished them all, viz., a determined hostility to the matrimonial state.

This hostility appears among the oldest of mediæval communistic sects—the Waldenses, which arose in the South of France in the second part of the twelfth century. They divided their adherents into two classes—the perfect (*perfecti*), and the novices (*discipuli*). For the first, communism and, perhaps, celibacy, also, was ordered; at all events, the latter state was deemed desirable. The novices (*discipuli*), on the contrary, were allowed to marry, and also to have worldly possessions. In return, it was the duty of the novices to support the *perfecti*, who were to consider themselves dead to the vanities of this world. This sort of communism reminds us of the platonic theory on the one hand, and of the Beggar monks on the other. In the Platonic republic, people were also divided into two classes—the ordinary people and the guardians. Communism and the avoidance of marriage were prescribed for the latter only. Like Plato, the

Waldenses proclaimed the equality of the sexes, one of their heretical opinions being that women could preach as well as men ; an opinion condemned by the Pope. Men and women went about together, giving umbrage to pious souls, who considered that, under such circumstances, celibacy was not synonymous with perpetual chastity.[1]

A similar account is given of the Apostolicans, a sect founded by Gerardo Segarelli at Alzano, near Parma, about 1260. They called each other brothers and sisters, after the manner of the early Christians. Living in strict poverty, they were not permitted to have either houses of their own, or provisions for the next morning, or anything that was comfortable or convenient. If hunger raged among them they begged for food from the first person they met, without specifying any article in particular, and ate without discrimination whatever any one gave them. If a wealthy man entered the community, he was obliged to renounce the possession of his property, resigning it for the common use of the Brotherhood.[2] Marriage was forbidden. " The Brothers who go into the world to preach repentance have power to take about with them a sister as an Apostle ; not as a wife, but as a helper. They call their female friends, who were allowed to accompany them, their sisters in Christ, and firmly denied that they lived with them in a conjugal or improper manner, although they shared the same bed.[3]

---

[1] *Hoc quoque probosum in eis videbatur, quod viri et mulieres simul ambulabant in via et plerumque simil manebant in una domo et de eis diceretur quod quandoque simul in lectulis accubabant.* (Chron. Urspug ad ann., 1212. See in Gieseler, *Kirchengeschichte*, vol. ii., book 11, p. 325.)

[2] Mosheim, *Versuch einer unparteiischen und gründlicher Ketzergeschichte.* Helmstadt, 1746, p. 224.

[3] Mosheim, *op. cit.*, p. 226, also p. 321. The same thing is related of the Waldenses, and of the holy men during the first few centuries of Christendom. " Disdaining an ignominious flight, the virgins of the warm climate of Africa encountered the enemy in the closest engagement ; they permitted priests and deacons to share their bed, and gloried amidst the flames of their unsullied purity. But insulted nature sometimes vindicated her rights, and this new species of martyrdom only served to introduce new scandal into the Church." (Gibbon, *Decline and Fall of the Roman Empire.* p. 381.)

Mosheim thinks (merely on the ground of probability, and unsupported by definite information) that this prohibition of marriage and possession of property referred only to the Apostles—*i.e.*, to the "agitators," and not to the common Brothers. If this be so, they would resemble the Waldenses very closely. Certain it is, however, that they declare communism to be an indispensable antecedent to perfection.

In the Netherlands and in Germany communistic sects were grouped together under the name of Beghards. This sect was at first, especially in the Netherlands, an association, or brotherhood, of unmarried craftsmen, living as we have seen, in common households. In the Beghard Houses celibacy was enforced.

While, however, all these sects comprehended, under the term "celibacy," the restraint from every kind of sexual intercourse, the "brothers and sisters of the Free Spirit" (a sect which sprang up in France in the fifteenth century) found a bolder and plainer solution of the matrimonial problem. Next to communism they claimed full, unbridled liberty for mankind, their conception of celibacy being complete sexual freedom, although marriage was prohibited.

VI. *The Mystic and the Ascetic.*

We must now deal with another characteristic which mediæval communism has in common with monasticism, and explain wherein both of these differ from modern socialism. We refer to its inclination to mysticism and asceticism.

One of the radical reasons for the tendency towards mysticism was the ignorance of the great masses of the people. As production and trade developed, the ascendency of social over individual life increased, social relations became more secluded and secret, and mankind was visited by terrible social evils. The people remained ignorant and helpless before these misfortunes, and the lower the rank of the people, the greater their ignorance and helplessness.

The ruling and rising classes, particularly the merchants

and princes, found their level under the new conditions by means of the political wisdom of ancient Greece and Rome and the Roman law. It was difficult for the lower classes to acquire this knowledge ; more difficult than in the present day, for at that time it was confined to its own languages, differing from the speech of the people—*i.e.*, Latin and Greek.

This was not, however, the chief reason why knowledge did not penetrate into the lower classes. The fact was that the people refused to receive it, because they thought it would be prejudicial to their interests.

Development of knowledge is as little independent as the development of art. That knowledge thrives is due not merely to definite previous conditions which scientific investigation first renders possible, but also to certain wants which urge on scientific research. Not every community and social class feels the need for deeper investigation into the real connection between things in nature and society, even if the necessary previous conditions are present. A class or community which is in process of decline, or hopelessly trodden down by others, will always oppose itself to the knowledge of truth. It will not use its intelligence to define clearly that which *is*, but will try to discover arguments by means of which it can pacify, console, and—deceive itself ; and this is quite apart from the necessity of deluding its opponents as to its strength and capabilities. In the society of the Middle Ages and of the Renaissance, the future did not belong to the poor and oppressed, but to the rich and powerful, to the nobles and capitalists. The latter classes had every reason to promote learning, which favoured the possessors of power in proportion to their comprehension of the truth. Even where learning was quite free and independent of them, it promoted their power.

The time was yet far distant when the visible future was to belong to communism—to the proletariat. The more the poor and oppressed thought they understood what was the truth, the more wretched must they have deemed it. Only a miracle could completely overthrow the big lords, and bring prosperity and freedom to the famishing classes. But they longed for that miracle from the very bottom of their hearts, and were *forced* to believe in it, if they would not despair. They began to detest the newly dawning culture, which did their tormentors such good service, quite as much as they hated the beliefs of the Papal Church which they were attacking. They turned away from the miserable and comfortless reality, and sought to lose themselves in brooding meditation, in order to derive some consolation and assurance. Against the arguments of science and truth, they set the voice from within—" God's voice," " Revelation," " Interior light "—expressions which mean, in reality, the voice of their longing and their wants. This inner voice resounds the louder and more triumphantly the more the contemplator secludes himself from mankind, keeps at a distance all disturbances, and fires his fancy by the various methods of ecstasy, and especially by hunger and prayer. Thus these enthusiasts arrived at a belief in miracles which finally developed into a faith as firm as a rock: so firm, indeed, that they became able to communicate it to others whom the same wants and the same longings made only too ready to receive it.

A characteristic example of this mode of thinking is presented to us in Thomas Münzer's writings, particularly in his explanation of the second chapter of Daniel, which treats of King Nebuchadnezzar's dream (the image of iron and gold with feet of common clay, which a stone shattered)— a highly profitable dream for revolutionary interpretation.

This is what Münzer says about the dream which the king's astrologers could not explain : " They were godless hypocrites and flatterers, who only spoke what their rulers wished to hear, like the theologians of our own times, who sacrifice their convictions for the sake of the loaves and fishes. These learned men were led astray by the notion that they could separate good from evil without the advent of the Holy Spirit. But the Gospel comes down from God into the heart. St. Paul, therefore, repeats the testimony of Moses and Isaiah (Rom. x.), and speaks of the inner ' Word,' to be heard in the lowest depths of the soul through the Revelation of God ; and whosoever does not become conscious of, and sensitive to, it through the living witness of

God (Rom. viii.), has no well-founded knowledge of God, though he may have devoured a hundred thousand Bibles."

" An elect who wishes to know whether a vision or dream comes from God, or from nature, or the devil, must also with his heart and soul and mind take leave of all the temporal comforts of his flesh."

In the most extravagant and millenarian fashion, Münzer pictured to himself the new society of the future as a paradise on earth. " Yes," he cries, " the advent of belief must touch us all, and be held fast in order that we, fleshly, earthly men may become gods through the incarnation of Christ, and therefore with Him be children of God, taught and sanctified by Himself. Yes, indeed, far rather be wholly and entirely transformed in Him in order that the earthly life may be changed into the heavenly." [1] This is a small specimen of Apocalyptic mysticism. In contrast to modern communism, asceticism was also a distinguishing feature of this period.

Production was not sufficiently developed to provide means for a refined enjoyment of life by the masses of the people. He, therefore, who desired equality among mankind, could see evils not only in luxury, but also in art and science, which, as a matter of fact, were often enough the handmaids of luxury. Communists, as a rule, went further than this. In the face of the vast amount of misery in the world, it seemed to them that not only were arrogance and frivolity sins, but that even the most harmless pleasures were sins also. Melancthon was very indignant over this mode of viewing things, and relates, in his *History of Thomas Münzer*, that the latter taught : that " one must attain to a right and Christian godliness in the following manner : Firstly, open vices must be abandoned, such as adultery, murder, blasphemy, &c. At the same time, the body must be mortified and subdued by fasting, bad clothing, speaking but little, looking morose, leaving the beard untrimmed. Such childish discipline as this he called mortification of the flesh and the cross as described in the Gospels. His whole preaching

[1] *Aussgestrickte emplössung des falschen Glaubens der ungetrewen Welt.* Muihaisen, 1524.

was based upon this." This gloomy Puritanism brought the communists into opposition, not merely with the ruling, but frequently also with the labouring classes of the day, who were still strong in their ancient love of life, and full of cheerful good-humour. In many places communists were hated by the peasants and workmen as hypocrites. It was when the progress of the Reformation led to the oppression and ill-treatment of the latter classes, and when the restoration of princely absolutism made their resistance appear hopeless, that the spirit of Puritanism began to take root among the peasants and petty traders. But this was after the rise of capitalist production, which made saving the favourite virtue of the small employers because it promised them the quickest advancement into the ranks of the great profit-winners.

Puritanism, however, differed in essential points from the asceticism of Christendom in the first centuries. The character of Christian asceticism in its beginning was chiefly determined by the ragged proletariat whose prominent peculiarities (moralists might call them vices) were idleness, dirt, and stupidity. Primitive Christian asceticism was nothing but a system of more refined methods to bring these peculiarities to the apex of perfection. It was the same with the Indian (Brahmin and Buddhist) asceticism, which developed under similar conditions.

The proletarians of mediæval times were, in a great measure, workmen, and could not permit themselves the luxury of such self-abnegation; they did not live on the liberality, *i.e.*, the gains, of others as did the anchorites, but on their own exertions; they were, therefore, obliged to bestir themselves in order to provide for their wants in the world, if they would not starve. Neither stupidity nor idleness was compatible with their existence; they were not degraded enough, and, moreover, stood too near a thriving and well-to-do peasantry and tradespeople to be able to reconcile themselves to dirt. Neither stupidity, idleness, nor dirt offered any attractions to those who were superior enough to be capable of adopting communistic ideas. All accounts unite in asserting that the members of the communistic sects of mediæval and Reformation times were distinguished above their fellows by diligence, respectability, and sobriety. By reason of these qualities they even received ready employment as workmen in some places.

One well-authenticated proof of this is offered by the Anabaptists, in Moravia, where they had succeeded in establishing themselves in various localities, and founding a few colonies of peace-loving folk, who were as communistic as the surroundings in which they lived permitted. Gindely, who by no means sympathises with them, says :—

"Among the various parties, Anabaptists were sporadic in Bohemia, but existed in great masses and in very many communes in Moravia. They had immigrated into the latter country before 1530 and had rapidly increased into more than seventy communities. The State persecuted them with more or less zeal, but they maintained themselves in spite of this, thanks to the protection of a few noble families, who had good grounds for what they did.

"Such was the position in which Maximilian found them in Moravia, though they had previously been frequently and in vain proscribed. Following his father's custom, he made a proposal to the Diet, in 1567, to expel this people within a short time. And now a new and entirely unexpected departure from old tradition took place on the part of the nobles. In union with the knights (the prelates and towns did not take part in this petition) they begged the emperor to allow the Anabaptists to remain in their own homes. Not because the people were still unconvicted heretics, nor because any one had an interest in their conversion ; no, it was set on foot on far more practical grounds, namely, that the Anabaptists were even more profitable subjects than the Jews, and could not be banished without great material injuries. Catholics, Utraquists, as well as Bohemian Brethren, bowed before the weight of their own argument. The Anabaptists were, in fact, everywhere extremely industrious, thrifty, and temperate, and, moreover, by far the cleverest workmen in Moravia."[1]

[1] A. Gindely, *Geschichte der böhmischen Brüder*. Prag., 1857, vol. ii. p. 19.

We hear of the same thing in the primitive communistic colonies of America where Nordhoff found many instances of communistic industry and sobriety, and his testimony has been corroborated by Professor Ely, Mr. E. B. Smalley, and others.   There is nothing more absurd than the idea that work is not carried on systematically in communistic associations; experience has long proved the contrary.

VII. *Internationalism and the Revolutionary Spirit.*

In one point early Christian, mediæval, and modern communism are in accord, *i.e.*, in their internationalism, in which they are quite distinct from Platonism, the latter being merely local.   Platonism was instituted for a few municipalities and their adjacent territories.   Ever since the Christian era, on the contrary, every communist has worked for the good of mankind in general, or at all events for the universal national sphere of civilisation in which he happened to live.   The local limitation of Plato's communism is in accord with the peculiar conditions of peasant and petty trade methods of production.

Capitalists and the proletarians overcome local limitations. The merchant does not live for his local customers alone, but principally to carry on business between home and foreign markets.   The more intimate and easy this traffic, the greater his prosperity.   Hence the merchant is international, or, to express it better, interlocal.   Wherever he can make a profit, he is at home.

The interlocalism of the merchant has its source in his commerce with foreign countries; and his position in the foreign market depends on the power of the State to which he belongs (whether it be an ancient city or a modern nation).   A strong governmental power is necessary to his prosperity, and, above all, a strong military power.   Hence he is always a patriot either at home or abroad, and particularly in the latter case.   We see that he has been, ever since mediæval days, on the side of princely power and Chauvinism in every place where the conditions are favourable to absolutism.

The interlocal feeling of the proletarian arises from other causes. He possesses nothing to chain him to the soil; his home offers him nothing but oppression and a short purse, and these he can find anywhere. The smallest prospect of bettering his lot in some other place is sufficient to make him pluck up stakes and journey thither. Governmental power is the strongest protector of those who ill-treat and despoil him. From the fall of the Roman Republic to the first decade of our century, the proletarian had no hope of overcoming the government, or of making it useful to him, or of influencing it the least in his favour. The State has been the proletarian's greatest enemy. Not much wonder, then, that he has found it easy to draw the conclusions natural to this state of things. The special characteristics of all sects of communists, from the early Christians down to our own century, has been not only indifference but undisguised aversion to the government, to participation in politics, and the defence of the country. Anarchism is a posthumous child of these conditions of society. This aversion could only be subdued in times of revolution, when it seemed as if the power of the State were tumbling to pieces, thus putting the proletariat in a position to secure that power for itself. In the time of reaction, however, a disgust for all politics would again set in with even greater force. We shall see that such was the case among the Bohemian Brethren after the downfall of Tabor, among the Anabaptists after the Peasant War, and among the Mennonites after the suppression of the Münster rising.

But, since the time of the early Christians, the communists have always, and under all circumstances, laid stress on the duties of international and interlocal solidarity.

In foreign lands the merchant steps forward as a competitor—as the opponent of the native born. He founds his aspirations not on their good-will, but on the power of his country to protect him. The proletarian on foreign soil shows himself as a struggler against the same spoliation as that from which he suffered at home. He cannot count upon the protection of his government, but he can very often rely on that of the proletarians in the regions into which he has wandered, and by whose side he is fighting a common enemy.

It must be admitted that where the proletarian looks upon himself rather as a seller of his labour-powers than as a combatant, he is more inclined to regard his proletarian associates as rivals than as brothers-in-arms, and, in such a case, the disposition towards international solidarity is overcome without much difficulty.

This, however, does not apply to communists : they are in the first line of combatants against exploitation and oppression, and, in every place, they encounter the same opponents, and suffer from the same persecution.   This it is which welds them together.   From the days of early Christendom there has always been one special peculiarity among communists, viz., that they form one all-embracing family, that the foreign comrade is just as much a brother as the native born ; and that, in whatever part of the world he may happen to be, if he finds comrades he is at home.   Thanks to this peculiarity and to the lack of possessions, it was easy for their leaders, their agitators, to go from place to place.   Poor they always were, for the man of property who joined them was obliged to distribute his means among the needy.   The protagonists of the sect were constantly travelling, sometimes displaying a power of locomotion and covering an extent of ground in their journeys which would be quite respectable even in these days of railways.   Thus, for example, the Waldenses of Bohemia were by this means able to keep up a constant communication with those of Southern France.

For this reason, communists became of the greatest importance in the conjoint revolutionary movements of the lower classes of their time.   The greatest check to their progress was the local narrow-mindedness of the peasantry and petty citizens, which did them enormous injury in the face of their well-organised enemies.   Wherever this narrow-mindedness was conquered and revolutionary risings in isolated localities were brought into communication with each other, it was essentially the work of the communist wandering preachers, and it was mainly due to their centralising influence that the peasant insurrection of 1381 in England and the Taborite movement in Bohemia were so successful. During the great Peasant War in Germany, in 1525, they were active in a similar way, but German particularism was too strong for them ; apart from the fact that this rebellion was in a great measure thwarted by the want of cohesion among the peasantry.

Here we must notice another important characteristic of heretical communism, the last which we desire to deal with in this connection—a characteristic which distinguishes it from early Christian communism, and makes it analogous with that of modern times : *its revolutionary spirit.*

The people of the Middle Ages, the exploited classes, *i.e.,* the peasantry, petty traders, and proletariats, were different from the population of declining Rome. Capable of carrying arms and boorishly insolent, they had no comprehension of the teaching which commands men that " Whosoever shall smite thee on thy right cheek, turn to him the other also ; " which interdicts the taking of the law into one's hands by " Vengeance is mine, saith the Lord," and " All they that take the sword shall perish with the sword ; " which advocates uncomplaining sorrow and suffering as a Christian duty. As soon as the populace in general could read the Bible for themselves (the Roman Catholic priesthood understood well why they wished to make the knowledge of this book their own privilege), they did not draw from the New Testament its lessons of humility and self-denial, but those of hatred to the rich. The favourite portion of the New Testament to the heretics of the lower classes was the Apocalypse, that revolutionary and blood-curdling imagination of an early Christian brain, in which the Apostle exultingly predicts the downfall of existing society amidst deeds of horror compared with which everything hitherto exhibited in acts and threats by the most debased anarchism appears mild. In addition to the Apocalypse, they zealously studied the Old Testament, which is full of examples of peasant democracy, and teaches not only hatred of tyrants, but also active and restless opposition to them, as well as to the rich and powerful. The adherents of the communistic sects were, in general, too weak to entertain, in times of peace, the thought that they could overthrow existing society by their own power, in order to set up communism in its place. If they were not servile and submissive like the baser proletariat of declining Rome, they were still a universally peace-loving folk up to the time of the Reformation, and such evidence as we have unanimously bears out the fact that love of peace and patience were as much their characteristics as were industry and sobriety.

But when insurrectionary times came, when peasant and trader rose around them, then revolutionary enthusiasm seized the communist also. It then appeared to them, or at least to a portion of them (for they were often divided over this question), that the time had come when God would show strength in weakness, and when no miracle seemed impossible. They threw themselves into the revolutionary movement to make it serve the purposes of communism, and having once cast in their lot with the rest, no compromise with the existing powers was possible. They soon obtained the upper hand over the vacillating and procrastinating factions, easily became leaders of movements (like the Taborites among the Hussites, Münzer and his adherents among the rebels of the Thüringian Peasant War), and gave even these a communistic colouring, thus lending to communism the appearance of a strength which in reality it did not possess. As a result, a combination of all the propertied classes rose against it, furious with rage, and completely shattered it.

It is this spirit of revolt in the communistic agitation of the lower classes which, in spite of many resemblances, most clearly distinguishes it from the communism of the early Christians, and bears the most important testimony to its kinship with modern proletarian-communistic movements.

Early Christian communism was unpolitical and passive. Proletarian communism, on the contrary, ever since the Middle Ages, has necessarily been political and rebellious when circumstances were favourable. Like the social democracy of the present day, its aim has been the dictatorship of the proletariat, as the most efficacious means of bringing about a communistic society.

CHAPTER II

I. *The Great Schism.*

IT was in Bohemia that the earliest successful movement of the Reformation occurred ; it was there that heretical communism found the first opportunity of clearly differentiating itself from the other heretical sects. The Bohemian movement was of great importance to the German communism of the Reformation as it was the forerunner of the latter. Hence our attention must be first directed to the Hussites.

How was it that the Reformation movement was first successful in Bohemia ?

German historians maintain that only Germanic nations possess the inward fervour, the true sense of religion, necessary to produce an urgent desire for reform.

As a matter of fact, however, we find that the first Reformation movement took place among the Latin nations in Italy and the South of France. We need only mention Arnold of Brescia, and the Albigenses. If these movements were not equally successful with that of Wycliffe, it must be attributed to other circumstances than the lack of religious fervour.

It is not within our province to explain how necessary the Papacy was for a long time to the nations of Christendom, and how many were the important functions which it fulfilled in their political life. These functions, however, became more and more superfluous from the beginning of the twelfth century, while, on the other hand, the Church of Rome was gaining more and more experience as to the ways and means by which it could tax the Christian nations, and render them contributors to its treasury.

The Church had become the largest landowner in all Western Christendom, nearly one third of all the land in Germany, France, and England belonging to her. But she did not derive her revenues from landed property only. She knew how to prey upon the faithful in every way. In proportion to the Church's growth in wealth, her centralisation and dependence on the Pope had increased. The greater the treasure she amassed, the larger was the portion which found its way to Rome.

But the opposition which raised its head in various Christian countries against the Papacy grew stronger, not only in the ranks of the working-classes producing the treasures the Romish Church attracted to itself, but also among all grades of the ruling classes, who looked covetously at the wealth which they would have liked to pocket themselves. Under these circumstances the desire for Church reform became more pronounced; *i.e.*, the desire for the abolition of Papal domination and the Church's power of taxation, and also for the secularisation of Church property. But it did not everywhere lead to a violent breach with Rome, or to the foundation of a separate Church. It was not to the interest of the ruling classes in every country to countenance so revolutionary an act against existing powers; a proceeding which might perhaps have endangered their own authority.

In Italy, no opposition to the Church arose. The large sums which the Popes extorted from Christendom flowed into that country, and became a means of advancing its commerce and industry. The Papal power was looked upon as a rampart against the enemies of the nation, preventing its neighbours, France and Germany, from making plundering raids; for these nations eagerly coveted its wealth. Thus the decline of Papal power portended the beginning of foreign rule. How could Italy, therefore, be expected to throw off the Papal yoke?

The kings of France were likewise not interested in such a movement. They had become much more powerful than the Pope himself, and were able to make tools of their former masters. To such an extent did the power of the French monarchs transcend that of the Popes, that in the fourteenth century they were able to force the latter to transfer their residence from Rome to Avignon.

Scarcely, however, had the Papacy fallen under French domination, when France was drawn into the great Hundred Years' War with England. In the latter country the King and Parliament had about this time become strong enough to resist Papal presumption ; and the fact that the Pope allowed himself to be made the tool of her national enemy was another reason which strengthened the anti-papal feelings in England. A fruitful soil was thus prepared for Wycliffe, who was constantly striving for the separation of England from the Roman Church, and for the secularisation of Church property.

Matters, however, did not reach this point, a compromise being effected between the Pope and the English upper classes. These became alarmed at the rising of the peasantry in 1381, and at the gradual strengthening of the Lollard movement, which contained in itself numerous communistic elements. With such a rebellious population threatening them, it appeared rather dangerous to both king and nobility to enter on any revolutionary action with the intention of rendering themselves independent of the Pope, and confiscating Church property. A compromise with the Papal See was all the more easily arrived at, as the latter was just then ceasing to be the tool of French policy ; having been warned by the rise of Wycliffeism that a continuance of its present subservience would inevitably jeopardise its position throughout Europe. Hence the longing of the Papal Court for a return to Rome, where it would be further removed from French influence.

The Wycliffe movement also showed the Papal authorities the danger threatening their position as Princes of the Church. It pointed out to them the necessity of seeking a firm support in their secular estates. The continued loss to the Papacy of its dominance and powers of exploitation in England, France, and the provinces of Castile and Aragon, reduced it to greater dependence upon the power and wealth of the Princes. All the more important, therefore, became the control of its own

territories in conjunction with its spiritual dominion of the
world at large, and all the more imperative the necessity of a
return to its native soil.

If the Papal Court had every reason to yearn for Rome, the
Italians had equal cause for desiring its return.   The " Babylonian Captivity " (as it was called) of the Pope in Avignon
had clearly proved how essential to their country was the
presence in Rome of the Head of the Church, the city of Rome
itself being the chief sufferer.

This passionate desire for the return of the Pope found its
grandest exponent in Petrarch.   In his letters and poems he
paints in vivid colours the misery and filth to which the
palaces and altars of the saints in Rome had sunk since the
removal of the Holy See, and how the Eternal City was falling to ruin, like a wife abandoned by her spouse.   The
presence of the righteous ruler would disperse the cloud
hanging over the seven hills.   It would redound to the everlasting fame of the Papal power, to the prosperity of Rome,
and to the peace of Italy, if a Pope had the courage to cut
himself loose from the enthralment of France.   In Avignon
the Papacy must, from the very nature of things, be stifled in
luxury and vice, and incur the hatred and contempt of the
whole world.   No one has more sharply criticised the Papal
power than Petrarch ; but his object in doing so was not to
weaken or destroy it, but to lure it back to Italy.   In his
opinion the depravity of the Curia did not lie in its shameless
spoliation, but in the fact that it spent the proceeds of its
cupidity in Avignon instead of Rome.   The climate of the
former was destructive to the moral health of the Papacy.
Once back in Rome its recovery would be immediate.

In addition to the economic reasons which influenced the
Italians there were others of a political character.

The awakening of a feeling of nationality is most intimately
connected with the development of industry.   If industry has
attained to the level of capitalisation, its interests, and above
all the interests of capitalists, demand a national, centralised
government with a monarch at its head ; a government which
can secure to capitalists the home market, and give them
sufficient scope and freedom of movement in the markets of

the world. This was first clearly shown in the seventeenth century ; but the first germs of the modern feelings of nationality can be traced back to the fourteenth century, when it had its rise under peculiar conditions, and did not for a long period acquire the strength of a self-evident instinct.

This feeling first manifested itself in the highly developed nation of Italy, which, in the fourteenth century, had, more than any other nation, the most pressing need of a union of its powers under one government. Such a union was absolutely necessary, if an end was to be put to the ceaseless internecine wars among its petty states, if quiet and order were to be restored, and if the country was not to remain a prey to foreigners, as in fact it had then become and continued to be until the second half of this century.

The only power seemingly in a position to give unity to Italy and to acquire ascendency over its different sovereigns was the Papacy, and hence on the first appearance of Wycliffeism the Pope began seriously to meditate a return to Rome. The time was opportune for such a step, as the war with England had terminated fatally for France, making her opposition appear less dangerous.

The first attempt to fly from Avignon was made by Urban V. In spite of the protest of Charles V. of France and the cardinals (for the most part creatures of the French throne), this Pope embarked at Marseilles and went *viâ* Genoa to Rome, where he was received with acclamations. But soon after, in 1370, the French cardinals, who had found more to amuse them in France, again became paramount, and Urban returned to Avignon. (Gibbon maintains that it was chiefly a question of Burgundy wine, which could not be procured in Italy.)

The second attempt was made in 1376, by Gregory XI., who remained in Rome until his death (1378). Fearing that the French cardinals would again elect a Pope friendly to France, the people of Rome rose in arms, surrounded the Conclave, and with a cry " Death, or an Italian Pope ! " forced the cardinals to elect an Italian, Urban VI. As soon as they were able, however, the French cardinals withdrew from

Rome, declared the election extorted and invalid, and chose another Pope, Clement VII.

This was the origin of the great schism in the Church ; and we have dealt thus fully with its causes, on account of its importance both in the history of the Papacy and of the heretical sects.

Two co-existent Popes were not an unheard-of thing, but it was a novelty that each Pope should exhibit a distinct national character. One was supported by France and Spain, the other by Italy, Germany, and England. A third subsequently appeared upon the scene, who was acknowledged almost solely by the Spaniards. Hence the disruption of Catholic Christendom at a later date into separate national Churches, found its prelude in this ecclesiastical schism. This was not a case of dogma, nor of purely personal effort, but of national and political antagonism.

A furious conflict ensued between the several Popes, in which neither of them, nor of their respective adherents, gained the upper hand. The whole Church was out of joint, and society bade fair to share the same fate. Society was indeed menaced by the bitterest antagonisms, as had been shown by the *Jacquerie* in France and the revolt of the peasantry in England. Hence it became a question of putting an end to this dislocation and of re-organising the Church, or as was said, of " reforming it in its head and in its limbs." As the Papacy was wholly incapable of such a task, it had to be carried out by other powers. A series of international Congresses were convened—Councils of the Church—at which, however, the delegates of the secular princes had quite as much to say as those of the ecclesiastical organisations.

The Papacy resulting from these Councils stood far below that which had once vanquished the Hohenstaufens. It is true that thenceforward the Popes were less under the influence of an individual nation than those of Avignon, but national churches had been formed virtually subject to the respective sovereigns. The Pope was thereafter compelled to share his rule and spoils, if he would not lose them altogether, and his share was limited and strictly defined by special treaties (concordats or pragmatic sanctions).

This was the condition of things in France, England, and Spain. In Italy the Romish Church was from the outset the national one.

Germany was the only country in which no national Church was formed at the period of the Councils. It was too much disrupted to be able to control and limit the spoliation and government of the German Church by the Pope. From that time Germany became the primary object of the Papal greed for power and wealth.

One member of the German Empire, however, formed an exception—the kingdom of Bohemia.

II. *Social Conditions in Bohemia before the Hussite Wars.*

With the exception of England, perhaps, no country exhibited so rapid an economic development during the fourteenth century as Bohemia. In England this was specially favoured by the wool trade, and by successful predatory incursions into France ; in Bohemia by its silver mines, in which that of Kuttenberg ranked foremost. Opened up in 1237, it continued until into the fifteenth century to be by far the richest silver mine of Europe, its annual yield, at the beginning of the fourteenth century, amounting to about 100,000 marks of silver (a mark=$\frac{1}{2}$ lb.).

The rapid development of Bohemia's power at that time, and the splendour of the reigns of Ottocar II. (1253–1278) and Charles I. (Charles IV. of Germany, 1346-1378) depended chiefly on those mines. Moreover, though they were supported by the Pope, both the latter king and his son Wenzel owed their succession to the imperial throne of Germany principally to the Kuttenberg mines, which supplied them with the means necessary for the purchase of electoral votes—a method often resorted to at that period.

Thanks to Kuttenberg's capacity of production, trade and industry, as well as the arts and sciences, flourished in Bohemia, and above all in Prague, which at that period had become "golden Prague," covered with splendid buildings and the seat of the first University of the German Empire (founded 1348). Nor did the Church go empty-handed.

Its greed great, its scent keen; it knew where there was anything to get, and moreover how to get it. Hence monasteries and churches in Bohemia were exceptionally wealthy, especially under Charles IV.

Æneas Sylvius, afterwards Pope Pius II., who was well informed concerning the possessions of the Church, writes in his *History of the Bohemiaus:* " I believe that in our age there was in all Europe no country in which so many and such magnificent and richly adorned places of worship were to be found as in Bohemia. The churches were heaven inspiring; . . . their high altars loaded with gold and silver, enclosed the relics of the saints; the priestly vestments richly ornamented and embroidered with pearls, and the vessels of the most costly description; . . . it was astonishing not only in the cities and market-towns, but even in the villages."

But the exceptional opulence of the Church in Bohemia only served to increase its spoliation by the Pope.

Next to the Church and the King and his courtiers, the shareholders of the Kuttenberg mines derived the greatest profits from land. In the fourteenth century these shareholders were no longer simple mine labourers, but merchants of Prague and Kuttenberg, and capitalists who employed labour.

It was natural that the development of manufacture and trade should give rise to the same phenomena in Bohemia as elsewhere. Together with the great antagonism between the Papal Church and the bulk of the population, there existed an antagonism between traders and consumers, between masters and journeymen, between capitalists and those engaged in house industries; while that between the large landed proprietors and small tenants was continually becoming more acute. It was not inconsistent with this antagonism that the universal tendency of that period should be towards raising the peasantry from serfdom by commuting labour-rents into money-rents, which existed even in Bohemia.

This phenomenon demands a more detailed examination. To make it comprehensible we must glance at the change in the condition of the peasantry which had been brought about by the development of the municipal system and of industry in Bohemia, as well as throughout Europe.

The growth of cities created a market not only for industrial but also for agricultural products. As towns increased in size, tradesmen and craftsmen became less able to produce all the necessary means of subsistence and raw materials. They purchased from the neighbouring farmers whatever these produced in excess of their own requirements, and in exchange gave their own or imported manufactures, or *money*. Thus the peasants became possessed of money. The natural result of this was an effort to convert their rents, which had hitherto been paid in produce and labour into money-rents, a change which would make them free men having complete control over their own possessions. The landowners themselves must often have wished for this change, as they also began to be in want of money.

It might be thought that this effort of the two classes towards the same goal would have produced only harmony and contentment.

Nothing can be less true. Under the system of payment in kind, farmers had no great incentive to increase their produce, as it was limited by the personal needs of the land-lords and their retainers. The greed for money, on the contrary, is limitless, since it is impossible ever to have too much of it. From that time we find a far stronger impulse among the owners of property to increase the burdens of the peasantry, while a counter pressure sprang up simultaneously on the part of the oppressed. So long as the peasants could not sell the excess of their natural produce, it was a small sacrifice for them to give it up; but when there existed a market for it, the relinquishment of it to the landlord, or the giving up of the proceeds of its sale, meant a renunciation of pleasures which soon became necessaries.

There was another conflicting element between the two classes. Before the development of the town, the peasant had no asylum to which he could flee from an oppressor. Now the town offered a place of refuge of which many a one availed himself. Well-to-do farmers contrived to profit by the pecuniary embarrassment of their landlords, and in this way free themselves completely from their burdens. Thus the number of forced labourers became smaller, and the business of the manorial farms often suffered in consequence. Hence when the peasants, under the ægis of the rising towns, increased their efforts to throw off or diminish their burdens, the landlords simultaneously exerted themselves strenuously to bind their serfs more firmly to the manor, and to augment their compulsory service.

There was still a third element of antagonism. The moment agricultural produce acquired a market value, all land, whether under cultivation at the moment or not, possessed a market value. As soon as the towns had attained to power and importance, the time had gone by when the population was so sparsely scattered that the land was looked upon as practically boundless, and every one wishing to possess it—were he simply peasant, or mighty landlord with his tenants, or an association of monks—could easily obtain as much as he wanted, either from the lord of the manor, or from the *Markgenossenschaft* (the primitive society of the members of a commune holding land in common). Now, although the stage had not yet been reached at which every tract of arable land had been put under cultivation, yet the population had already become so dense that land no longer seemed inexhaustible. The possession of it began to be a privilege, and indeed a privilege so valuable that the most violent conflicts broke out concerning it. The *Markgenossenschaft* now proclaimed their *collective* land to be the *private* joint property of the families constituting the corporation. Side by side with the members of the *Markgenossenschaft* a class soon began to form itself, composed of the less privileged inhabitants of the commune.

On the other hand, however, endeavours were made by the lords of the manor, whose power in the commune was indeed preponderant, to seize these lands and convert them into their own private property, at the same time graciously conceding usufructuary rights to the fellows of the *Markgenossenschaft*.

The greater the strides made in economic development,

the more intense became all these antagonisms, and the greater the embitterment between landlords and peasants. Conflicts were more easily excited between these two classes —conflicts which, in the majority of cases, were only local, but which in some cases broke forth simultaneously throughout whole provinces and even whole countries, growing finally into regular wars—peasant wars.

The fortunes of war sometimes favoured one side and sometimes the other. In general, however, it may be said that in spite of isolated defeats, the peasantry of the thirteenth and fourteenth centuries (earlier still in Italy) had permanently bettered their position.

The causes of this improvement may be understood in part from what has already been said. Legal methods, and even physical compulsion, were of little use when the towns lent their protection and shelter to the fugitive peasants. In order to retain for their own benefit the labour power of the peasantry, the lords of the soil were compelled, therefore, to treat them better, and make their existence endurable.

The financial embarrassment of the landlords also frequently aided the peasants. In the twelfth century Christendom had grown sufficiently strong, not only to defend itself against its enemies, but even to assume the offensive against the Orientals, whose wealth and high culture had excited the greed for plunder of the military and priestly castes of the Christian world. The Crusades began with the most vigorous union of the feudal lords of all lands, those adventure-seeking and booty-craving members of the higher classes. But initiated amidst great illusions, these wars ended lamentably, their results bearing no fit ratio to the sacrifices they entailed. They enriched many towns, especially in Italy, but they caused the ruin of a large part of the European nobility, and instilled into the rest of the higher classes those longings for the productions of a higher culture, which in Europe were not to be obtained without great expenditure. It is not surprising, therefore, that the financial embarrassment of the nobility rapidly increased. If in some cases this led to an effort to extort still more from the peasant, it often burdened the landlord also with a load of debt, and forced him to agree to absolve the peasant from his burdens upon the payment of a round sum. The higher nobility suffered comparatively little from these conditions, but the inferior ranks were rapidly ruined, and to all intents and purposes lost their independence.

One more circumstance must finally be noticed. While the population was increasing, the closing of the land-corporations and their absorption by the lords of the manor made it exceedingly difficult to find room for new settlers. The surplus population was, in consequence, compelled to seek a livelihood outside of agricultural pursuits, and especially in urban handicrafts, or in *war-service*. Together with the ruined lower nobility, sturdy country youths, whose services were not required at home, gave themselves up to the trade of soldiering, and flocked to the well-to-do towns, or to those nobles who paid them well and held out the prospect of rich booty. They sought service under princes, or such fortunate army-leaders as were beginning to make a business of war, and to contract for troops.[1]

Side by side with the army of the feudal caste (the *mounted men*, or knights), another was now formed consisting of paid peasants, and *foot-bands* once more assumed a military importance.

But these levied peasants had not as yet become proletarians. They were farmers' sons who, after completing their war-service, returned home to take part in the labours of the family, or to set up their own firesides. They brought with them the implements and weapons of war, and the veteran's skill in the use of them. French knights of the fourteenth and fifteenth centuries often enough had a taste of the quality of the English bow and the Swiss pike.

At the end of the fourteenth and beginning of the fifteenth centuries serfdom had in fact ceased in Bohemia as well as in England, but attempts were not wanting among the landlords

---

[1] Mercenary armies existed in Italy as early as the thirteenth century. According to Sismondi, the first paid troops consisted of men who had been banished and proscribed ; of which the urban party-strifes supplied a large number. (Sismonde de Sismondi, *Histoire des républiques italiennes du moyen âge.* Paris, 182, vol. iii. p. 260.)

to re-inaugurate the system ; attempts which were a fruitful source of social discontent.[1]

But the greatest discontent must have been among the members of the inferior nobility who, themselves not much above the higher class of peasants, possessed very limited sources of revenue and could not, like the great barons, squeeze anything of importance out of their tenants, but who, unfortunately, had formed their standard of life on the pattern of the great barons and wealthy merchants. At the end of the fourteenth century this class went rapidly to ruin. The royal power was already too strong in Bohemia to permit the formation of a body of robber-knights, although many earnest attempts were made to that end.

As Bohemia was a part of the German Empire, a profitable national war was impossible, hence the members of the Bohemian knighthood were driven almost exclusively to mercenary war-service as a means of retrieving their fortunes.

The development of silver mining was not only a potent factor in the encouragement of manufacture and trade, and, through these, in the growth of the above-mentioned antagonisms, but it produced, as a necessary consequence, *a revolution in prices*, by which they were especially embittered.

The discovery and working of the rich silver mines of Bohemia must have brought about a *rise* in the prices of all goods. It must have had the same effect in that country as was caused in Germany at the end of the fifteenth century by the rich yield of the Saxon and Tyrolese mines, and has been produced throughout Europe since the middle of the sixteenth century by the discovery and development of the gold and silver deposits in America. We have not been able to find proofs of this in the various histories of Bohemia, but if in this matter, as in others, the axiom holds good, that under the same conditions like causes produce like effects, there can be no doubt that in the fourteenth century there was a complete revolution of prices in Bohemia.

It was inevitable that the different classes should be affected

[1] Palacky, *Geschichte von Böhmen*, i. 2 p. 34, sqq. ; ii. 2 p. 30 ; iii. 2 p. 38.

in various ways by this revolution. Some were injured, others benefited ; some were merely touched by it, others completely shattered ; but in every circumstance of social intercourse in which a money payment was the medium, the social antagonism comprised in it could not fail to be intensified by this rise in prices. The greatest sufferers must have been those classes who received their incomes in money and did not possess the power to increase those incomes proportionately to its decreased value. In the towns these classes formed the lowest strata of the wage-earning population ; in the country they were the petty nobility.

But above all these social antagonisms stood another still more potent—the national. In Bohemia the hatred of Germany was combined with that felt for the Papal Church. In the thirteenth century Bohemia was economically far behind the times. Its Western German neighbours were much in advance of it in social development. After the opening of the Kuttenberg mines, the marvellous progress in industry, trade, art, and science had been made possible in Bohemia only by the fact that its rulers attracted German emigrants thither. The two favourite monarchs of Bohemian patriots, Ottocar II. and Charles I., were the very ones who most encouraged the immigration of German peasants, craftsmen, and merchants, as well as German artists and savants.

Kuttenberg was a purely German town, and quite as much so were the other mining towns, such as Deutschbrod and Iglau. Together with these, however, numerous other towns had been either founded by Germans, or were so largely peopled by them, that the municipal authority fell into their hands, and this the more readily as they represented the well-to-do classes—the merchants and prominent handicraftsmen. The petty craftsmen, the mass of day-labourers, and other of the lower urban population, were native-born Czechs.

The University was also under the control of the Germans. It was a self-governing institution, modelled after the University of Paris, and divided into four "nations," each of which had a vote in the management. The Bohemians, however, were always in a hopeless minority, as they were opposed by the Bavarian, Saxon, and Polish "nations," the last named being composed chiefly of Germans (Silesians, &c.). This is not an insignificant fact. In those times a university was a scientific and political power of the first rank, and had an importance equal to that possessed by the press and universities combined at the present day. Externally, also, it was a mighty organisation. Like those of Paris, the buildings of the University of Prague, together with the residences of the professors and students, formed a distinct quarter of the town, having probably its own surrounding walls,[1] and as early as the beginning of the fifteenth century the number of students amounted to many thousands. Æneas Sylvius tells us in his *History of the Bohemians* that when, in 1409, the German students quitted the town, two thousand left in one day. Three thousand followed a few days later, and founded the University of Leipzig. It can be safely assumed, therefore, that the total number of students at that time in the university was not less than ten thousand.

There were also numerous establishments connected with the university, such as lands and buildings endowed for the use and enjoyment of the professors and poorer students; and all this wealth and power was in the hands of the Germans. Bitterly did the Czech professors complain that they were forced to starve as country schoolmasters, while their German colleagues obtained all the fat appointments in the University; and that whenever the interests of the Czech "nation" clashed with those of the German, the authorities invariably sided with the latter.

To all this was added the fact that the Church had become an institution of spoliation for the benefit of the Germans. The poor livings were, it is true, turned over to the Czechs; but the monasteries were for the most part in the possession of the Germans, as well as the higher appointments of the secular clergy.

Thus the animosity to the Church conspired with the hatred of the Germans in uniting the whole Czech nation in solid phalanx against those two spoilers.

This gave rise to the national feeling which suddenly

[1] Maurer, *Stadteverfassung*, ii. p. 37.

appeared in Bohemia in the fourteenth century.   But in its beginnings this feeling assumed the most diverse forms in different countries, being determined in each case by the special circumstances which called it forth.   In Italy and Germany it sprang chiefly from a longing for political unity. Among the patriots of the former country it led to an adulation of the Papacy; in those of Germany to an enthusiasm for a powerful empire.   In France and England the most prominent national feeling was a reciprocal hatred between the two countries.   In Bohemia, on the contrary, it made its appearance as a special kind of class antagonism.

The peculiar form assumed by this antagonism can be easily understood from what has been said.   The Germans expected and received the most lucrative appointments among the secular clergy, in the monasteries and in the University, the latter at that time an essentially theological institution. If the Czechs had every reason for rearing a barrier against the spoliation carried on by the Church, and for craving its possession, the Germans had quite as good grounds for resisting their efforts.

Such was the atmosphere in which the movement against the Pope and the Germans had its birth, a movement which has received the name of the Hussite War from its most prominent literary advocate, Johannes Huss.

III. *The Beginning of the Hussite Movement.*

In its beginnings the Hussite movement borrowed the most weighty of its arguments and claims from Wycliffeism, for as soon as the doctrines of the English reformer reached Bohemia they were eagerly seized upon and propagated. But while Huss adhered closely to Wycliffe's teachings, it is a gross exaggeration to assert that those teachings produced the Hussite movement.   They supplied the Hussites with arguments of the greatest utility, and influenced the formulation of the demands put forward by them ; but the cause, strength, and aim of the movement had their roots deep in circumstances which were wholly indigenous to Bohemia.   In the reign of Charles I. they had already found expression in Milic of Kremsier and Mathias of Janow, long before Wycliffeistic writings had penetrated to Bohemia, which did not take place till about 1380, in the last years of the curate of Lutterworth.

Wenzel, son of Charles I., and the fourth Bohemian king of that name (1378–1419), endeavoured as far as possible to suppress existing antagonisms. As he was repugnant to accepting the German crown on account of his powerlessness, it was not necessary for him to be a "parson-king" like his father. Although he endeavoured to subjugate the Church to his own control, and was thus put in touch with the efforts of the Czech patriots and Church reformers, he was forced to recognise the fact that Bohemia's flourishing economic condition, and with it the greater part of his power, depended on Germans. While favouring the strivings of the Czechs, he did not wish the Germans to be injured thereby. To this highly contradictory situation we must ascribe the vacillating policy of Wenzel, who one day encouraged the Czechs and the friends of reform (*e.g.*, in the question of the University), and the next day endeavoured to repress them—sometimes in vain. Although the Germanic spirit and influence declined in power and importance under his rule, his wavering, contradictory, and frequently capricious policy succeeded almost to the end of his life in preventing any violent encounter between the antagonistic parties.

The explosion came only when Bohemian affairs were interfered with by foreign powers, who, instead of a policy of vacillation and compromise, preferred that of a strong hand, and, by their attempt to stamp out the brand with a firm foot, caused the whole structure to burst into flame.

Johannes Huss (from 1398 professor in Prague University, and from 1402 pastor of Bethlehem Chapel), the most prominent literary representative of the anti-Papal and anti-German movement, enjoyed the favour of Wenzel, who appointed him father-confessor to Queen Sophia. The University, which was at that time in the hands of the Germans, turned at first against Huss and Wycliffe, whose doctrines Huss propagated, and pronounced forty-five of Wycliffe's Theses to be heretical. The quarrel of the

University became more and more a national one, in which the Czechs and the friends of reform were in the minority. Wenzel finally interposed and gave three of the four votes of the University to the Bohemian "nation," and the remaining one to the other nations combined, whereupon the majority of German professors and students left the country. The University now declared for Huss, and appointed him Rector.

Huss had then to deal with the Archbishop of Prague, and, lastly, with the Pope himself. Fiercer and fiercer grew the struggle, and wider and wider the gulf between Huss and the Church. The conflict became especially sharp when, in 1411, Pope John XXIII., being in want of money, again made preparations for the sale of Indulgences, which took place in Prague in 1412.

Huss raised the most violent opposition to this sale, as well as to the money-seeking Pope, whom he denounced as anti-Christ. It soon culminated in a severe encounter between the Catholic Germans and the Hussite Czechs, the latter of whom burnt the Papal Bull, and even threatened the priesthood.

It seemed, indeed, at that time, as if these bitter antagonisms were about to measure their strength in open conflict; but Wenzel was once again able to preserve peace by a cold-blooded neutrality. In December, 1412, he expelled Huss from Prague, and soon afterwards prepared the same fate for four papistically-minded theologians; he simultaneously destroyed the preponderance of the Germans in Prague by decreeing that in future half of the town-councillors should be Czechs.

In 1414, the great Church Council assembled in Constance. Its mission was to reunite and reorganise the Papal Church— a task which involved not only the setting aside of the three existing Popes and the installation of a new one, but also the suppression of Bohemian heresy. Wenzel had been deprived of the imperial crown by the German Electors in 1400, and his brother Sigismund (who, since 1410, had been Emperor of Germany and was heir presumptive to the throne of Bohemia) had special interest in the suppression of Hussism, as this sect threatened the defection of Bohemia not only from the Church but also from his Empire.

Huss was cited before the Council. Full of confidence, he set out on the journey to Constance, relying, not on the letter of safe-conduct given him by Sigismund, but on his good cause. Like so many idealists before and after him, he saw only differences of opinion and misapprehension where there were actually irreconcilable antagonisms. If he could only clear up these misapprehensions and refute these opinions, the irresistible strength of his ideas would, he thought, be manifest. But he failed to convince the pious fathers, either that Apostolic poverty was enjoined upon the followers of Christ, or of the truth of his dictum that a spiritual or secular ruler, be he Pope or King, ceases to be lawful the moment he incurs the guilt of a deadly sin.

This democratic principle seriously offended Sigismund as well as the Council.

That Bohemia arose in its might in favour of Huss only bore witness to his dangerous power, and was one more reason why the Council should render him harmless. After it had vainly sought by threats and long imprisonment to induce him to recant, it condemned the reformer and his doctrines on July 6, 1415, and handed him over to the secular judges. Sigismund was sufficiently devoid of character to break his word; and, in spite of the letter of safe-conduct, Huss was sentenced to the stake.

This reduced the Bohemians to the alternative of rebellion, or subjection to the Church and the Germans. They chose rebellion.

A few of the more resolute among the followers of Huss had already openly renounced the Church. They upheld the claim previously raised by Mathias of Janow, that the Holy Sacrament should be administered to the people in both kinds. The use of the chalice had hitherto been confined to the priests. It was quite in accordance with their doctrine which had, as one of its aims, the abolition of the privileges of the priesthood, that it should also declaim against the external sign of their privileged condition. The chalice, *i.e.*, the *lay* chalice, became from that time the symbol of the Hussites. According to the usual popular representation of history, the only question at issue during the gigantic struggles of the Hussite war, was essentially whether or not the Holy Communion ought to be administered in both kinds ; and in this connection "enlightened minds" never tire of pointing out, with much self-satisfaction, how narrow-minded the people of that time were, and how luminous, on the contrary, are the free-thinkers of the present day.

This picture of the Hussite movement is about as true and well founded as would be a representation in coming centuries of the revolutionary conflicts of our times, in which it should be made to appear that the people of the nineteenth century were so ignorant as to attribute a superstitious importance to particular colours, so that the bloodiest battles raged over the questions whether the French colours should be white, red white and blue, or red ; those of Hungary black and yellow, or red white and green ; and that for a long time a wearer of a black red and gold ribbon was punished by severe imprisonment in Germany.

What the various flags are to the nations of to-day, the chalice was to the Hussites. It was their *standard*, round which they rallied, and which they defended to the last ; but it was not an *object* of strife.

It was precisely the same with the different forms of the Holy Communion which made their appearance in the Reformation of the sixteenth century.

The casting off of the fetters of the Catholic Church—an act of which the symbol was the acceptance of the lay chalice—became universal after the execution of Johannes Huss. The ice was broken, and the practical consequences of renouncing the Church soon ensued—those consequences which were fundamentally the object of the whole conflict. Masses of the lower population in Prague now began to rise from time to time, not merely in demonstrations, but sometimes to expel the secular clergy and monks, and plunder the churches and monasteries ; the greatest gainers by these uprisings being the nobility. Not in vain had they become the most zealous advocates of Hussite doctrines. To revenge the death of Huss, and, of course, out of pure enthusiasm for the faith (?), they now sent challenges to bishops and monasteries, and began, wherever possible, to seize the possessions of the Church.

Wenzel was powerless in the face of the storm. In vain did Sigismund and the Pope endeavour to goad him into energetic measures against the rebels. The Bohemian king deemed it most prudent to act as if he saw nothing. Matters finally went so far that Sigismund threatened his brother with war if he did not interpose in the Hussite revolt. The threat was effective : Wenzel turned against the Hussites, and tried to bring back the exiled clergy. Thereupon a tumult arose in Prague, during which the masses of the lower population, led by Johann Ziska, seized the town on July 30, 1419.

The king had fled before the threatening catastrophe to his stronghold in Wenzelstein, and when the dire news was brought to him fell into the most ungovernable rage. This was the probable cause of the attack of apoplexy which followed and from which he died a few days afterwards.

Bohemia was left without a king, a prey to the Hussite heresy.

IV. *The Internal Parties of the Hussite Movement.*

So long as the heresy in Bohemia was kept under by Church and State, it displayed only its national and ecclesiastical characteristic. For the mass of the people the national enemy and the clerical enemy were one and the same person, and a common hatred had united the different social strata.

Now that the enemy had been repelled, and the " pure Word of God " was triumphant, it soon became evident that this Word, though equally applicable to all, was viewed in the most diverse lights by the various classes, according to their respective interests.

Hussism divided itself, in general, into two great parties, each of which had its centre in a town, viz., Prague and Tabor ; while Kuttenberg became the head-quarters of the scanty remnant of Catholicism.

Next to Prague, Kuttenberg was at that time the largest and most powerful town in Bohemia, and the German shareholders and labourers in its mines had every reason for remaining Catholic, as no one had more to lose by the success of the Hussites. Nowhere else, therefore, did the Catholics display so much fanaticism. They put to death every Hussite who fell into their power—and their victims were numerous. Indeed, the Bohemians affirmed that the Kuttenbergers had established a prize fund for the capture of Hussites, sixty Prague groschen being paid for an ordinary heretic, and three hundred for a heretic priest.

In addition to Kuttenberg, there were a few small towns in which the Germans had succeeded in maintaining themselves and which remained true to the Catholic cause. In the course of the Hussite wars, however, the greater number of these towns, and even Kuttenberg itself, fell into the hands of the Hussites, and became Bohemianised. After Kuttenberg had been definitely lost to Catholicism, the centre of the party gravitated to Pilsen.

Together with these few towns, a small fraction of the nobility still remained true to the old faith, partly because they hoped to fare better with the monarchical court, and partly through disgust for the democratic tendencies which were developing in Hussism.

The majority of the nobility, however, held fast to the Hussite cause, being induced to do so by the Church possessions which they seized. Their ideal government (especially among the higher ranks) was an aristocratic republic, with a mock king at its head. As Sigismund was not available for that purpose, they sought a substitute in Poland and Lithuania ; but no prince of any importance cared to put his head into the wasp's nest.

The larger portion of the population of Prague sided with the aristocratic party. In a series of revolts in that town, the lower classes had taken the reins of government into their own hands, after having expelled the German priests and aristocrats. In addition to the Council, there now existed the assembly of the entire commune, in which every man had a vote who carried on an independent business. The Councillors were probably chosen from this assembly.

A new municipal aristocracy, however, soon came into existence. Like the nobility, this powerful town naturally profited by the opportunity to seize the property of the Church. Men of a speculative turn of mind found a good instrument for raising themselves above the masses, in such of the confiscated property as was sold, divided, or squandered, and in the spoils of churches and monasteries. After the capture of Kuttenberg, the profits of its mines fell to the lot of the Praguers, and formed a considerable part of their incomes, a circumstance which must also have been favourable to cunning speculators. Thus a new urban aristocracy was formed composed of Czechs, which soon sympathised with the nobility, and most unwillingly submitted to the domination of the "great assembly" of the town.

There was still another reason for the growth of aristocratic sympathies among craftsmen and even among the very lowest classes in Prague. Their industries and trade flourished, so long as the Court and the upper nobility dissipated what they squeezed out of the whole country. The Praguers consequently began to look upon a monarchy and spoliating nobility as the most highly necessary requisites of society. The democratic elements in the community continued to lose strength, while the aristocratic sentiment, as continually, gained in power. Revolts, intrigues, and foreign intervention strengthened first one and then the other of these elements; but Prague as a friend to the democrats was always untrustworthy, while as their enemy it was most determined. In the second half of the Hussite wars it was unceasingly opposed to them.

The Praguers and nobility (especially the upper ranks) united in forming the "moderate party," apparently so called because their confiscation of Church property was most *immoderate*. This party went under the name of the Calixtines or Utraquists.[1]

Opposed to these was another movement, which in its composition and general tendencies may well be designated as democratic.

---

[1] "Calixtines," from *Calix*—the Chalice; "Utraquists," because they received the Holy Communion in both kinds—*sub utraque specie.*

It found its most numerous adherents among the peasantry in Bohemia, and formed by far the largest class of the population.

The Hussite revolution caused a violent outburst of antagonism between the peasantry and the lords of the soil. The confiscated lands of the Church were useless to the nobility without the *people* of the Church, who supplied rent and forced labour. These toilers, however, had not risen against the Church, merely to exchange one master for another still harsher. They wished to become free peasants and owners of property; and the same desire for freedom prevailed among other classes. The revolution from above necessarily called for a revolution from below. All barriers were swept away which had hitherto in a measure prevented the violent collision between the opposing elements. Custom, which had subjected employer and employed to rigid rules, was cast to the winds, and the throne set aside, which had to some extent controlled the barons and peasants. The latter felt that if they did not succeed in making government by the nobility impossible, and in wholly destroying its power, they would be crushed by its unlimited mastery. They now had to choose between complete freedom and abject servitude.

A part of the petty citizens and proletarians of Prague sided with the peasants; but the number of their partisans was greater in the small towns, in which those classes had succeeded in getting rid of the German " honourables," who formed the higher ranks of citizens. All these towns were far behind Prague in power. They were not, like the capital, in a position to resist the superior power of the greedy barons single-handed. Like the towns of Germany, whom the weakness of the throne had at an earlier date forced to unite in leagues in order to resist the robber knights, the towns of Bohemia now combined against their enemies, with the exception of the few still remaining Catholic.

The lower nobility at that time occupied an economic position between the peasantry and the higher nobility, similar to that now held by the small tradesmen, who stand between the capitalist class and the proletariat. They were quite as vacillating and untrustworthy as their representatives of the present day. The lower nobles, who were hardly more than large free farmers, had something to lose and something to gain on both sides. The liberation of the peasants threatened them with a further diminution of their income from rent and forced labour; but, on the other hand, the overthrow of the upper nobility would rid them of dangerous competitors and opponents, who were continually pressing them further down. Hence the spoliation of the higher nobility must have been quite as much desired by the knights as by the peasants. Some of the inferior nobility made common cause with the aristocratic party, some with the democratic; while the larger part oscillated hither and thither, inclining in the direction whence at the moment victory and booty appeared most certain.

Among the knights who remained inviolably true to the democratic party, the most prominent was Ziska von Trocnow, who had fought as a mercenary against the Poles and Turks, and in the service of the English against the French. He placed his military experience at the disposal of the democrats, and became their most dreaded and noted leader. But however firmly he may have held to them, he was their partisan only in the capacity of *soldier* and not of *politician*. As a soldier, he was the organiser and leader of an army without its equal. As a politician, he stood midway between the democrats and Calixtines, like many other knights and a large part of the humbler citizens of Prague.

After Ziska's death his special adherents separated themselves from the democrats, and formed a distinct middle party, calling itself "The Orphans," because its members had lost their father, Ziska.

The democrats, on the contrary, were named Taborites, after their political and military centre, the communist town of Tabor. These communists were the vanguard of the democratic movement.

V. *The Communists in Tabor.*

In Bohemia, as elsewhere, the development of industry and

trade necessarily produced a growth of communistic ideas. The inception and dissemination of these ideas must have been specially encouraged by the extension in the fourteenth century of woollen manufacture, which in Bohemia began in the towns of Prague, Iglau, and Pilsen.[1]

The close connection of the woollen trade with communistic ideas is a remarkable fact which can be traced through the course of the Middle Ages. The woollen craft in the towns of that time was the one in which the features of capitalism were first and most sharply developed, while in many places in Italy, the Netherlands, France, and Germany it expanded into an export industry. Capital was needed to carry it on, and hence the woollen worker became either a sweated workman, receiving the raw material from the dealer and delivering to him the manufactured article, or a cloth producer turned capitalist himself, and employing a large number of journeymen.

It is a remarkable coincidence that the same industry became the very hearthstone of the social revolutionary struggle of the Reformation period ; that in every conflict with the then existing municipal and State powers the weavers fought in the front ranks, and that they were inclined to welcome any new departure which proclaimed war against the whole reigning order of society. " Not without good reason," says Schmoller, " has language, identifying the weaver and conspirator, drawn from the warp of a loom *(Zettel)* the idea of the way in which disturbances are plotted or *warped (angezettelt)*." [2]

" In the eyes of many contemporaries," says Professor Hildebrand, " the guild of clothmakers occupied a position

---

[1] As early as 1337 we find workmen in cloths who manufactured them entirely unaided. There must therefore have existed larger manufacturers employing journeymen as houseworkers. (Hildebrand, *Zur geschichte der deutschen Wollenindustrie.* Hildebrand's *Jahrbücher*, vii. p. 104.)

[2] Schmoller, *Die Strassburger Tucher- und Weberzun.* Strassburg, 1879, p. 460. The word "warp" had the same meaning in Old English as in German. Thomas Sternhold (died 1549) wrote in his Psalmes, 7, "While he doth mischief *warp*." Psa. 52, " Such wicked wiles to *warp*."

similar to that which some parties in 1848 sought to confer on the privileged (!) class of working men." [1]

The oldest heretical sect of the Middle Ages brought into unison with communistic tendencies was, as has already been said, that of the *Waldenses*. About the year 1250 one of their enemies, " pseudo Reiner," a Roman Inquisitor, gave a description of the Waldenses in the book, *De Catharis et Leonistis*. To make them appear contemptible, he emphasises the fact that their leaders were workmen in crafts, such as shoemakers and *weavers*. Weavers were also frequently mentioned elsewhere as members of the sect.[2]

In Northern France the *Apostolicans* (a sect allied to the Waldenses) also had communistic tendencies, or at least primitive Christian principles, which among proletarians amounted to the same thing. Their aim was to re-establish the apostolic manner of life. " They were already well known in the twelfth century, in the time of St. Bernard, who sharply refuted them in two of his discourses on the *Song of Solomon*. . . . They worked hard and gained their bread by the labour of their hands. They were craft-workers, chiefly *weavers*, as can be seen from St. Bernard." [3]

In the Netherlands and in Germany, communistic ideas were developed among the *Beghards*. Their association was composed chiefly of *weavers*, and acquired such importance in some towns that the master-weavers waged war against the "weaver-brothers." Mosheim [1] informs us that in consequence of the pressure brought to bear upon them by the guilds of weavers, the authorities at Ghent and other towns were often forced to " check the industry of the Beghards."

In England, mediæval, sectarian communism found its representatives among the *Lollards*. It has already occurred to Thorold Rogers that Norfolk, the centre of the woollen industry, was also the centre of Lollardism. Weavers were the protectors and the trustiest adherents of the poor priests.

---

[1] *Op. cit.*, p. 115.

[2] Compare L. Keller, *Die Reformation und die älteren Reformparteien*, Leipzig, 1885, pp. 18, 33, 120.

[3] Mosheim, *Ketzergeschichte*, p. 380.

[4] *De Beghardis et Beguinabus Commentarius*, Leipzig, 1790, p. 182.

We think it, therefore, no mere accident that weavers were also found in the front rank of the communistic movement in Bohemia.

In addition to the economic condition of Bohemia itself, there were external influences that helped the spread of communistic ideas. Beghards made their appearance in the land, where they were called *Picards*. The immigration of German craftsman, so much encouraged by the kings of Bohemia, was also not without its effect on the penetration of Beghardism to that country.

Waldenses are said to have fled from Southern France to Bohemia at the time of the first persecution, and to have found an asylum, keeping themselves hidden and propagating their doctrines secretly.[1]

While the antagonism between the Bohemians and the Church was gaining strength, and the opponents of the latter were not only tolerated, but received encouragement, the communistic heresy naturally reared its head, and proscribed communists from adjacent countries sought safety in Bohemia. Communism could be the more easily developed, as, in its arguments, and even in many of its claims, it was in sympathy with the other heretical movements. They were unanimous in wishing for a return to primitive Christianity, and the restoration of pure Christian doctrine. Disagreements regarding the manner in which this was to be consummated did not begin until later.

The declaration of war by the Church and the German Empire against Bohemia, brought about by the burning of Johannes Huss, led to the overthrow of the traditional rules regulating property and society by the confiscation and robbery of the Church's possessions. This was the golden moment for the communistic sects, who now openly declared themselves. Hitherto they had dragged on their existence in secrecy and without recognition, and only now and then had the world heard of them through the treachery of some member,[2] but the relatively wide extension they had

---

[1] F. Bender, *Geschichte der Waldenser*, Ulm, 1850, p. 46, *sqq.*

[2] At the close of the fourteenth century two preachers came to visit the Waldenses of Bohemia from the valleys of Piedmont, where that

acquired became evident as soon as they were able openly to avow themselves.

The communists in Prague were too weak, or their opponents were too strong, to allow of their free development, whereas in smaller towns they had more scope.

Communist preachers now proclaimed that the Millennium had come. Prague was to be consumed by fire from heaven, but the elect would find protection and safety in other towns. Christ would descend in power, and establish a kingdom in which there should be no masters or servants, no sin or penury, nor any other law than that given by the free Spirit. The survivors of that time, translated to a condition of Paradisaical innocence, should know no more bodily suffering and want, and no longer need the sacraments of the Church for their salvation.[1]

Matters progressed so far that communistic associations were organised which, in the absence of evidence to the contrary, were presumably limited to the towns, the most important of these being Pisek, Wodrian, and Tabor ; in the last of which the communists succeeded in obtaining complete mastery.

Tabor was founded in the neighbourhood of the small town of Austi, on the Luznic River, famous for its gold washings. The abundance of gold may well have exercised an important influence on the development of trade and industry, as well as on the antagonisms connected with these. It is certain that from the year 1415 communist agitators found protection and shelter in Tabor, principally, as the story goes, through the agency of Pytel, a rich cloth manufacturer and merchant, and the employer of a large number of journeymen weavers.

---

sect still maintained itself. In his *History of the Waldenses*, from which we derive this information, Bender gives no definite date ; but it was certainly during the reign of Charles I. of Bohemia. The two Italians proved traitors, for they disclosed to the Catholic clergy the spot where the Waldenses used to assemble, and thereby caused a rigorous persecution of their fellow-associates.

[1] Compare Palacky, *op. cit.*, iii. 2, p. 81. The chief source from which Palacky draws his information concerning the communism of the Taborites is J. Pribram's *Proti knezin Taborskyn*, a disputation against the Taborite priests, unfortunately existing only in manuscript.

According to a letter of Æneas Sylvius, the later inhabitants
of the town were for the greater part weavers. During the
few reactionary attempts made by Wenzel in 1419, these
communist agitators were driven out of Austi, where there
was a strong Catholic party. They established themselves
in the neighbourhood, on a broad hill overlooking the
Luznic River and forming a peninsula with steep declivities,
which was connected with the bank by a very narrow neck of
land. Here they made their stronghold, and named it Tabor,
in the style of the Old Testament, for which, like the later
Anabaptists and Puritans, they showed a great predilection.

Communists streamed there from all sides in order to hold
their meetings undisturbed. On July 22, 1419, no less than
42,000 persons from Bohemia and Moravia took part in one
of these assemblages. This indicated a remarkable dissemination of communistic ideas.

" The whole incident was depicted even by their opponents
as a great popular festival of a religio-idyllic character,
elevating both to the soul and heart. Perfect quiet and
order reigned throughout. The throngs of pilgrims marching
thitherwards in procession with banners flying, and preceded
by the Holy Sacrament, were quite as festally welcomed by
those living on the spot, who received them with jubilations,
and directed them to their proper places on the hill. Every
one who came was ' brother ' or ' sister,' as all social distinctions
were unrecognised. The priests shared the work among
themselves ; some preaching in designated places (men and
women being kept apart), others hearing confessions, while a
third part communicated in both kinds. Thus it went on till
noon. Then came the consumption in common of the food
brought by the guests, which was divided among them, the
want of one being made good by the superabundance of
another ; for the brothers and sisters of Mount Tabor knew
no difference between *mine* and *thine*. As the emotions of
the entire assembly were of a religious character, there was
no violation of the strictest modesty and propriety ; all music,
dancing, and play being unthought of." [1]

Eight days after this gathering, the riot broke out in Prague

[1] Palacky, *op. cit.*, iii. 1, p. 417, *sqq.*

which put an end to the Catholic reaction, caused Wenzel's death, and led to the Hussite War. It was no longer a question of mere demonstrations and communist picnics.

The fundamental principles of the Taborites are comprehensively set forth in a document drawn up by the Prague University. After the fashion of the day, a disputation was held December 10, 1420, when it was hoped that the antagonism between the Praguers and that sect would be smoothed away. To this end the professors had made a schedule of not less than seventy-six points, in which, according to their opinions, Taborite doctrines were either heretical or, at least, erroneous. In conformity with the tastes of the professors and the tone of thought of the age, the majority of these points were of a theological nature ; but two of them contained the germs of republicanism and communism. The Taborites taught—

" In these days there shall be no king, ruler, or subject on the earth, and all imposts and taxes shall cease ; no one shall force another to do anything, for all shall be equal brothers and sisters.

" As in the town of Tabor there is no mine or thine, but all is held in common, so shall everything be common to all, and no one own anything for himself alone. Whoever does so commits a deadly sin."

As a consequence of these propositions, the Taborites concluded that it was no longer seemly to have a king, but that God Himself should be king over mankind, and the government be put into the hands of the people. All princes, nobles, and knights were to be uprooted as weeds and utterly exterminated. Imposts, taxes, and payments were to cease, and all laws of princes, nations, towns, and peasants be abrogated as inventions of men and not of God.

The purely ecclesiastical points relate, among other things, to a summons to the razing of all the churches, the prohibition of Divine worship in a church, and making or reverencing sacred pictures, &c. The Taborites also inveighed against erudition (or perhaps science). " Nothing shall be believed or held concerning Christ but that which is expressly said

or written in the Bible ; and besides the Bible no writings
of doctors of divinity, professors, or learned men of any
kind shall ever be read, taught, or propagated. Whosoever,
therefore, shall devote himself to the study of the seven
sciences, or accept, or cause himself to be appointed to a
professorship in them, resembles the heathen ; he is a vainglorious person, and commits a deadly sin." This doctrine
must have been especially obnoxious to the professors of
Prague. The opposition among Christian communities to
science has been treated of in a former chapter (p. 19, *sqq*).

It was natural that in its realisation communism should
assume the forms handed down by tradition from primitive
Christianity, and that it should accord with the existing
conditions of production.

Each community had a common box called " coop," to
which every one brought what he called his own.   There
were three such boxes, one in each of the towns of Pisek,
Tabor, and Wonian. The brothers and sisters sold all their
possessions and laid them at the feet of the comptrollers
of these coops.

Pibram writes in his work against the sect (1429) : " The
Taborites contrived another monstrous trick, in that they
enjoined and commanded all the people of Pisek, who had
betaken themselves to the hill, to bring each one all that he
possessed, and thus almost completely filled one or two coops
which they had set up. The comptroller of these coops was
the dishonest Mathias Lauda of Pisek, and he, with the other
managers as well as the priests, suffered no loss from this
arrangement. This dastardly proceeding shows how dis-
gracefully the people were robbed of their possessions and
earnings, and how the managers enriched and fattened
themselves." [1]

Palacky was himself forced to admit that this was a
despicable calumniation.

Meanwhile, however honest and unselfish the comptrollers
of the coops might be, this kind of communism could not
be carried on for any considerable length of time. Labour
would become impossible if every one were to sell his means

[1] Quoted by Palacky, *op. cit.*, iii. 2, p. 297.

of production and carry the proceeds to the common coop, in order that articles of consumption might be bought with money from the common treasury. We do not believe that this procedure was at any time universal among the Taborite communists. It is certain, at all events, that it was soon abandoned. Practically, communism fashioned itself as follows—Each family worked for itself in its own private house and private field, with its own means of production, and kept for itself all that was necessary for its own wants. The superfluity alone belonged to the community.

This change was not brought about without earnest protest from the more zealous and pronounced faction. Under existing circumstances communism merely in articles of consumption was realisable only in the form just mentioned. For this reason the extremists demanded the introduction of pure communism and the abolition of the family. This is possible in two ways : through celibacy, or through the suspension of strict monogamy, *i.e.*, by the so-called community in wives. Ultra-communists among the Taborites chose the latter form, being induced to do so partly by their determined opposition to the Catholic Church and monasticism, which led to a condemnation of priests' celibacy.

The efforts of the stricter party found their clearest and most decided expression in the sect of the brothers and sisters of the *Free-Spirit*. They had found entrance into Bohemia, and when in that country Picards (Beghards) were spoken of, it was always understood that reference was made to this community. The Hussitic variety of the brothers and sisters of the Free-Spirit were also called Nicolaitans, after the peasant Nicholas, who was the chief expounder of their doctrines ; but they were best known under the name of *Adamites*, because they regarded the Adamitic state (the state of nature as it was called in the eighteenth century), as the only one of sinless innocence. In their places of assembly, which they named Paradises, they are said to have gone about naked, but we are unable to determine whether this statement is based on rumour only, or on malevolent calumny.

Æneas Sylvius tells us that the Adamites lived on an island

in the River Luznic, and went about in a state of nudity.
"They held their wives in common (*connubia eis promiscua
fuere*); but no one could have a wife without the consent of
their chief elder, Adam.   When, seized with ardent desire, a
brother burned for a sister, he took her by the hand and went
with her to the chief elder, to whom he said : 'My soul is
aflame with love for her.'   Thereupon the elder answered
him : 'Go, be fruitful and multiply and replenish the
earth.' " [1]

This kind of avoidance of marriage was too much opposed
to the moral views of a period when monogamy and the
separate family life (institutions handed down from antiquity,
and deeply rooted in the popular feeling) were most impera-
tively demanded both by the needs of society and of the
existing methods of production.   The abolition of marriage
was, it is true, a logical consequence of the communism of the
time, but this very fact shows that this communism was not
in accordance with the wants of a society in which monogamy
was a necessity, and itself proves that the communism of the
day was condemned to be confined to small associations and
communities.   The bulk of the Taborites offered a most
determined resistance to the efforts of the extreme party.

In the spring of 1421 an open conflict broke out between
the two factions.   Priest Martinck Hauska, one of the head
elders of the more advanced enthusiasts, had been taken
prisoner by a knight, but at the intercession of many friends
he was released.   He afterwards preached his doctrines with
all the more zeal, and his partisans became so threatening
that the Taborite bishop, Nicholas, appealed for help to
Prague, where communistic heresy had gained a foothold.
The Town Council immediately recommended severe measures and, in accordance with the pleasant custom of that
period, two burgesses were condemned to death and burnt.
Simultaneously, an open rupture took place between the two
parties at Tabor ; the ultra-communists were driven out, and,
to the number of three hundred, sought safety in the woods
bordering on the Luznic (March, 1421).

Priest Martinck soon broke loose from them and renounced

---

[1] Æneas Sylvius, *De ortu et historia Bohemorum. Opera omnia,* p. 109.

his "heresies"; but his associates remained firm. Ziska, who was at heart inclined towards the Praguers, and to whom the " Picard heresy" must have been an abomination, marched out against the refugees, surprised them in the forest, and took a number of prisoners, of whom fifty were burnt at the stake by his orders as they absolutely refused to recant.

No longer feeling at ease among the Taborites, Martinck resolved to betake himself to Moravia. On his way thither he was taken prisoner at Chrudim, together with his companion, Prolop the one-eyed, and handed over to Archbishop Conrad in Raudnitz. Ziska demanded of the Praguers that they should have these dangerous persons brought to Prague, and there burnt alive as an example ; but the Town Council feared the lower classes, among whom Martinck's views were strongly advocated, and accordingly sent an executioner to Raudnitz, by whom the prisoners were so long tortured that they betrayed the names of some of their associates in Prague. Thereupon they were placed in barrels and burnt (August 21, 1421).

But the Picard heresy was not yet wholly suppressed. A band of Adamites had established themselves on an island in the River Nezarka, an affluent of the Luznia, against whom Ziska sent four hundred armed men, with orders for their complete extermination. Although taken by surprise, the heretics defended themselves with desperation, and slew a large number of their enemies, but finally had to yield to superior force. Those whom the sword had spared, the fire consumed (October 21, 1421).

The more advanced faction of communism was now completely crushed, and the small fighting power necessary to subdue it shows that its tenets had not been widely adopted. In fact, only a few particularly bold, or particularly one-sided men, prejudiced in favour of communism, dared at that time to so far overstep the limitations of their age. They are interesting to the history of communistic thought, but acquired no importance to general history.

The Adamites were crushed and rendered powerless, but Ziska, who persecuted them with singular animosity, did not succeed in wholly destroying them, as remnants of the sect continued to drag on an existence among the Taborites. In the last decade of the fifteenth century they reappeared, and endeavoured to amalgamate with the Bohemian Brethren, of whom we shall treat further on.

After the overthrow of the Adamites, there was no other noteworthy effort to establish the more radical form of communism ; but the milder kind (communistic more in intention than in reality) maintained itself in Tabor for nearly a generation.

What use, it may be asked, was made of the revenues of the common coops (or rather storehouses, since the contributions were chiefly in kind)?

In the early Christian community, the superfluity of one served to lessen the deficiencies of another. There was no occasion for this in Tabor, where a nearly complete equality in the conditions of life existed among all members of the community. This equality was easily brought about by spoils from the Church and from the properties of opposing nobles and towns, which proved sufficient to enable each person to establish himself comfortably.

The Taborites did not need to expend anything for the care of the poor ; but the wants of the clergy had to be supplied, as they had no priestly aristocracy with its own possessions. Any layman might become a priest. The members of that order were chosen from the community, and they in turn elected the bishops; but they were financially dependent on the community. Their functions, like those of the mediæval priesthood in general, were in the main similar to those of the present state and municipal officials and teachers in Germany. Their duties were to organise and manage the various institutions of the Brotherhood, and regulate the connection between the several communities, as well as the relations of these with the outer world. One of their chief vocations was the instruction of children. The Taborites set great store by a general and good popular education. This was one of their most striking characteristics, and was to be found nowhere else at that time. In this respect they resembled the Brothers-of-the-Life-in-Common more than any other sect ; but the monastic and Catholic tendencies of the latter fraternity gave quite a different character to their activity. Education among the Taborites must, of course, be measured by the standard prevailing at the time, and was chiefly theological in tone.

Æneas Sylvius says in one place : " The Italian priests may well be ashamed of themselves, for it is certain that not one among them has even once read the New Testament. Among the Taborites, on the contrary, you will find hardly one young woman who is not versed in both the Old and New Testament." He remarks elsewhere : " That malignant race has only one good trait, viz., their love of education " (*literas*).

This solicitude with regard to popular education was in apparent, though only apparent, contradiction to the repugnance of the Taborites to erudition, which they evidenced not only by the previously mentioned injunction, but by forcing all learned men who joined them to take up some handicraft. The learning which they opposed was that from which the lower population was cut off, and which was inimical to their community; *i.e.*, the culture which had become a privilege of the upper classes, but which, from the existing standpoint of production, was incompatible with universal equality. The methods of production among the handicrafts and small farmers laid too great demands on the strength and time of their workmen to allow these to acquire a higher education without stepping out of their class. On the other hand, however, the tenet of equality imposed the obligation of making every authorised means of self-culture [1] available to all.

Their war system was, however, of far more importance to them than their educational arrangements. This tiny community, which declared war so boldly against the whole

---

[1] It is worthy of remark that the Waldenses were also famed for their zeal in the cause of popular education. The Roman Inquisitor known under the name of Reiner, says of them : " All this people, without exception, men as well as women, are unceasingly engaged in teaching and learning. The labourer who works by day learns and teaches by night ; and as they study much, they pray but little. They teach without books. . . . He who has been learning for seven days looks out for a pupil whom he in turn may teach." The last statement indicates that they had invented a peculiar method of instruction.

existing order of society, could maintain its existence only so long as it remained unconquered in the field; and it enjoyed no peace nor even a single truce, for it was in direct antagonism to the interests of the ruling powers. On the other hand, the community was never able to gain a single decisive victory. It could defeat its enemies but not overthrow them; for the opinions of these enemies were in harmony with the existing conditions of production, while the communism of the Taborites was an artificial growth grafted on those conditions, and could never become the universal form of society of the age.

But if the perpetual war, in which the Taborites were engaged, redounded to their glory, it also led to their doom.

Their entire organisation was modelled for the purposes of war. They divided themselves into two groups, of which one remained at home and laboured for the other whose functions were exclusively military, and who were always under arms. With wife and child they marched out against the foe, like the ancient Germans; whom they also emulated in savage fierceness and impetuosity. The two groups apparently alternated in their duties, the returning warriors taking up the handicrafts, while those who had been engaged in the latter went forth to fight. This is only conjectural, for on this, as on other points relating to the Taborites, we are unfortunately reduced to surmise, and however copious the information concerning their deeds of war, but little can be ascertained about their internal affairs.

From a military point of view the organisation of this war-community is of great historical moment. It is customary to trace the origin of standing armies in the declining years of the Middle Ages to Charles VII. of France, who, in the middle of the fifteenth century, kept up a permanent military force of fifteen companies of mercenaries. As a matter of fact, the first standing army was formed by the Taborites, who, moreover, had an advantage over the French in that they relied on a universal liability to war service, and not on paid levies. It was to this organisation that they owed their great military superiority over their enemies.

Discipline and skill in manœuvres were wholly wanting in the armies of that period ; for whence were these qualities to come in those disorderly crowds of vassals and mercenaries who to-day were summoned together and to-morrow were again dispersed if the war chest was empty, or anything else aroused their displeasure ?

The Taborite army was the first since the downfall of ancient Rome, which was regularly organised, and did not consist of a mere mass of untrained warriors. It was divided into differently armed bodies, which were well drilled in scientific manœuvres, all systematically controlled from a centre and harmonising with each other. The Taborites were also the first to employ artillery to good purpose in the field, and, finally, to perfect the science of marching, their forced marches alone gaining them many a victory over the unwieldy armies of their opponents.

In all these points they show themselves to have been the creators of a more modern army system so far as the Middle Ages were concerned.

It may perhaps be with truth asserted that in the military, as in other spheres, all great advances have been brought about by social revolutions, and that the most successful military leaders of the last five centuries have been those who best knew how to recognise these advances and use them for their own advantage, *e.g.*, Ziska, Cromwell, and Napoleon.

The military strength of the Taborites was enhanced by their enthusiasm and scorn of death. For them there was no compromise—no halting in the path once taken ; they had only one choice—victory or death. Thus they became the most dreaded warriors of Europe, and through their military terrorism saved the Hussite revolution ; as, in 1793, the *sans-culottes*, by their terrorism, saved the bourgeois revolution of 1789.

VI. *The Downfall of Tabor.*

After the death of Wenzel, the Calixtines, *i.e.*, the nobility and Praguers, entered into negotiations with Sigismund.

They were not altogether pleased by the thought that they were about to take up the cudgels against Emperor and Pope, and, in fact, against all Europe ; hence the dangerous strength already acquired by the Taborites urged them to a compromise. Had it only been a question of the lay chalice, this compromise might easily have been effected, but it was more ; it was a question of the lands and money of the Church, and upon that point no agreement could be reached. The Church, however, and her servant Sigismund, showed themselves quite as implacable as the Taborites, and the rupture resulted in a fight to the death, in which the Calixtines, the robbers of the Church, driven by necessity, fought on the side of the Taborites, but only half-heartedly.

This is not the place for a history of the Hussite wars. Suffice it to say that after Pope Martin V., in his Bull "*Omnium plasmatoris Domini*" of March 1, 1420, had summoned united Christendom against the Hussites, one plunder-loving army of the Cross after another was formed to stamp out the heresy ; that in every one of the five Crusades, between 1420 and 1431, the army of the Crusaders was wofully defeated ; that the fame of the invincibility of the Taborite hosts continued to increase, until finally (as in the fourth Crusade at Mies, 1427, and in the fifth at Tauss, 1431) large armies scattered merely at the news of the approach of the Hussites, flying in a panic without even having seen the enemy. Neither can we follow the internal conflicts between Calixtines and Taborites, which were fought out in the intervals between the wars against the crusading armies.

After the great day at Tauss, there no longer seemed to be an enemy capable of resisting the Taborites. No foreign army dared again attack them, while at home the power of their opponents (the nobility and a few towns) was vanishing faster and faster, and was threatened with complete destruction by the continuance of the Taborite reign of terror.

It now became evident, however, how little military victories avail, if the aims of the conquerors are in contradiction to those of economic development.

A complete military overthrow of the Taborites would

naturally have been followed by their extinction. But even their victories gave rise to elements which led to their ruin. Their greatest triumph was immediately followed by their fall.

The greater the success of the Taborites, the more intolerable became the position of their foes in Bohemia (the Calixtines), to say nothing of the Catholics. The nobility were reduced to a condition of absolute insignificance, and would long before have willingly made peace with the Church, if they, the robbers of the Church, had not feared its greed and thirst for revenge. After the victory at Tauss, they showed themselves to be more amenable than ever.

Meanwhile the Pope and Emperor, together with their adherents among the spiritual and secular princes, had been made more pliant by the Hussite victories. Their intrigues and conspiracies with the Calixtines had never totally ceased, and after the triumph at Tauss were carried on more energetically than ever. An agreement was finally arrived at, by which the Papal Church, in the persons of delegates from the Council of Bâle, even consented to wink at the possession of Church property, and, instead of taking anything from the Bohemians, actually gave them something. It sent agents to Bohemia well supplied with money to enable its new allies, the Calixtines, to regain their power of withstanding the Taborites. When the nobility, who " had for many years disappeared from the scene " (Palacky), felt themselves backed up by the Emperor, and especially by the wealth and power of the Church, they began to pluck up heart for a war, for convening assemblies and organising themselves, in order to recover their lost power with the secular aid of the Praguers and the ecclesiastical, but exceedingly worldly, methods of Catholicism.

The situation is well described by Æneas Sylvius in his *History of Bohemia;* but it must be remarked that the *rôle* ascribed by him to Prokop (the most important of the Taborite leaders after Ziska's death) is entirely unsubstantiated by facts, for Prokop never possessed the unlimited power assigned to him by Sylvius. Wherever, in what follows, Prokop's reign of terror is spoken of, it would be more correct to substitute the *Taborite* reign of terror. Æneas tells us that : " The Bohemian barons often met together and admitted the error they had committed and the danger they had incurred in casting off the dominion of their king, only to wear the heavy yoke of Prokop. They pondered facts ; and these told them that Prokop alone was master ; that he ruled and governed the land as best pleased him, levying tolls, imposing taxes and contributions, dragging the people to war, leading the troops whithersoever he liked, robbing and murdering, tolerating no opposition to his commands, and treating the highest as well as the lowest like slaves and servants. They saw that the Bohemians were.the most unhappy people under heaven ; that they were always in the field, living summer and winter in tents, lying on the hard ground, and forced to constant military service. The people were worn out with home and foreign wars, which kept them for ever either fighting or anxiously awaiting a fight. The barons at length realised that it was time to shake off the cruel tyrant's yoke under which, after overcoming other nations, they now groaned. They resolved to summon all barons, knights, and towns to a general *Landtag*, which should take into its consideration a suitable organisation of the whole kingdom. When this Landtag had assembled, Herr Meinhard drew a picture of the happiness of that kingdom which was neither addicted to sloth nor worn out by war. He set forth that Bohemia, on the contrary, had hitherto enjoyed no rest, and that their country, if not cared for in time, must, wasted by unceasing war, soon crumble into dust; that the untilled fields were lying fallow, while men and beasts were in some places dying from starvation," &c., &c. ; all of which evils could, of course, be brought to an end only by a re-instatement of the nobility in their ancient power.

While the different opponents of the Taborites were thus ignoring their individual interests in presence of the common antagonism to Taboritism, and uniting in a coalition against it, changes were in progress among the Taborites themselves which were much more threatening than the intrigues and conspiracies of their enemies.

The communists of Tabor had always formed only a fraction of the democratic party bearing the name of Taborites, although they constituted the most energetic, implacable, and in every way most advanced portion, and were by far the most capable in military affairs. The bulk of the adherents of that party were petty citizens of towns and peasants to whom the communistic programme was rather a matter of indifference, but whose sufferings were being continually increased by the prolongation of the war.

Although victorious, the Bohemians were for a long time too weak to keep the enemy far from their lands. At the outset, they confined themselves to the defensive, and it was only at a comparatively late date (1427) that they were able to devastate foreign countries in the manner prescribed by the mode of war at that time, its essential features being plunder and destruction—approximately the same as attend the spread of European civilisation in Africa to-day. But war on the offensive in no way secured Bohemia from being ravaged by neighbouring foreign enemies. Meanwhile the civil war continued, and the country became yearly more exhausted; commerce, as well as agriculture and the handicrafts, suffered, and the nobility and wealthy Praguers, together with the humbler citizens and peasants from all parts, were sinking into ruin. All classes of society experienced a profound weariness of war and a yearning for peace; and in proportion as the implacable Taborites figured as the sole obstacle to peace, the number of their adherents dwindled away, and the voice of the people cried out against them. In order to maintain its power in the land the little band of Taborites was driven, therefore, to measures of increased severity. The antagonism between them and the masses of the people grew more and more bitter, until at length the nobility were usually supported by the populace in their rising against the sect.

Moreover, in the strict sense of the word, the Taborites were no longer the Taborites of old.

The fate of Tabor is of the greatest interest; for it shows what would have been the outcome of the Münzer movement in Mühlhausen, and of the Anabaptist movement in

Münster, if they had remained unconquered by military force.

Taborite communism was based upon the needs of the poor, and not on those of production. The social democracy of to-day relies for its hope of success on the fact that the requirements of production and those of the proletariat lie in the same direction. It was otherwise in the fifteenth century. While the needs of the poor engendered the struggle for communism, those of production demanded the existence of private proprietorship. Hence communism could never become the universal form of society in those days, as the necessity for it among the poor must have ceased the moment they had established it, *i.e.*, as soon as they ceased to be poor, especially if the only means by which its long continuance could be ensured were abandoned—at any rate for small communities—namely, the abolition of the separate family and of separate marriage. As we have seen, the Taborites did relinquish this. They practically exterminated the Adamites, and in so doing again opened the path for the re-establishment of private proprietorship in the community. The rapid growth of competence and even wealth in their midst, due to the spoils they acquired, soon caused greed and envy to supplant the modes of thought essential to communism and brotherhood. Equality in the conditions of existence began to cease ; there began to be richer and poorer brothers in Tabor, and the former became constantly less willing to relinquish their overplus for the benefit of the latter.

The downfall of the Taborites was also hastened by the incursion of foreign elements. The man who has so wholly given himself up to an idea that he is willing to risk his life in its defence will not readily prove untrue to it, even if he comes under conditions which tend to weaken its power over him. The original Taborites would have held fast to the faith for whose cause they had endured so many persecutions and dangers.

But the many years of war of which the burden lay especially heavy on this community, must have fearfully thinned their ranks. From a military point of view, this was not noticeable, for the loss was quickly made good from among the communist enthusiasts from far and wide to whom Tabor had become a Mecca. Even the most distant nations, *e.g.*, England, were represented in the town. No great difficulty seems to have been made about admission to the brotherhood. Æneas Sylvius, who visited the place, was surprised at the number of different sects living together in peace. " They are not all of one faith," he tells us, " for every one in Tabor may believe as best pleases him. Nicolaitans, Arians, Manicheists, Arminians, Nestorians, Berengarians, and Poor of Lyons are all to be found among them. The most highly esteemed, however, are the Waldenses, those arch-enemies of the Roman See."

Another increase which Tabor received was much more doubtful in its influence. The success of its armies had attracted thither a large number of adventure-loving folk, to whom the Taborite ideal was a matter of indifference, but who longed for fame and still more for booty.

The armies of the Taborites would not at first have materially suffered in a military sense from this cause, though the elements of enthusiasm, devotion, and voluntary discipline must necessarily have gradually disappeared. They must, however, have largely lost in trustworthiness. The bankrupt nobility had placed themselves in the service of this community for the same reason as the mercenaries, for the landlords had been able, in a measure, to maintain themselves only by becoming to a certain extent the vassals of the Taborites, to whom they paid imposts, and by whose side they were compelled to fight. (Compare on this point the complaint of the Bohemian barons concerning Prokop's tyranny, recounted by Æneas Sylvius.)

As soon as the nobility rose against the sect and began to enlist mercenaries, to whom (thanks to the wealth of the Catholic Church) it was able to offer momentarily better conditions, treachery became rife in all nooks and corners of the Taborite armies.

Hence it is comprehensible that when civil war once more broke out, and Calixtines and Taborites measured their strength in desperate conflict, the latter, deserted by peasants and townsmen, and betrayed by a part of their own troop, should succumb to their enemies, who, setting aside their own internal animosities, had formed an overpowering alliance against the remnant of the democratic party still true to the one remaining communistic brotherhood, more in obedience to necessity than to their own impulses.

On May 30, 1434, a decisive battle was fought at the village of Lipau, near Brod, in Bohemia. The forces of the nobility outnumbered those of the Taborites, the former having 25,000 men, while the latter had about 18,000. For a long time the fight wavered doubtfully hither and thither, but at last victory inclined to the side of the nobility. This was much less due to their skill and bravery than to the treachery of the Taborite general, Johann Capek, commanding the cavalry, who, in the midst of the battle, instead of cutting his way into the ranks of the enemy, took to flight. A frightful slaughter ensued, no quarter being given. Out of 18,000 Taborite soldiers, 13,000 were cut down and killed! This fearful defeat broke for ever the strength of the Taborites.

Tabor ceased to rule Bohemia. Democracy was overthrown, and the nobility, in union with the upper classes of trade, thereupon set about re-arranging for the exploitation of the country. After endless negotiations between the king and his "true subjects," among whom each faction feared (and rightly) that the other was only thinking out a way of betraying it, Sigismund was at last acknowledged king in 1536. He had previously consented to a universal amnesty; and as regards the property of the Church which had been stolen, had conceded to all nobles and communes the right to dispose of it as they might think best.

The power of the Taborites, however, was not completely annihilated at the battle of Lipau. They continued the struggle a short time longer, but ever more feebly and ineffectually, until, in 1436, they were glad to obtain an agreement from Sigismund assuring them at least of the independence of their town.

Tabor remained in this condition until after the beginning of the fifth decade of the fifteenth century. At that time Æneas Sylvius visited the place and reported on it in a letter to Cardinal Carvajal. This is one of the few extant communications from an eye-witness concerning the internal affairs of the sect. A few significant passages may be reproduced, as they give a very good characterisation of life in a Taborite community. According to Æneas, the houses in Tabor were built of wood or clay, and were placed without any regard to order. "This people possess abundant and costly household effects and extraordinary wealth, as they have gathered into one place the spoils from many nations. They wished at one time to live in all things in conformity with the primitive Church, and held all their possessions in common ; each called the other brother, and what one lacked he received from the others. Now, however, each lives for himself alone, and some hunger while others revel [*alius quidem esurit, alius autem ebrius est*]. Shortlived was the fire of neighbourly love, short the imitation [of the Apostolic community]. . . . The Taborites robbed strangers of their possessions, and what they had acquired by violence became common property [*hæc tantum in commune dederunt*]. But they could not maintain this state of things. Nature gained the upper hand ; already they are all given over to greed ; and, as they can no longer rob as of yore, being enervated and in fear of their neighbours, they snatch what they can from the profits of trade [*lucris inhiant mercaturæ*], and give themselves up to the lowest pursuits. There are 4,000 men in the town capable of bearing arms, but they have become craftsmen, and *for the most part gain their living by the weaving of wool* [*lana ac tela ex magna parte victum quærentes*], so that they are valueless in war." [1]

It is worthy of remark that the majority of Taborites were wool-weavers.

Æneas Sylvius visited Tabor in 1451. According to his description, the military strength of the town had completely vanished, as well as its communism. But even the ruins of its revolutionary past appeared to the rulers of Bohemia to be still dangerous. One year after the above-mentioned visit, Georg von Podiebrad, then administrator of Bohemia, appeared

[1] Æneas Sylvius Piccolomini, *opera omnia*, p. 662.

before the place, and demanded the surrender of the whole body of Taborite priests. After a delay of only three days the town yielded, and gave them up, those not "converted" being thrown in prison till their death. Thus the peculiar position of republican Tabor and every form of its independence came to an end.

This pitiful termination of a once haughty communistic commonwealth, before which half Europe had trembled, makes it hardly possible to suppress the wish that, like Münster, Tabor had fallen in the brilliancy of its communistic youth, and had not languished in the wretchedness of bourgeois senility.

With the overthrow of Tabor the last asylum of democracy in Bohemia was destroyed.

The fate of the Taborites, exhibiting as it does many analogies with that of the Jacobins, resembles the latter also in the circumstance that it was they who by their reckless heroism saved the revolution—not for themselves, but for the exploiters of that revolution. In France, these were the great capitalists and knights of industry ; in Bohemia they were the upper nobility, who acquired an almost unlimited mastery both in State and society. The petty nobility gained nothing by the Hussite wars, which accelerated rather than checked their downfall, as the upper nobles, to whom the lion's share of the Church's possessions fell, enriched themselves also at the cost of the lower ranks of their class by buying up their properties.

The peasants and petty townsmen were, however, the chief sufferers by the wars. The exhaustion of the country and the diminution of the population, reducing as they did the power of resistance among the peasants and small townsmen to the lowest point, became inducements to the lords of the soil to increase very largely their demands on the petty rent-paying citizens, and also the burdens imposed on the peasants. These burdens became heavier and heavier. The feeble attempts at resistance and revolt, here and there ventured on by the ill-used peasantry, were easily overcome. Where, however, in spite of the increase of forced labour, the supply of labour was insufficient, the landlord recouped himself by substituting for agriculture a branch of business requiring only a small number of labourers. In some instances the extension of this new industry not only counterbalanced the want of peasants, but even drove peasants away from their situations. In England, the want of labour (originating, it is true, from causes different from those active in Bohemia) gave an important impetus to the development of sheep-raising. This pursuit was finally so general in that country, that it became the chief means of expropriating the peasantry and creating a proletariat. A similar, though less influential part was played in many districts of Bohemia by the *fish-ponds* constructed by the landlords. If, as Thomas More said, the *sheep* ate up the peasants of England, those of Bohemia were equally devoured by *carp*.

At the beginning of the fifteenth century serfdom had almost completely disappeared in Bohemia. At the close of that century it was already again the universal condition of the peasantry.

It is absurd to hold the Hussite Wars responsible for this. Whether social development be brought about by peaceful means or by violent struggles, is immaterial to the direction it takes, that being necessarily determined by the progress and needs of production. When the results of violent revolutionary conflicts are not in accordance with the intentions of the revolutionists, it is a proof that these intentions are in contradiction to the requirements of production. Violent revolutions can never give direction to social development ; they can, under definite conditions, only hasten it, at the same time, however, intensifying the evil for the defeated. This was one of the results of the Hussite Wars. From the fifteenth century onwards a deterioration in the condition of the peasantry set in throughout Europe, though later in some countries than in others. That Bohemia, notwithstanding its backward economic position, was one of the first lands in which this deterioration appeared, and that it there made the most rapid progress, were consequences of the Hussite Wars. But for these the decisive change might not perhaps have occurred until a century later, after the German Peasant Wars.

CHAPTER III

THE BOHEMIAN BRETHREN

TABOR had fallen, but it did not disappear without leaving a trace of its existence. This communistic military town had been so brilliant in its achievements, and its operations had been so intimately connected with the wants of some classes of the lower population, that the principles on which it was based necessarily survived, though under changed conditions and in more suitable forms.

The successors of the Taborites were the *Bohemian Brethren*.

We have already remarked that the communists of the Middle Ages loved peace and abhorred violence ; sentiments which were quite as much in harmony with the helplessness of the poor in that age as with the traditions of primitive Christianity. At the beginning of the Hussite revolution, when the time-honoured authorities were overthrown and the lower classes arose in victorious insurrection, the mass of communists were hurled along with it ; and once it had gained momentum, the logic of facts necessarily forced to the summit of power those who were its most advanced and war-like partisans.

But the peace-loving fraction of communists, who condemned all war, violence, and force, did not wholly cease to exist even during the brilliant triumph of the Taborite power. Their foremost representative was Peter of Chelcic—Peter Chelcicky. Born about the year 1390, and, as it would appear, an impoverished knight, he lived in quiet retirement in the village of Chelcic, near Wodnian, one of the Taborite towns, and there produced a series of writings which aroused universal attention. As early as 1420 he had maintained that no violence should be employed in religious matters ; and this conviction was strengthened during the wars of the revolution. He branded war as the most horrible of all evil, while in his opinion soldiers were not a hair better than murderers.

Chelcicky was a communist in the primitive Christian sense. But not through war and not by State compulsion should equality be forced upon society ; it should be realised as it were behind the back of State and society. The true believer must have no part in the State, for this is sinful and heathenish. Social inequalities such as wealth, standing, and rank were created by the State, and can only disappear with it. The sole Christian method of destroying the State, however, is to ignore it ; hence the true believer is forbidden not only to accept a government office, but also to invoke the power of the State. For him police and judges are non-existent. The Christian strives after goodness of his own free will, and must not force others to be good, for God demands that goodness should be voluntary, and all compulsion is an outcome of evil.

For the true Christian there is no place in the State and in society outside of the lowest social strata, who are allowed to obey and serve, but not to command and rule. As the Christian must not rule, so also he is forbidden to accumulate wealth, and for this reason is prohibited from engaging in trade, since this is allied with fraud. Towns, the seats of trade, are a product of evil devised by Cain. He it was who transformed the primitive simplicity of life into deceit, by devising measures and weights, people having previously bartered without measuring or weighing. Chelcicky's greatest rage, however, was directed against the nobility.[1]

This anarchistic though peaceable communism gained in adherents in proportion to the increase of the general weariness with war, and the defection of the lower classes from the Taborite *régime*.

After the fall of Tabor the *Chelcicky Brethren* became the

---

[1] Compare on this point Jaroslab Goll, *Quellen und Untersuchungen zur Geschichte der Böhmischen Brüder*, II. *Peter Chelcicky und seiner Lehre*. Prague, 1882.

most important of all the sects existing in Bohemia, which were in part composed of the scattered Taboristic elements.

Among the partisans of Peter Chelcicky the most prominent was Brother Gregory, who, although a nobleman, was so impoverished that he was forced to support himself as a journeyman tailor. When some of the old Taborites established a colony in the village of Kunwald, near Seftenberg (a district in which Taboristic views had maintained themselves), they elected Gregory as their head and organiser (1457), to whom it was due that the colonists adopted Chelcicky's principles, and lived up to them in all respects.

The nature of the first organisation of the Bohemian Brethren is not at all clear, as the later Brothers were ashamed of their communistic origin, and endeavoured to conceal it in every possible way. If, however, we examine the organisation of the later Brotherhood (made clearer by that of the well-known Herrnhuters, which is of cognate character), and if we take into consideration the internal conflicts from which that organisation resulted, we shall obtain the following facts.[1]

Every member of the Brotherhood was, of course, most strictly forbidden to participate in the State Government through the acceptance of any post either in the general or communal departments, or in military service, as well as by any appeal or complaint to the Government.

Complete equality was to prevail in the community ; there were to be no poor and no rich. Before being admitted to the community every wealthy person, or member of a privileged class, must relinquish his property and his privileges. No " Brother " was to engage in trade, lend money on interest, or keep an inn. On the other hand, the rules of the fraternity made it obligatory on each member to assist any Brother who might be in want.

---

[1] A good insight into the later organisation of the Bohemian Brethren can be obtained from the work by J. U. Comenius on the Church history of the Brotherhood, from their Church ordinance of 1609, and from the confession of faith which they presented to King Ferdinand in 1535. These are all contained in the German edition of *Kurzgefassten Kirchen-Historie der Böhmischen Bruder.* Comenius, Schwabach, 1739.

Private proprietorship and the separate family were not prohibited. As regards family life, communism displayed itself chiefly in the accentuation of brotherly feeling, the joyous participation in all things by the members, and in efforts to maintain equality so that no one should rise above, or sink below the others. If the right to private property were to be preserved, this state of things would be possible only in conjunction with the prevalence of the strictest discipline, permeating the whole life of the community. Hence, even the most intimate circumstances of family life were not exempt from this discipline.

In marked contrast to the anarchistic theories of Peter Chelcicky which repudiated every act of compulsion as un-Christian and heathenish, the priests and elders exercised a disciplinary power which in modern times would seem intolerable, and the more so as among the Bohemian Brethren there was a particularly prominent exhibition of that gloomy and sullen frame of mind, already pointed out by us as a universal peculiarity of mediæval communism. This feature was a natural consequence of the unspeakable misery and wretchedness resulting from the Hussite Wars.

Every kind of amusement and dance was forbidden as a snare laid for believers by the devil. To live, work, and suffer in silence were the sole duties imposed upon the pious Christian. In its observance of the Sabbath, the community was strictly puritanical.

Although private proprietorship and the separate family were not prohibited, celibacy was regarded as a higher and holier state than that of marriage, while poverty and celibacy were required of the clergy. The unmarried members lived in brother-houses and sister-houses (the sexes being kept apart), where they worked and lived in common. We may assume that these establishments were organised similarly to the Beghard houses.

Like the Taborites, the Bohemian Brethren would not tolerate erudition, and regarded learned men as a privileged class. Up to the time of his death in 1473, Brother Gregory cautioned the community against men of learning. On the other hand, the Brethren, like the Taborites, laid great stress on a solid popular education, and moreover devoted themselves enthusiastically to the democratic art of printing from its inception. " Very rarely," says Gindely (*op. cit.,* i. p. 39), " has a Christian sect sent into the world so many writings in its defence." The number of their works, from their foundation to their almost complete extinction, after the death of Comenius in 1670, is much larger than that of all other contemporary literature combined. They boast of being the first to have the Bible printed in the mother tongue (in Venice), so that in this respect the Bohemians took precedence of all other nations.[1] At the beginning of the sixteenth century there were five printing establishments in Bohemia—one Catholic in Pilsen, one Utraquist in Prague, and three belonging to the Bohemian Brethren in Jungbunzlau, Leitomischl, and Weisswasser respectively. Even these three could not always meet the demands made on them, and occasionally had their books printed in Nurenberg.

Peculiar, but strictly in accord with their severe discipline, was the regulation that no member should write and publish a book without the consent of the community. " No one with us," says their Church ordinance, " has permission to publish books unless they are previously examined by the other members of the community, and authorised by their unanimous approval."[2]

Johannes Lasitzki, a Pole, who visited the Brotherhood in 1571, writes as follows in his work, *De origine et rebus jestis fratrum Bohemorum* : " No book appears without a previous examination by several elders and Church officials, chosen and appointed for the purpose. . . . It is also the custom not to allow any work to be published in one member's name only (except under special conditions), but in the name of the whole Brotherhood. Thus each member of the spiritual body gets quite as much honour from the work as any other, and every opportunity is removed for the indulgence of the vain thirst for fame which as a rule titilates the minds of authors, while the writings themselves acquire so much the greater weight and esteem."[3]

---

[1] Comenius, *op. cit.,* p. 57.   [2] Comenius, *op. cit.,* p. 296.

[3] Cited by Comenius, *op. cit.,* p. 328.

In spite of these regulations what a colossal productivity they exhibited!

It is not surprising that the new community, which included so many former Taboristic elements, should, in spite of its peaceable and submissive character, seem highly suspicious and dangerous to the reigning powers. As early as 1461 a violent persecution broke out against them under Georg von Podiebrad, already known to us as the destroyer of the independence of Tabor. Still administrator of the country in 1452, he was elected King of Bohemia in 1458, after the death of King Ladislaus. One of the first acts of his reign was the persecution of the Bohemian Brethren, which began with the imprisonment of Brother Gregory and other members of the sect. The community in Kunwald was afterwards broken up, and its members driven out, all assemblages being at the same time prohibited.

Comenius tells us that, "through this rigorous inquisition, which was everywhere directed against the Brethren, it came about that most of them, and especially the leaders, were scattered through the woods and mountains, where they were forced to live in caves, which, however, by no means secured them from danger. From this living in caves they were called by their enemies *Jamnici*, or cave-dwellers." [1]

It is possible that the appellation of *Jamnici* may have originated previous to this persecution. As early as the fourteenth century the Beghard sectaries of Western Germany bore the nickname of "Nookers" (*Winkler*), on account of the secrecy of their meetings; while in East Germany they were called "Hole-dwellers" (*Grubenheimer*). The word *Jamnici* (from the Bohemian *Jama*, a hole or cave) is a translation of the German *Grubenheimer*, and perhaps indicates that the Beghard tradition was active among the Bohemian Brethren. Common people called them *Picards* as well as *Jamnici*.

With the death of Podiebrad the first persecution came to an end.

The Brethren underwent occasional subsequent persecutions, from which, however, they did not on the whole suffer

[1] Comenius, *op. cit.*, pp. 45, 46.

much. The power of the government was still weak in Bohemia, and the Brethren found influential protectors in individual nobles in towns ; for persons of intelligence soon perceived that there was no harm in the enmity to government advocated by this sect, and in their efforts in the direction of equality, but at the same time they recognised how easy it would be to exploit a people who preached the obligation of industry, renunciation, and toleration.

It was in no small measure due to this protection that the community rapidly increased in numbers even during the first severe persecution. Their proselytism was also favoured by the circumstance that, like the Taborites, they proclaimed the greatest tolerance in matters of belief, impossible in other Church organisations which had been instituted for the purpose of dominating the people. At the very first congress of the Brethren, held among the hills of Reichenau, in 1464, to which delegates were sent not only from Bohemia, but even from Moravia, it was decreed that the question of social organisation should take precedence of all others, and that matters of belief should occupy a secondary position.

Thanks to this tolerance, they succeeded in attracting many kindred communities. It made them, however, all the more rigid where differences of a practical nature existed. At the second congress, in Lhota, 1467, which gave the community a definite organisation, just as that at Reichenau had (to use a modern expression) given it a programme, certain delegates from the remnants of the Adamites presented themselves with proposals for a union with the Brotherhood. These proposals were rejected. The communism of the Adamites was too far-reaching ; hence only a few members of that sect were admitted, after having abjured their " errors."

The negotiations for a union with the Waldenses were also broken off, that community having become too opportunist and bourgeois in character. In his tract upon the attitude which should be maintained towards the Romish Church, Brother Gregory writes as follows :—" Certain Waldenses admitted that they had strayed from the paths of their predecessors, and that there existed among them the iniquity of taking money away from the people, amassing wealth, and neglecting the poor; whereas it is certainly opposed to Christian belief that a priest should heap up treasure, since he should employ his own worldly possessions, and even those inherited from his parents, in the giving of alms, and not leave the poor in their necessity," &c.[1]

But the Bohemian Brethren were destined soon to meet the same fate as the Waldenses.

The puritanism, by means of which the fraternity protested against existing society, and which was the cause of its separation from that society, was, as a matter of fact, an excellent aid to social advancement. We have already pointed out (p. 22) how, in spite of many external resemblances, this puritanism differed from the asceticism of primitive Christianity. Although both proclaimed the vanity, nay, the wickedness of life's pleasures of every kind, yet primitive Christian asceticism was allied with stupid indolence, while, on the contrary, the puritanism of the Reformation was united in its professors with indefatigable and cautious industry. At that time, when capitalised industry on a large scale was not yet developed, and capitalism was only budding, this industrious puritanism was an exceedingly effective means of turning small traders into capitalists. This means became more effective the more the masses of the people yielded to the instinct of a native joy in life connected with the primitive modes of production, which had for their object not sale, but personal consumption; not accumulation, but enjoyment. In addition to the aid derived from their puritanism, the Brethren must have been much favoured from a business point of view by their good popular education, and especially by the firm cohesion—the solidarity—resulting from their communistic tendencies. This solidarity must have been as great a help to them in business as it has sometimes been to the Jews.

If among the Taborites the spoils of war had produced a condition of opulence (which their communism put an end

---

[1] An extract from the Czech original, with German translation, is to be found in Goll's *Quellen und untersuchungen zur Geschichte der Böhmischen Brüder*, Ch. I. *Der Verkehr der Brüder mit den Waldensern*, Prague, 1878, p. 98.

to), wealth also soon became common among the Bohemian Brethren, as a consequence of their industry, frugality, and thrift, together with their intelligence and the assistance they rendered each other. Actuated by very worldly motives and attracted by their wealth, large numbers from all classes now joined their ranks.

With the increase of opulence, however, many of the older members began to feel fettered by the severe discipline which was enforced. In the interests of equality this discipline allowed no member to be richer than the others, and also forbade the investment of accumulated money in any trade or at interest. Moreover, with the increase of wealth, conflicts sometimes arose regarding property ; lawsuits became necessary, and the power of State was needed for the protection of the surplus belonging to individual members.

Thus a more moderate party was gradually formed among the Brethren, which dared not disavow the original precepts of the fraternity, but strove to have those precepts interpreted as merely embodying the *ideal* of a higher and altogether exceptional sanctity, and not as universally binding principles.

The split between the two parties first showed itself at the end of the seventh decade of the fifteenth century, when two barons and several knights applied for admission to the Brotherhood. The stricter party consented to receive them only on the condition of their relinquishing their property and rank, while the moderate section wished to dispense with this renunciation. The extremists gained the victory, and those alone of the candidates were admitted who acquiesced in all the demands of the community.

Evidence of the influence of the moderate party was furnished in 1480, when admission was granted to a *savant* named Lukas, to be followed by others. If the acceptance of these members was a success to the moderates, the erudite element in return contributed to the strength of that party. In vain did the strict faction, with the weaver Gregory of Wotic at their head, combat the lukewarmness which was gaining the upper hand. In the synod which was held at Brandeis, on the Adler, in 1491, the moderates gained the day ; for it was resolved that, in future, persons of wealth and high standing might be admitted without giving up their riches and rank. They were only to be reminded how easily, without this renunciation, they might forfeit the salvation of their souls. Thus the demand for equality, if not quite cast aside, was now confined merely to holy aspirations.

The pious Brethren also discovered the way to a participation in State government. At the same congress it was agreed :—" If through worldly power it should fall to the lot of any Brother to be a judge, juryman, or guildmaster, or to go to the wars ; or if he, in combination with others, should have to give his consent to the torture or execution of a criminal, we now declare that these be things to which a repentant person should not hasten of his own good free-will, but rather flee from and avoid. But if he cannot evade them, either by persistent entreaty or by any other means, then shall he yield to the powers that be." The Brethren, moreover, were not only allowed to take part in criminal prosecutions by the Government, to accept office or fight in the wars if compelled to do so, but they might in future even appeal to the compulsory powers of the State or to the judges ; nay, it was permissible to carry on any profitable business, such as inn-keeping or any trade—of course, *only in case of necessity.*

The stricter party were infuriated by this decree, which cast to the winds the equality, freedom, and brotherhood hitherto existing in the community. They raised an energetic counter-agitation, and succeeded in winning over their Bishop Mathias, of Kunwald, and in intimidating the waverers or urging them onwards. On their compulsion, Mathias soon convened another synod, which annulled the Brandeis decrees and pronounced for an unconditional return to old and fundamental principles.

But the delight of victory was of short duration. The extremists had won the day, not by internal strength, but by a surprise. At the synod of Reichenau, in 1494, they were again in the minority, and finally recognised that they had lost all prospect of vindicating their views in the community. A division in the Brotherhood was the natural consequence, and the attempt at re-union, in 1496, only led to reciprocal reproaches and to the intensification of the antagonism.

The rigorous section was called the " Smaller Party." It was inferior in numbers and composed of uneducated peasants and handicraftsmen, and being in antagonism with the needs of social development, languished away. After several of its members had been burnt at the stake in Prague (1527), it vanished from public ken.

The moderate section, on the contrary, strengthened by rich and powerful adherents, with liberty to take part in the State government and utilise it for their own purposes, having, moreover, an organisation in harmony with the requirements of social progress, advanced rapidly in prosperity. In 1500, they already possessed two hundred churches, and, during the sixteenth century they became an important factor in politics and economics. How largely the nobility was represented among them, may be gathered from a petition, presented in 1575 to the Emperor by the nobles of the Brotherhood, and signed by seventeen barons and one hundred and forty-one knights.

Every trace of a communistic origin disappeared, and, as has already been remarked, all communistic traditions were carefully expunged from their literature. Moreover, although they had admitted persons of wealth into their ranks, they now on the other hand went so far as to tolerate mendicity. "*As far as possible,*" says their Church ordinance of 1609, " we secure our people against beggary "; hence there was no longer an unconditional obligation among the Brethren to help each other.

Gindely says (*op. cit.*, ii. p. 312) :—" The Bohemian Puritans, nay, even the fanatics who adhered to Peter Chelcicky more than to Huss, and in conformity with Pauline doctrines favoured celibacy, accepted no office, allowed themselves no luxury, tolerated no wealth, put no money out at interest, and abhorred war—these men produced very wealthy capitalists, very honourable husbands, very decorous burgomasters and jurymen, as well as very skilful generals and statesmen."

Success attended the Brotherhood until the Thirty Years' War, and the Battle of White Mountain in 1631. This battle, which decided the long struggle between the intractable Bohemian nobility and Hapsburg absolutism, and led to the extinction of the former, the confiscation of their properties and the distribution of these among the Jesuits and sycophants of the Court, also brought about the downfall of the Bohemian Brethren. The scanty remnant dragged on a painful existence, until they finally founded an asylum on the Saxon estates of the pietist, Count Zinzendorf (1722).

But neither the communistic enthusiasm of the extremists, nor the worldly wisdom of the moderates long survived among the Herrnhuters. Poor, miserable peasants and handicraftsmen, who had escaped the persecution only by living in the most isolated and uncivilised corners of the land, they had lost all traces of an identity with the original Brotherhood.

In the sixteenth century the Bohemian Brethren ceased to play a part in the history of socialism. In the seventeenth century, they also lost their importance to general history.

CHAPTER IV

THE GERMAN REFORMATION AND THOMAS MÜNZER

I. *The German Reformation*

ÆNEAS SYLVIUS PICCOLOMINI (so often quoted by us), formerly an enthusiast in the cause of Church reform, had made peace with the Roman Pope, and, as a reward, had been given the Cardinal's hat, 1456.[1] A letter was addressed to the newly-created Cardinal by Martin Mayer (a native of Heidelberg and Chancellor to the Archbishop of Mayence, Ditrich von Erbach), in which, among other things, he says :—" There are thousands of ways in which the Roman See robs us of our gold as if we were a nation of barbarians. From this it has come about that our country, once so famed, which by its courage and blood founded the Roman kingdom and was the king and queen of the world, is now sunk in poverty, a servile and tribute-paying land, and, grovelling in the dust, has for long years been bewailing its misery and indigence. Our rulers, however, have at length awakened from their sleep, and have begun to ponder how they can oppose this evil ; aye, they have resolved to shake off the yoke and regain their old freedom, and the Roman Curia will suffer not a little if its princes carry out what they have in their minds." [2]

In refutation of Martin's charges Æneas Sylvius deemed it necessary to write a book on the condition of Germany, which

---

[1] Two years later he was made Pope, Pius II., and in that capacity saw fit to condemn his earlier writings as heretical.

[2] Ullman, *Reformatoren, &c.*, p. 214.

appeared in 1458, shortly before his election to the Papal throne.[1] "He were indeed wanting in mental gifts," he sets forth, "who should assert that Germany is poor." He endeavours to prove this by a reference to the commerce and mining industry which at that time flourished in Germany and brought in great wealth. "If it be true," he exclaims, "that where there are merchants there is always great wealth, then must it be conceded that the Germans are a very rich people, since the greater part of them thirst after profits in trade and roam through the most distant lands. . . . And then consider the veins of silver that have been discovered among you. Kuttenberg in Bohemia, Rankberg in Saxony, and Freiberg in Meissen possess inexhaustible silver mines on their dizzy heights." He then points to the gold and silver mines in the valleys of the Inn, and Enns; to the gold washings on the Rhine and in Bohemia ; and finally asks :—" Where in your land is there an inn (*diversorium*) which has not its drinking cups of silver ? What woman, not only among the nobility but among the plebeians, does not glitter with gold ? Shall I make mention of the neck-chains of the knights and bridles of the horses, embossed with purest gold ; of the spurs and scabbards garnished with precious stones ; of the finger-rings and shoulder-belts, the armour and helmets, sparkling with gold ? And how beautiful are the utensils of the churches ? What number of reliquaries do we find encrusted with pearls and gold ? how rich the vesture of the altars and priests ! "

Hence Germany was well able to contribute to the support of the Roman See. But what would happen to the Pontificate if Germany should cease to fulfil her mission ? It would become poor and wretched and incapable of performing its high duties, since the small and uncertain revenues of the Papal States were insufficient for its needs. Without wealth it were impossible to be intelligent and highly esteemed. Moreover the laws of all societies (*in omni lege*) recognised the necessity of a wealthy priesthood.

There could be no greater contradiction between two statements than is here exhibited. It might be said that

---

[1] We avail ourselves of the Leipzig edition of 1496 :—*Enee Sylvii. de Ritu. Situ. Moribus ac Conditione alemanie. Lyptzick.*

only one could be true, the other must be false; and yet both are true. Each by itself gives an incomplete picture of Germany's condition in the second half of the fifteenth century. They are both true precisely *because* they are in irreconcilable contradiction; the great antagonism of the time is, indeed, accurately reflected by the discrepancy between these statements. It was precisely because this antagonism was irreconcilable, that it could be terminated only by the conflict of the two opposing elements, and the triumph of one.

Mayer's letter and the reply by Æneas Sylvius show us in the clearest light the pivot on which the Reformation turned, freed from the confused heap of theological wranglings concerning predestination, the Holy Communion, &c., with which it was afterwards overlaid by the Church reformers of various parties.

Æneas Sylvius was right; Germany in the fifteenth century was flourishing through its mining and trade. He was also right in affirming that the Papal See was chiefly dependent on the revenues it obtained from Germany; for the other great civilised nations of Europe had already to a great extent freed themselves from Papal spoliation.

For this reason the Vatican was obliged to exercise all its powers of extortion upon the German nation, and obstinately refuse even the smallest concession. No relief, therefore, from the Papal exactions could be expected. Germany must either suffer submissively, or throw off the Roman yoke completely.

This conviction continued to acquire strength, for Martin Mayer's statement was also correct. Although the wealth of Germany was undoubtedly increasing, the Papal claims were nevertheless most oppressively burdensome and very obstructive to economic development.

It was a sufficient injury that she had to bear a burden from which the rest of the civilised nations were free. It is true that in France, England, and Spain the population was taxed for the Church, but the most substantial part of the revenues derived from such taxation remained in those countries and benefited the ruling classes. These seized upon all the lucrative benefices for the members of their own order, or for creatures and parasites from other classes. In Germany, on the contrary, many benefices fell to the share of foreigners—tools, not of the German princes, but of the Pope. All the lucrative clerical appointments in Germany were moreover articles of commerce, which the Pope sold to the highest bidder.[1] Enormous sums flowed into Rome year in year out, and were lost to the great extortioners in Germany —its princes and merchants. Moreover, great as the profits from trading and mining might be, and rapid as was the increase of wealth in Germany, the necessity for money and the greed for gold among the ruling classes augmented in like proportion.

In the fifteenth century the production of commodities for the market had already attained remarkable dimensions, while that for home consumption as the exclusive form of production was, even in country places, in the course of rapid decline. Money began to play a great part in economic life. The necessity for it was ever greater on all sides, but chiefly among the upper classes, not only because their mode of life had reached a most extravagant degree of luxury, but also because money alone could satisfy the constantly increasing demands upon them. Money was also required to pay the mercenaries and officials who supported the absolute monarchy, at that time developing itself; funds were needed to attract the independent nobles to its Court and induce them to serve its purposes; and lastly means were necessary to bribe the tools of its adversaries. All this implied imposts, raking and scraping townsmen and peasants in order to extract from them all that they could yield, the ordinary revenue rarely proving sufficient; and it meant moreover incurring debts—debts the interest of which enforced fresh

---

[1] " It is not easy to get a lucrative benefice here," said Hutten once, " unless one has been of service to the Holy See, or has sent large sums of money to Rome for bribery, or bought the living through the direct mediation of the Fugger family." (*Die römische Dreifaltigkeit.* Speeches by Ulrich v. Hutten, translated and edited by David F. R. Strauss, Leipzig, p. 106.) The Fuggers were indeed zealous Catholics, and did not spare money in the conflict with Luther.

expenditure. In spite of all exactions and all loans, only a few princes were in a satisfactory financial condition, and hence they felt, as did their subjects, upon whom these and other burdens rested, that they were becoming impoverished in spite of Germany's increasing wealth, and that it was unbearable to look on quietly while the Pope, for no reason whatever, carried off the cream of the profits and left them the skimmed milk. It was nevertheless by no means a very simple matter to rid themselves of papistical demands.

Undoubtedly the mass of the people suffered like the princes, and indeed even more than they; the lower classes, the peasants, the town proletarians and the class immediately above them, together with the burgesses and the lower nobility, groaned under the dominion of Rome. Even before the days of Wycliffe and Huss they had shown themselves disposed, under Louis the Bavarian, to enter upon a struggle against the Papal Church, though they had, perhaps, to endure quite as much under the increasing demands of the higher nobility, the great merchants and princes; and with this state of feeling among them, Bohemia was to learn, as England had done, how dangerous it was for the princes to undermine one of the great powers in the community.

The Revolution of 1789 in France brought about a period of reaction in Europe, and cooled the desire of the bourgeoisie for a revolutionary struggle, which could only be carried on with the assistance of small traders and the proletariat, against princely autocracy and the aristocratic landed proprietors. In the same way the Hussite war produced a period of reaction not only in Bohemia but in Germany also, and it required a long time for the idea of casting off the yoke of Rome to gain any influence among the upper classes of the Empire.

Then again there was the alliance between the Emperor and the Pope. The Imperial authority was declining very fast in Germany, and the Emperors were afraid that it would diminish still more rapidly if the other traditional authority of the Empire—the Papal—were shaken or destroyed. Moreover there was the danger from Turkey, which directly threatened the Imperial (*i.e.* the Hapsburg) possessions, a danger which could apparently be averted only by one of the Pope's organised Crusades.

If one adds to all this the fatal disruption of Germany, which certainly reduced the power of the Emperor to a minimum, but at the same time made concerted action among the opponents of the Pope and Emperor very difficult, it is comprehensible that the Reformation movement in Germany only became strongly pronounced in the century after the Hussite War.

Meantime development was spreading far and wide in all spheres. The means for a religious and military conflict had greatly improved. The art of printing had been invented and artillery had been made more perfect, while the facilities for commerce, and especially for maritime intercommunication, had considerably increased. Shortly before the Reformation, bold navigators had sailed directly across the Atlantic Ocean, for the first time in the world's history.

The advance of the Turks and nations of Central Asia was the incentive to these voyages, for these nations barred the old paths of commerce to the East. Thanks to the greater perfection attained by European navigation, this did not lead to any interruption in the trade between Western Asia and Europe, but rather to the search for new ways to India— along the coast of Africa on one side, and across the ocean on the other. The age of discovery had begun ; modern colonial policy took its rise.

By these means not only was the horizon of mankind vastly widened, and a complete revolution of human knowledge initiated, but an economic change was also inaugurated. The commercial centre of Europe was transferred from the basin of the Mediterranean to the shores of the Atlantic. The economic development of Italy was bound down and hemmed in, while on the contrary that of Western Europe was suddenly accelerated by a powerful impetus. Existing antagonisms, as much between classes as between nations, were brought to a climax, and fresh antagonisms were engendered, till the passions peculiar to the new capitalistic form of exaction were unfettered and exhibited with all the strength and recklessness of the Middle Ages, out of the barbarism of which society had just stepped. All traditional, social, and political relations were overthrown; all prevailing codes of morality proved unstable. For a whole century a series of terrible wars raged throughout Europe in which the thirst for gold, the lust of murder, and the madness of despair were rampant. Who has not heard of the Eve of St. Bartholomew? Who does not know the deeds of the heroes of the Thirty Years' War in Germany, of Alva in the Netherlands, and of Cromwell in Ireland? There is no need to mention the abominations of contemporary colonial policy.

This mighty revolution, the greatest which Europe had seen since the migration of nations, found its termination in some measure (except in the case of England) in the Peace of Westphalia, in 1648. It arose from the German Reformation, which agitated the whole of Europe and supplied the catch-words and arguments for the combatants till the middle of the seventeenth century, so that to the superficial observer it might seem that in all these struggles religion was the only object in question: indeed, they are called the Religious Wars.

Taking all this into consideration, it is not surprising that the German Reformation movement was vastly more important in historic significance than the earlier agitations of this kind; that it has come to be known in general as *the* Reformation and that the Germans, though they halted so long after the other civilised nations of Europe in the revolt against Rome, were regarded as the chosen people of religious freedom, destined to carry it to other countries.

II. *The Rich Product of the Saxon Mines.*

The land from which the spark was to fly forth that should kindle the whole world into flame was Saxony. We have seen how important the silver mines were for Bohemia in the fourteenth century; how they had intensified social antagonisms and increased the power of the country and its rulers. In the fifteenth century the produce of the Bohemian mines diminished, while, on the other hand, those of Saxony—namely, in Meissen and Thuringia—reached a dizzy height of prosperity. The silver wealth of Freiberg had been well known in 1171, its mining laws becoming the foundation of mining legislation throughout the whole of Germany. At the close of the fifteenth century, however, it was outdone by Schneeberg, where, in 1471, fresh veins of ore were discovered, which for some time were the most productive of all German silver mines. In 1492 mining was started at Schreckenstein, and in 1496 the foundation-stone was laid of the mining town of Annaberg. In 1516 the mines of Joachimsthal came into prominence (they were partly Bohemian and partly Saxon); in 1519 those of Marienberg.

In Thuringia the most important mine was at Mansfeld. It had been worked since the twelfth century, and yielded copper as well as silver and gold, the bituminous marl-slate being conveyed to Venice, where the process of separation was better understood than in Germany.

The rapidly increasing wealth in the precious metals promoted production and trade in Saxon cities. Erfurt became rich and powerful as the Saxon emporium for trade to the south (Venice), while Halle and, later, Leipzig were the chief marts for the north. North and south, commerce developed most actively in the direction both of production and trade. The line commercial intercourse took from Saxony to Italy passed through Nurenberg and Augsburg, and contributed much to the powerful position taken by these towns from the fourteenth to the sixteenth centuries.

With commerce, production also developed, while art and local trade flourished in the above-mentioned towns.

But it was not only town life that was influenced by the rich mines of Saxony; their effect in the country was perhaps even greater.

The demand for wood at the mines was an important item ; it was required partly as timber in the construction of the shafts, for the laying of tracks (with wooden rails, as we see them represented in Agricola's book *On Mines*), &c., and partly and especially for fuel in smelting the ore. A regular traffic in wood became quite necessary, and we find that it was already the object of many commercial treaties in Saxony even in the beginning of the sixteenth century.

Other natural products were required in the mining districts, which lay, as a rule, in unproductive mountainous regions at a high altitude, where but little corn grew—much too little to support the crowd of people who gathered about a large mine. The mountain peasants being unable to cultivate the corn for themselves, were forced to buy it. The development of the mines, therefore, greatly promoted the commerce in wheat as well as in wood. It formed, for example, the chief revenues of Zwickau, which lay on the road from the Saxon " Lowlands " to the " Highlands."

Hence at a very early date the peasants and lords of the soil in Saxony became producers of commodities for the market ; and, having once found a market for their produce, it was a matter of indifference to them what they cultivated, provided their productions were saleable. It was not even necessary that it should be wheat, the market for which was circumscribed, while that for plants used in manufacture was much more extensive, e.g., woad, which was used for blue dyes. Nowhere in Germany was this cultivation so widely developed as in Saxony, especially in Thuringia, the centre of the industry being Erfurt. Even at the beginning of the seventeenth century, woad is said to have been cultivated in three hundred villages of Thuringia, though the competition from indigo was already very strong. The antagonism between the territorial lords and the peasants which was engendered by this development must, consequently, have reached a great height at the beginning of the Reformation in Saxony. The value of land was very great, and so was the greed of the nobles for it. The system of money duties and the avarice shown by the princes and nobility were most remarkable, as was also the great dependence of the peasantry on the merchants and cultivators. Capitalists, princes, and nobles seized upon the whole profits arising from this commercial prosperity. Thanks to the rapid increase of the precious metals, and the decrease in the cost of production, the price of agricultural produce arose enormously. In Saxony, the centre of the mining wealth, the rise in prices must have been particularly mischievous, for it did not in the least benefit the peasantry, while in the cities it was the cause of serious strikes.

For this reason, we find that class antagonism at the beginning of the Reformation was peculiarly bitter in Saxony, exactly as it had been a hundred years before in the neighbouring country of Bohemia. But in the latter country the mining population had represented a conservative power. Their proletarianism was only in its infancy; the miners were counted among the privileged classes, and, being Germans, were necessarily regarded as partisans of the traditional order of things, i.e., of the sovereign and the Pope.

Since that time the proletariat element among miners, and the working of mines by capitalists, had made enormous strides; but in Saxony the miners were not strangers to the country; they possessed no privileges which the overthrow of the existing order of things could affect, but, on the contrary, came more and more into conflict with the ruling powers during the last decade before the Reformation. Far from opposing any revolutionary movement, they were quite ready to join any such that broke out, and their numbers, their aptitude for arms, and the economic importance of their profession, gave them a power with which statesmen had to reckon.

The class, however, which derived the greatest increase of strength from the wealth of the mines was the absolute monarchy, a class which, besides being the most revolutionary of any, was most favoured by all the tendencies of the age.

Although the eager rush for gold and silver was increasing, most of the princes found difficulty in satisfying their need for money by means of taxes and imposts. It was different, however, with the princes within whose territories lay the rich silver and gold mines. Of these the best-filled coffers were possessed by the sovereigns of Saxony. The inheritance of the two brothers, Ernest and Albrecht (1485), had been divided into two parts, Ernest receiving the chief portion, Thuringia; Albrecht the lesser, Meissen. But the silver mines in the mountains had not been divided; they remained the common property of both houses, the revenues being simply shared. Thanks to these revenues, the Saxon princes of the sixteenth century played a prominent part in Germany, taking precedence after the Emperor of Germany.

Paradoxical as it may appear, the residue of the Imperial power at that time rested to a great extent only upon the impecuniosity and avarice of the German princes, especially of the Prince-Electors. The latter had, in reality, become independent sovereigns. If they tolerated the Imperial dignity, it was chiefly in order to find a purchaser to whom they could sell a part, and in truth a very trifling part, of their sovereign rights. The same *rôle* which was played at the close of the old Roman Republic, first by the rabble of the capital, and subsequently by the Pretorian mob, was enacted by the Prince-Electors of the fifteenth and sixteenth centuries. Every Imperial election was to them a most profitable business, the noble lords taking money in bribes from all the candidates, and finally giving their votes to the highest bidder.

Perhaps the most disgraceful episode in this traffic of elections occurred when the nomination of a successor to Maximilian I. was in view, an episode which began during this Emperor's lifetime and lasted from 1516 to 1519. The two dynasties which had been contending for predominance in Europe, and had alternately made a tool of the pontifical power, now sued also for the Imperial crown—the French dynasty of Valois, and the House of Hapsburg, the centre of whose dominion had slipped away from Germany to Spain.

Nearly all the Electors accepted money from both Francis I. of France and Charles V. of Spain.

The only prince who took no money was the Elector Frederick of Saxony (of the Ernestinian line, to whom Thuringia had fallen). The other Electors, hankering after the treasures of the joint possessors of the silver mines in Meissen, offered the Imperial crown to him—of course for corresponding fees. But Frederick rejected the offer, well knowing it was not worth the price, and turned the choice upon the House of Hapsburg. Notwithstanding the Tyrolean mines and the flourishing commerce of the Hapsburg Netherlands, in spite also of the might of Spain at their back, the Hapsburgs appeared to threaten the independence of the German princes less than did Francis I., who already possessed a well-organised and compact France.

We will not enter upon the other considerations which demanded the election of Charles, such as the danger from Turkey, &c.

The Elector of Saxony not only became the emperor-maker by virtue of his riches and power, but he was also the centre of the opposition made by the German princes against the Emperor and Pope in their struggle for independence.

The University of Wittenberg, founded by Frederick in 1502, undertook the intellectual guidance of the movement, which was at once inimical to the Pope and friendly to the princes. Luther, who had been a professor in this school since 1508, and had fallen under its influence, finally became its spokesman and the confidential friend and *protégé* of the Prince-Elector. These events are too well known to require being dealt with in detail. Every one knows how, in 1517, Tetzel came to Saxony to extort money from the people for Pope Leo X. by the sale of indulgences; how Luther attacked him, quarrelled with him, and was carried further than he at first intended by the intervention of the Vatican; how out of the "monk's quarrel" arose the rebellion of the whole nation against the Pope, and how the latter tried to intimidate the former by his anathemas (1520). But Luther, feeling sure of his prince's aid, defied the Pope and burnt his Bull; he dared even to defy the newly-elected Emperor, Charles V., who summoned him before the Imperial Diet at Worms (1521). Charles, however, could not deal with him as Sigismund had dealt with Huss, for he knew that the monk was supported by the greater part of the German nation, and particularly by the powerful Frederick of Saxony. Hence the monarch upon whose dominion the sun never set did not dare to interfere openly with Frederick and Luther.

Thus Saxony became the intellectual centre both of the aristocratic opposition to Rome, which proved victorious, and

of the democratic, which was crushed.   In Thuringia a number of small towns, such as Mühlhausen and Nordhausen,
succeeded in maintaining their freedom from princely rule.
Erfurt also could count itself a free town.   At the beginning
of the Reformation it was the chief commercial city of
Central Germany, though it was soon to yield its place to
aspiring Leipzig, which had already surpassed the old trading
town of Halle.   The Erfurt University was considered the
most eminent in Germany.   It became the seat of the new
German Humanism, which united itself to the kindred movements in Italy and France, and sought to emulate them in
spirited contempt for traditional beliefs.

It was, however, not only the learned and civic, but also
the communistic, opposition, that found its greatest support
in Saxon towns.

III. *The Enthusiasts of Zwickau.*

The Hussite War was not without its influence upon the
obscure and feeble beginning of the communistic movement
of Germany which was comprised under the name of the
" Beghard doctrine."   The ruling classes were stimulated by
this war to a greater mistrust of, and severity towards, all
the suspicious agitations among the lower orders, while, on
the other hand, Bohemia became an asylum from which the
German emigrants could exert their influence on their own
country.   Czech Taborites zealously supported the propaganda in foreign lands, and to them also the Hussite
propaganda in Germany can almost always be traced back.
The Hussite spirit in the armies of the " Brethren " grew
so strong that they desired to spread its doctrine over the
whole world ; and the bold thought was more than once
expressed that all Christendom should, either by force of
arms or by the path of peaceful teaching, be brought to
accept the Truth.   The so-called letters of heretics, those
popular manifestoes of the Taborites, wherein they summoned all Christians, without distinction of nation or rank,
to free themselves from priestly domination and to confiscate
Church property, were carried to England and Spain, while

in Dauphiné the people sent contributions in money to Bohemia, and began in good Taborite fashion to murder their lords. In the south of Germany we find the Taborite emissaries more active than any others. Two facts in particular did great service to the propaganda—the existence of the numerous Waldenses congregations, and the strong socialistic tendency which made itself noticeable, especially among the lower strata of the town folk, and threatened the rich hierarchy quite as much as it did the Jews.[1]

Of course the communistic sects could only exist in the form of secret societies. The Brethren, therefore, usually resided in out-of-the-way mills, hamlets, and farms, and assembled in small numbers when they held their services, thus avoiding every sort of notice.

After the futile attempt of the Pope and the Emperor to crush Luther, after the burning of the Papal Bull by the latter, and still more after the Imperial Diet at Worms, the cave-dwellers, like other rebellious spirits, plucked up courage to make an advance.

When social and political powers have lost their material foundation, their best support is their traditional credit and prestige. By means of these they can, under certain circumstances, maintain themselves for a long time against superior opponents. But the longer they do so the more terrible is the downfall when, in a trial of strength, this prestige proves to be merely a hollow show.

The Emperor and Pope experienced the truth of this during the years 1520 and 1521. Hitherto no one had ever defied them both at the same time with impunity. The less the lower strata of the people recognised that the princes and knights were in reality supporting Luther, the more isolated he appeared to be ; consequently the result of the Diet must have influenced the great masses most powerfully. If the truth were so strong that a single monk could defend it, undismayed and unpunished, before the greatest rulers of Christendom, then all who had a good cause to defend might unhesitatingly venture to step forward.

[1] Fr. b. Bezold, *Geschichte der deutschen Reformation*, pp. 127, 128.

Saxony was the first to move. A few weeks after the declaration of the Diet against Luther and his friends (June, 1521) the people of Erfurt rose in a series of insurrections and put an end to the Catholic Church government. In Wittenberg also there were disturbances ; but the agitations in Zwickau, which began in the year 1520, are of the most importance to us. From very ancient times and until the Thirty Years' War, cloth weaving was the chief trade. As early as 1348, when statutes were enacted respecting this industry, the clothmakers formed a guild, which was the most important, and apparently the oldest in the place ; and in the second half of the fifteenth century Zwickau, next to Oschatz, supplied the largest amount and the best quality of cloth in Meissen, although it did not always come up to the standard of the much admired material from London and the Netherlands. In 1540, two hundred and thirty clothmakers might be counted among the householders ; but an old and not unfounded tradition tells us that at that flourishing period their numbers amounted to six hundred.[1]

It is with this " flourishing period " that we are now dealing. During the ten years of the Peasant War, from 15,000 to 20,000 stone of wool were used in manufacture, and from 10,000 to 20,000 pieces of cloth were produced annually.

The clothmakers had something more than an economic importance. From their numbers they formed a considerable portion of the population of the town, which at that time contained nearly 1,000 houses ; so that in the " flourishing period " from one-quarter to one-half of the houses belonged to the clothmaker masters ; in any case they possessed more than 230, and probably nearer 600.

The manufacture of cloth had become an important industry, and the trade was in the hands of great merchants. This was nothing unusual ; but the proximity of the Zwickau weavers to the workers in the Saxon mines was a unique circumstance, and the rebellious, defiant spirit of the latter must have given courage to the journeymen clothmakers, while the communistic enthusiasm of the latter must in its

[1] E. Herzog, *Chronik der Kreisstadt Zwickau*, vol. i. p. 234.

turn have infected the miners. We cannot wonder therefore that the communists in and about Zwickau were
the first during the Reformation in Germany to dare to
assert themselves openly. As early as 1520 we find an
organised community there with chiefs, called " Apostles," as
among the Waldenses. The long yearning for the millennium now appeared to them to be on the eve of gratification,
through the medium of a frightful visitation from God—
a violent revolution. Though their principal adherents were
the clothmakers of the town, they gained followers from
among the miners, and many persons of education also
joined them, of whom we may mention Max Stübner, who
had studied at Wittenberg with one of the " Apostles."
Their leader was the weaver Nicholas Storch.

They also acquired some influence beyond Zwickau, and
even in Wittenberg itself, where, besides the lower classes,
some idealists joined the agitation. At that time class
antagonism in the Reformation had not shown themselves;
it still bore the aspect, on the one hand, of a national movement without distinction of class, while, on the other hand,
it appeared as a purely religious struggle for the purification
of the Church and the re-establishment of evangelical Christianity.

We have pointed out how easy it was for the idealists
(who were not directly interested in exploiting the lower
classes) to show their sympathy with the communistic movement at this stage, supported as it was by early Christian
tradition.

The enthusiasts of Zwickau made a deep impression even
upon Melancthon, Luther's friend and fellow-worker. " One
sees by many signs," said he, " that firm spirits dwell in
them." He wrote to the Elector Frederick about Nicholas
Storch :—" I have observed about him thus much, that he
has the true conception of the Scriptures, with the noblest
and highest articles of the faith ; he has also a great gift of
speaking." Frederick himself, in consequence of the demean-
our of the theologians, did not know rightly what to think of
the enthusiasts. Melancthon was clever enough not to compromise himself, but to leave to Luther the decision upon

the true character of these enthusiastic spirits. But he felt himself so drawn towards them that he took one of the "Apostles" (the Stübner mentioned above) into his house. Luther could not tell him much about the Zwickau sect at first; he lived on the Wartburg, where he was awaiting the results of the ban of the Empire which had been promulgated against him. What the Brethren were driving at however was made clear to him soon enough, and he came forward energetically against them.

Luther's friend and colleague, Karlstadt, favoured these enthusiasts far more decidedly than did Melancthon. The Lutheran movement advanced much too slowly for Karlstadt's revolutionary vehemence. He took up the contest against the celibacy of the priests and the Latin Mass much earlier than Luther, who only followed his lead with hesitation. He went further than merely denouncing sacred pictures and the keeping of Lent. Quite in the Beghard and Taborite manner, the learned Professor condemned every form of scholarship, declaring that it was not the learned, but the working classes, who should preach the gospel ; the former should learn from the latter, and the high-schools ought to be shut.

By far the most prominent among the adherents of the Apostle of Zwickau, however, was Thomas Münzer. From the year 1521 to 1525 he was the centre of the whole communistic movement in Germany. His figure rises so conspicuously in all its concerns, its history is so closely connected with him, and all contemporary evidence about it refers so exclusively to him, that we will follow the usual method and relate Münzer's history, as the history of the communistic movement in the first years of the Reformation.

IV. *Münzer's Biographers.*

Our information about Münzer is very scanty, as is the case with so many unsuccessful revolutionists both before and after him. Notices of him are not lacking, but they come chiefly from his enemies, and are consequently malicious and untrustworthy. The best-known sources of enlightenment are the passages in Melancthon's *Historie Thome Müntzers, des anfengers der Doringischen vffrur, sehr nützlich zu lesen,* &c., which seems to have been published in the same year (1525) in which the insurrection was suppressed. This account is given in nearly all the editions containing a full collection of Luther's works. We all know how a time-serving dependent of a prince of that epoch would be likely to write about the prince's most dangerous enemy. Melancthon had special cause for animosity, since he had long coquetted with the associates of Münzer as we have already seen; he had even received and answered letters from Münzer himself, and was obliged to expiate his offence by redoubled indignation.

Accuracy was not the chief object of the "gentle Melancthon," his only desire being to abuse Münzer. Even on matters of indifferent interest, his statements are wholly untrustworthy.

Sleidan and Gnodalius have simply copied these statements, and from them they have been repeated in the later histories of that period. Münzer was only seen in a true light after the French Revolution, which roused the Pastor G. Th. Strobel, of Wöhrdt (Bavaria) to a study of the Peasant War, and particularly of the Münzer sedition. This led to the discovery of the omissions and contradictions in Melancthon's statements, which Strobel sought as much as possible to rectify in his own writings (*Leben, Schriften, und Lehren Thomae Müntzers, des Urhebers des Bauernaufstandes in Thuringen.* Nurenberg and Altorf, 1795). This work is the first scientific monograph on Münzer, and that written by Pastor Seidemann (who published a memoir in 1842) can alone be compared with it. (*Thomas Münzer, eine Biographie, nach den im königlich sächsischen Hauptstaatsarchiv zu Dresden vorhandenen Quellen bearbeitet.* Dresden and Leipzic.) Seidemann has brought forward a number of new arguments; but in the title of his work he promises more than he performs, for in most of the particulars he relies upon Strobel, from whom he frequently takes excerpts without mentioning their author.

The most recent work on Münzer is by O. Merx (*Thomas*

Münzer und Heinrich Pfeifer, 1523–1525. Göttingen, 1889),
a doctor's dissertation, the author of which misses no opportunity of bringing his loyal opinions to light. This brief
memoir gives a few details and some chronologically accurate
statements, which till then had been buried in contemporary
writings or in collections of scattered materials. But it deals
wholly with the mere surface of events, and displays no comprehension whatever of Münzer's purpose or achievements.

All the other monographs on Münzer which we have come
across are scientifically worthless ; but the most pitiable of
all is a discourse by Professor Leo, *Thomas Münzer*, given by
order of the Evangelical Society in Berlin, 1856. He has
merely copied Seidemann, but has interlarded his statements
with servile malevolence. The spirit of Melancthon's writings
appears throughout his discourse, as it does in most of the
records of that period down to Janssen and Lamprecht.

We have met with but one among the independent
accounts of Münzer, which has correctly estimated the
historical importance of the man and his personality. It is
that which Zimmermann gives us in his *Geschichte des Grossen
Bauernkrieges*, a work never yet equalled, much less surpassed, in spite of the fact that more than half a century has
elapsed since its publication, and although a few of its details
were already well known.

Friedrich Engels has given an account of the Peasant War
based upon Zimmermann's work, and with it also a narrative
of Thomas Münzer's deeds, in a publication which first
appeared in the sixth number of the review, *Die Neue
Rheinische Zeitung*, Hamburg, 1880, and which since then
has repeatedly appeared in pamphlet form under the title of
Der Deutsche Bauernkrieg. Although (as he admits in his
preface) Engels gathered his data from Zimmermann, he
elaborated them independently on the basis of the materialistic conception of history, and with the recent experience
furnished him by the revolution of 1848, by which means he
acquired a great many new and important glimpses into the
causes of the Peasant War, which we have found of the
utmost importance in the following account.

On one point—and that certainly an essential one—we

cannot agree with Zimmermann. He holds that Münzer was ahead of his age and superior to it. "Münzer was three centuries in advance of his time, not only in his political but also in his religious views." [1]

Zimmermann came to this conviction after comparing Münzer's opinions with those of more modern thinkers, such as Penn, Zinzendorf, Rousseau, &c. Had he compared them with the earlier communistic sects, he would have found that Münzer moved entirely within their sphere of thought; indeed we have not succeeded in discovering a single new idea in him.

In our judgment also the importance of the man as an organiser and propagandist has been much overrated. The persecution of the Beghards and Waldenses, which had not ceased, indicates that not only the opinions, but also the organisations of the communistic sects, had been preserved up to the time of the Reformation. We may assume that, contemporaneously with Münzer, perhaps indeed before him, as was notorious in Zwickau, countless agitators and organisers were active in promulgating the same opinions, and that in many places secret associations were already in existence, upon whom they could rely for support.

Münzer surpassed his communistic confederates not only in philosophic conceptions and in the talent for organising, but in his revolutionary energy, and especially in his statesmanlike discernment. The communists in the Middle Ages were universally inclined to peace. In revolutionary times it is true they were easily carried away by the fever of sedition. When the Reformation set the whole of Germany in a mighty blaze the communists did not remain unaffected by it, but many of them appeared to doubt the efficacy of violent measures—the South Germans in particular, as they were influenced by the Swiss Anabaptists, who were decidedly opposed to Münzer's opinion that force alone could procure the spread of the gospel. They wanted to fight with spiritual weapons only—to "conquer the world with the Word of God," as they expressed it at the time. We shall revert to this in the chapter which deals with the Anabaptists.

[1] *Op. cit.* 2nd ed., vol. i. p. 162.

Münzer was very far from displaying this peaceful disposition. His vehemence and energy could not be surpassed, though at the same time he was anything but a simpleton or narrow-minded sectarian. He had a very good knowledge of the existing situation, and amidst all his mystical enthusiasm did not fail to reckon with facts. Moreover, very far from limiting his operations to a small community of true believers, he appealed to all the revolutionary elements of his time, and sought to make them serve his purpose.

He failed in his purpose it is true, but his failure was due to circumstances beyond his control. He did what he could with the means at his command, and that an insurrection of unarmed peasants in Thuringia, in 1525, could for a time threaten the very foundations of existing society was owing, in no small degree, to Thomas Münzer—to his extravagant communistic enthusiasm, combined with an iron determination, passionate impetuosity, and statesmanlike sagacity.

V. *Münzer's Early Years.*

Münzer was born at Stolberg, at the foot of the Hartz Mountains, in 1490 or 1493.[1] All information as to his youth and early studies is lacking. It is certain that he pursued a literary course with success, as he obtained a Doctor's degree. He became a priest, but his rebellious nature soon declared itself; for in Halle, where he worked as a teacher, he instituted a league against Ernest II., Archbishop of Magdeburg and Primate of Germany; and when this high functionary died, in 1513, Münzer could not have been more than twenty-three years old. In 1515 we find him Provost in Frohsa, near Aschensleben, apparently in a nunnery, where, however, he did not remain long. After numerous journeyings in all directions, he finally arrived at a convent in Beutitz, near Weissenfels, to which he had been appointed confessor. Even there he seems to have soon lost patience and to have left the place; for in 1520 he became a preacher in Zwickau, with the consent of Luther, whose

---

[1] Seidemann says it was in 1490, but Zimmermann has found it also stated as occurring in 1493.

struggle against Rome was taken up passionately by the young enthusiast and reformer. This residence in Zwickau decided his future career.

At first he was a preacher at the Church of St. Mary, and subsequently at St. Catherine's, in which, as Seidemann says, "he was an interloper." This fact has seemed very unimportant hitherto, but it does not appear so to us, for the Church of St. Catherine was, to a certain extent, the centre of the journeymen clothmakers' quarter. They had set up their own altar there in 1475, and the guild had endowed the benefice with a dwelling-house and a yearly stipend of thirty-five florins for the priest. The weavers held their assemblies in the churchyard. The Church of St. Mary, on the other hand, appears to have been the place of worship for the moneyed classes.

Whether a leaning towards the journeymen clothmakers prompted Münzer to solicit the post of preacher in their church, or whether his opinions were the consequence of that step, cannot now be decided. It is certain that, as their preacher, he came into the closest intercourse with them, learned their views, and was immediately influenced in the highest degree by them. A report [1] of his dealings with the journeymen clothmakers was published in 1523, in which we are told that "the journeymen cling to him, and he has held more meetings with them than with the esteemed priesthood. Thus it appears that Master Thomas has shown preference for the journeymen, chiefly for one named Nicholas Storch, whom he praised highly from the pulpit, and has depicted in glowing colours, exalting him above the priests as if he was the only one who had a knowledge of the Bible and was deeply imbued with its spirit. Master Thomas at the same time extolled himself, declaring that he was eager for the truth and possessed the Holy Spirit. It is in consequence of this unseemly conduct that Storch as well as Thomas has dared to establish conventicles after the manner of the Beghards, who set up a cobbler or a tailor to preach. Hence the choice of Nicholas Storch arose through the in-

[1] To be found in the Appendix of Seidemann's work, *Münzer*, p. 109, *sqq.*

fluence of Master Thomas, who declared his approval of the doctrine that the laity ought to become our prelates and pastors, and be responsible for the faith. Such was the origin of the Storchists, a sect which increased so much among the laity that it was openly said they had formed an association of twelve apostles and seventy-two disciples."

This was a bold step of the communists, and necessarily led to a conflict. So long as Münzer had thundered against the rich priests he had won the applause of the municipal council and the citizens, but now things were to be changed.

The contest shortly assumed the aspect of a religious war between the two churches—the weavers' church, St. Catherine, and that of the moneyed class, St. Mary; as a matter of fact, it was a conflict between their respective preachers, Münzer and Johann Wildenau von Eger (Egranus). A dispute between the two began in the year 1520. Either Wildenau was really the debauched person described by his adversary, or else he did not find sufficient support among the citizens; in any case, he gave way to Münzer in the spring of 1521.

This success made the journeymen clothmakers bolder, but it must also have made the municipal council and the burgesses more uneasy, and in consequence more inclined to use forcible measures. An opportunity for these was soon found in a weavers' riot, in which, however, Münzer was not in the least interested, if we are to credit his letter to Luther of July 9, 1523. Fifty-five journeymen clothmakers were put in prison, while those who were most implicated fled, and Münzer was banished. Nicholas Storch and others left Zwickau also, either at the same time or soon after, as the place had become too hot for them. Going to Wittenberg, where they arrived in December, 1521, they entered into correspondence with Melancthon and Karlstadt, as we have seen. Münzer, on the contrary, turned towards Prague, where he hoped to find associates in the land of the Taborites and a fruitful soil for his ministry.

But Bohemia had become a worse soil for Taborite teachings than even Saxony. The valiant democracy had long since been crushed in decisive battles with the great aristocracy, and the last remnant of the democratic communism which had influenced the Bohemian Brethren had been distorted beyond recognition, the middle-class interest having overpowered the proletariat.

Prague was the last place in the world for a man like Münzer. Even at the time when the power of the Taborites was at its highest point, the town proved at best but a lukewarm friend, while, as a rule, it was a decided enemy to Taboritism. Now it had become a strong pillar of the ruling classes.

Münzer reached Prague in the autumn, and after having posted up an appeal to the Bohemians, began preaching with the help of an interpreter. Scarcely had he become the object of attention, however, when his freedom as a preacher came to an abrupt end. He was placed under police supervision (being accompanied by four guards at a time), and was soon afterwards banished from the town, which he quitted January 25, 1522.

VI. *Münzer in Allstätt.*

From Bohemia Münzer returned to Saxony, staying a short time in Nordhausen, and finally going to Allstätt. Like Zwickau, this place was situated close to a great mining district—the copper, silver, and gold mines of Mansfeld. We may assume that the miners, bold and trained to the use of arms, supported the proletarian tendencies of Allstätt, and that Münzer's agitation was favoured by their proximity. Hunted as he was from place to place, Münzer certainly found Allstätt a spot where he could work under encouraging conditions. He soon gained a firm footing as a preacher, and we may consider it as a sign of his confidence in the future that he married one of the nuns, named Otilie von Gersen, who had quitted the cloister (Easter, 1523).

In the midst of these personal matters, however, Münzer did not forget the object to which he had devoted himself. He arranged an order of Divine Service entirely in German, being the first among the German reformers who did so, and permitted all the books of the Bible to be read aloud and taken as subjects for sermons, and not the New Testament only. The Old Testament, republican as it is in many of its parts, suited the democratic sects better than the New Testament, which is the product of a Roman imperial association.; and this predilection for the Old Testament can be traced from the Taborites down to the Puritans.

The "hypocritical papistic confessional" was abolished, and the Holy Communion administered in both kinds.

The whole of the congregation were to assist in Divine Service, the privileged position of the priest being done away with. "Our adversaries say that we teach the plough-boys from the field to celebrate Mass," says Münzer himself.

We find this remark in the first extant pamphlet of his which treats of the new order of Divine Service just mentioned: *Ordnung und Berechnung des teutschen ampts zu Alstädt durch Toman Münzer*, &c. Alstedt, 1524.

Two other publications deal with the same subject, the *Deutsch Evangelische Messe* and *Deutzsch Kirchenampt*, &c. Alstedt, probably 1524. In addition to these, Münzer published in Allstätt two propagandist pamphlets, the *Protestation* and *Erdichteten Glauben*.

There are also two letters of that time worthy of mention. One (which was to be circulated), dated the 18th of July, 1523: "an earnest epistle to his dear brother at Stolberg to avoid unbecoming tumult," and exhorting the Fraternity to be patient, as they had not yet attained to a right frame of mind. "It is an exceeding folly that so many of the chosen friends of God should suppose that He would haste to do good to Christendom and come instantly to its help, when no one longs for it, or is really striving to become poor in spirit through suffering and steadfastness." The people were still too well off. It must be worse with them before it could be better, for "God ordains that tyrants should rage in order that the elect may be filled with a fervent desire to seek Him. The man who has not believed against belief, hoped against hope, hated contrary to the love of God, knows not that God Himself will show mankind what is necessary for them." In conclusion, he blames the brothers for their luxury and want of firmness. "I understand that you are vainglorious, idle in study, and are shirking your duties. When you drink, you chatter about our cause, but when you are sober you are as frightened as cowards. Mend your lives, dearest brothers, in these things. Shun riotous living ; flee the flesh with all its desires ; be bolder than you have been, and write to me how you have traded with your pound."

The other letter, an exposition of the 19th Psalm, he wrote in May, 1524 ; and it was published in 1525 by Johannes Agricola of Eisleben, in order to prejudice the people against Münzer and prove to them " that all the world may perceive how the devil intends to make himself equal with God." [1] It does not contain any remarkable ideas which had not been expressed under different forms in Münzer's writings at that time.

The exposition of the second chapter of Daniel, which also appeared at Allstätt, will be noticed in due course.

The first of these publications (the *Ordnung des deutschen Amts*) contains all the essential characteristics of the Münzer philosophy ; his mysticism, disdain of the Bible, contempt of learned men, and finally his pantheism and religious tolerance. But he disdained the Bible only in so far as it is not supported by the voice of interior revelation, which could only be won through suffering—through asceticism.

We have already given examples of his mysticism.

The following passage shows his pantheism clearly enough : " He " (man) " must and ought to know that God is in him ; he is not to imagine Him to be a thousand miles away, but that heaven and earth are full, full of God ; that the Father unceasingly forms the Son in us ; and the Holy Spirit, through heart-felt sorrow, interprets in us none other than the Crucified."

Münzer's religious tolerance is evident from the following injunction : " No one ought to be surprised that we celebrate the Mass in German at Allstätt. We are not the only ones who make use of a ritual differing from the Roman ; at Mediolan [Milan] in Lombardy, many have a mode of celebrating Mass different from that in use at Rome. The Croats, Bohemians, Armenians, &c., celebrate Mass in their own

---

[1] *Ausslegung des XIX. Psalms Coeli enarrant durch Thomas Müntzer an syner ersten Jünger ainen.* Wittenberg, 1525.

tongue ; the Russians have quite other genuflexions, and yet they are not devils on that account. Ah! what blind, ignorant beings we are, that we should dare to be Christians in external pomp only, and quarrel with one another over it, like mad, brute creatures." Even the heathen and Turk are not worse than Christians. God will "not despise our retrograde, dull Roman brothers."

These are assuredly great and deep thoughts for that era ; but they are not peculiar to Münzer. We find pantheistic mysticism in earlier times among the brothers and sisters of the Free-Spirit.

Even Münzer's religious tolerance had its forerunners, for we know that it had astonished Æneas Sylvius among the Taborites, and was also advocated by the Bohemian Fraternity. This religious tolerance was, nevertheless, interpreted in a very limited sense. It was impossible that it could extend to every religious question, at an epoch when all the great causes of contentions in the State and in society appeared under the garb of religion. Münzer hated all hypocritical tolerance behind which timidity and lack of character concealed themselves. "There is nothing upon earth," he exclaims, "that has a better shape and mask than imaginary goodness, and this is the reason why all corners of the earth are full of hypocrites, amongst whom none are bold enough to venture to speak the truth. *The godless have no right to live, except in so far as they are permitted to do so by the elect.*" [1] This passage seems a contradiction to the other which shows Münzer's toleration, but the contradiction vanishes when one considers to what this toleration is applied. It applies simply to international relations ; it is the result of his acknowledgment of the sovereignty of the people. Every nation, he declares, may organise its religion as it thinks proper ; it is a matter of indifference to us. What concern is it of ours if the Turks and heathen believe what they please, or if the " retrograde Roman brothers " celebrate the Mass in their own way. We wish for nothing except that we should be allowed to regulate our own affairs according to our necessities. No

---

[1] Exposition of the second mystery of Daniel (*Ausmegung des andern Unterschiedes Daniels*).

animosity therefore ought to exist against foreign nations. Münzer's proclamation of relentless class-war in their own country is not by any means in contradiction to this opinion.

But this statement is taken from one of his later writings ; those hitherto given are of a peaceful character—as peaceful as is possible to a fiery soul. They are propagandist writings, dealing principally with questions of religion and church organisation, and containing no revolutionary threats or appeals. Münzer was not yet a rebel, nor even in open opposition to authority. He had, however, quarrelled with Luther, personal rivalry being apparently the cause.

Perhaps no period proved so distinctly how little Luther's personal initiative gave rise to the Reformation as the years 1522 and 1523.

He not only allowed himself to be driven by circumstances without recognising their inner connection, but he was even outstripped in the career on which he had entered by others. While he remained in quiet contemplation on the Wartburg and translated the Bible, the energetic elements of Witten- berg, led by Karlstadt, and influenced by the Zwickau enthusiasts who happened to be in that town, forestalled the practical results of a conflict with Rome by abolishing celibacy, monastic vows, fasting, the adoration of pictures, private Masses, &c., so that later on Luther had nothing to do but to accept and sanction these reforms ; that is in so far as he did not abrogate them.

One year after these occurrences at Wittenberg, the man who already considered himself to be the leader in the struggle for " Gospel truth," allowed himself to be surpassed by Münzer in one matter—the order of Divine Service in German ; for the latter introduced it into Allstätt and with such success that there was nothing for Luther to do but to copy it. He did not wish, however, to appear before the world as an imitator ; Münzer's innovation must be kept out of sight till his own copy of it was established. There was a simple way of securing this end, of which Münzer himself speaks in his apology (*Schutzrede*) wherein he accuses Luther of having, through jealousy, " induced his Prince not to permit my Service to be printed."

This accusation Luther never answered.

The rivalry of the two reformers did not tend to make their intercourse more friendly.   But the true ground of their differences lay deeper.

Luther had not yet taken any decided action with regard to the democracy, not being certain of the side to which the reins of power would fall.   But his civic instinct was too much developed for him not to see *that communistic sectarians should in no case be permitted to thrive.*

He had recognised this as early as 1522, when the Zwickau enthusiasts had begun to gain influence in Wittenberg ; but as neither Melancthon nor the Prince Elector had taken any decided stand, it became impossible for him to remain any longer on the Wartburg.   Hastening, therefore, to Wittenberg early in 1522, he dispersed these dangerous people, Storch going to South Germany, where he disappeared. Luther sought to silence Karlstadt in the same way as he had silenced Münzer, and caused his writings to be confiscated by the authorities.   In consequence of this, Karlstadt betook himself first to the country near Wittenberg, where he bought a property and wished to live as a peasant among peasants, desiring them no longer to call him doctor, but neighbour Andreas.   We soon find him again, however, actively agitating and organising with great success in Orlamünda, where he regulated the Church community on wholly democratic principles, and made a clean sweep of all Catholic ceremonies.

When Münzer appeared again in Allstätt, Luther, who knew of his connection with the people of Zwickau, could not but look upon him with distrust, which increased in proportion to Münzer's importance.   Moreover, the stings of jealousy contributed greatly to render Luther extremely indignant.   But the man was difficult to get at.   In vain Luther summoned him to Wittenberg for the purpose of examining him ; Münzer declared that he would only appear among a community in which he was in no danger.

Since Münzer would not go to Wittenberg, the Saxon Princes (Frederick, with his brother and co-regent, the Duke John) came to Allstätt, induced to do so by the disturbances which had taken place in the neighbourhood of that town. They not only attempted nothing against Münzer, however, but even permitted him to deliver an oration before them, which was bolder than had ever been made before reigning princes. This speech alone suffices to contradict the gossip about Münzer's cowardice, which is traceable through all the anti-democratic statements concerning his movements.

Far from disavowing his revolutionary views, Münzer in his oration declared revolution necessary, adding that it was best for the Princes to place themselves at its head, otherwise the rebellious people would stride over them. This discourse displayed no very great confidence that the reigning Princes would act upon the appeal, but it nevertheless proves that Münzer did not consider it as wholly impossible to gain at least the Prince Elector to his side.[1]

The Prince Elector indeed showed great indulgence towards these popular movements, as we have seen in the case of the Zwickau enthusiasts. To this circumstance it is possibly due that Münzer was dismissed unhurt by the Regents, though perhaps this may have been also owing to the consideration which Münzer enjoyed in Allstätt. Duke John possessed far more class-feeling than his brother Frederick, and when Münzer published his discourse [2] fell into such a rage that he exiled Nicholas Widemar of Eilenburg, the printer of Münzer's pamphlets, from Saxon territories. In vain Münzer protested against this in a letter dated July 13th. Widemar was prohibited from printing anything whatsoever without the sanction of the authorities at Weimar.

[1] " If you would be a true regent, you must begin your government at the roots." The roots of idolatry must be destroyed. The sword is the means of exterminating the godless. " In order that this should be done honestly and in accordance with the law, it must be done by our dear fathers, the Princes who profess Christ with us. If, however, they do not do it, the sword will be taken from them (Daniel vii.), for they profess Him with their lips and deny Him by their deeds." After this he spoke against hypocritical tolerance, concluding with the appeal : " Only be bold ! He Himself will rule to whom all power is given in heaven and in earth, as St. Matthew says in his last chapter. May He keep and guard you to all eternity. Amen."

[2] *Ausslegung des andern untersyds Danielis des propheten.*

The only effect on Münzer's resolute nature was that he had a new propagandist pamphlet printed in the neighbouring town of Mühlhausen, where a popular movement had just been victorious ; it was entitled, "An unveiling of the False Beliefs of the Faithless World."[1]

On the title-page he calls himself "Münzer with the Hammer," in allusion to a passage in Jeremiah xxiii. 29, in which the Lord says, "Is not My word . . . like a hammer that breaketh the rock in pieces?" "Dear brethren," he continues, further on in the title-page, "let us also make the hole wider, to the end that all the world may see and understand who are those great ones of the earth who talk so blasphemously of God, and have made Him like to a painted dummy."

This shows the whole character of the pamphlet. It begins with a polemic against the clergy, who deceive the poor ; and advises the latter to emancipate themselves from priestly rule. "Ye cannot serve God and Mammon. Whoever taketh honours and goods into possession will be eternally lost to God at the last, as God declares in the 5th Psalm, that their heart 'is very wickedness.' *For this shall the violent and sullen men be thrust from their seats.* The government and authority of godless, foolish men storm and rage against God and His Anointed," yea, some few are now beginning to "put their people into the stocks, into the pillory, and to scourge and flog them, and, worse than all, to threaten all Christians, and to torture and ignominiously put to death their own people as well as strangers, so that, after all the troubles of the elect, God will neither be able nor willing to behold such misery any longer." God puts more on His own people than they are able to bear, and it must and will end very soon.

The Princes are the scourges with which God punishes the world in His wrath. "Therefore they are nothing else than executioners and warders. That is their whole office."

It is not they who are to be feared, but God. But no one need despair of God. With Him nothing is impossible,

---

[1] *Aussgetruckte emplössung des falschen Glaubens der vngetrewen Welt. Thomas Münzer mit Hammer.* Mühlhausen, 1524.

not even the triumph of communistic revolution. "Many people may fancy it to be a very wild delusion. It seems to them impossible that such an undertaking should be set on foot and accomplished as the putting down the godless from the seat of judgment, and exalting them of low degree. Indeed it is a grand belief notwithstanding, and will yet do a great deal of good." The impossible will become possible, "and it may establish a refined society such as was contemplated by Plato the Philosopher (*De Republica*), and Apuleius of the Golden Ass."

The remainder of the pamphlet is only repetition. If we compare it with Münzer's earlier publications in Allstätt, a marked difference is observable. The *Exposition of the second chapter of Daniel* forms a transition stage between the latter and the former. The question now for Münzer was rather how to urge on and incite his associates, than to convince and persuade those who did not share his views. And it is no longer ecclesiastical, but political and social revolution to which he attaches the greater importance. The *Exposition* was an attempt to enlist the Princes in favour of the subject of revolution; but now the Princes are the chief enemy and not the Pope, and the question was no longer of vague conceptions of the "Gospel," but of pure communism "such as was contemplated by Plato the Philosopher," whose work on the State, Münzer must therefore have known.

This change of purport and tone in Münzer's agitation had certainly been brought about in part through his conflict with the Princes, which plainly showed him that he could accomplish his designs only by resisting his rulers. But perhaps in a considerably greater degree the cause for this change probably lies deeper still, being based upon the general change of conditions; for just at that time the first feeble flicker of the Peasant War was showing itself. It was now becoming a question of acting, not merely of preaching.

VII. *The Origin of the Great Peasant War.*

We have already had occasion to speak of the antagonisms which led to the peasant wars, but it now becomes necessary to point out how the position of the German peasantry at the beginning of the sixteenth century differed from that of their predecessors.

The period of the Hussite Wars may be fairly considered as approximately the line of demarcation at which the decline of the peasantry began, not only at different periods and in isolated localities, but universally.

We see the principal cause of this in the growth of capital, and in the autocratic power of princes with which it was allied.

The inevitable consequence of the development of production and trade in commodities was the increase of capital: Capital, and above all commercial capital, requires a strong government to ensure the home market and to make competition in the world's emporiums possible. Hence the capitalists supported the development of autocratic princely power, with its two great tools, bureaucracy and mercenary troops. They assisted the princes in their conflicts with the undisciplined masses not with their persons, but rather with their purses, while the latter on their part sought to maintain their hard-won freedom and rights; the nobles and the Church being ranged on one side and the peasants and petty townsmen on the other. In this struggle it was very much to the advantage of the princes and capitalists that the antagonistic classes themselves thus stood in sharp opposition to each other, and were in a state of embittered conflict.

Capitalists and princes managed to make all these classes more and more dependent on them. Every one sought to throw off his own burden, which thus fell finally with redoubled weight on the lowest ranks of the people; *i.e.*, the city proletarians and the peasants, these forming the great mass of the population. The revolution in prices increased the effect of these burdens.

But while the pressure on the lower classes was augmented, their power of resistance was at the same time diminished. If the position of the peasants themselves was improved in the thirteenth and fourteenth centuries, they did not owe it to the flourishing condition of the towns, particularly the numerous small country towns, in which they found a support against the common enemy. During the fifteenth century, in Germany, the towns fell more and more into dependence on the princes, their independence being finally lost by the end of the century. The comparatively small number which had managed to guard their freedom were mostly large cities, the ruling classes of which had themselves taken the most active interest in the peasant exploitation. These republican cities (and among them Nurenberg was by far the most important) were as much in favour of the princes as Prague had been during the Hussite Wars; but the small town-bourgeois had been the backbone of democracy, and in proportion as these lost their independence the democratic parties lost their strength also.

But the modification of town life made the position of the peasants worse in yet another way during the fifteenth century. Till the fourteenth century, the towns had been the places of refuge which stood open to the peasantry. This compelled the landowners, if they did not wish to lose their labourers, to attach the peasants to themselves; when possible by force, but where force would have failed by kind treatment.

All this was now changed. In the fifteenth century the closing of the guilds against the far too great influx of labourers became more general. This led to the oppression not only of the unorganised town proletariat, but of the peasantry likewise. The path to prosperity in the towns being thus closed to them, it is not surprising that antagonisms should spring up between the petty citizens and the towns and the peasantry, sometimes indeed bridged over by alliances against their common enemies—the Church, the nobles, princes, capitalists—alliances which, however, made their friendship even then a very cool one.

The more the towns ceased to be places of refuge for the peasantry, the less necessity there was for the landowners to be careful of them, for they felt they had a hold on them, since they had nothing to gain in the towns and were not completely destitute in the country. The towns were becoming more and more closed even to the proletarians. A country proletariat now came into existence, which was increased by the diminution and dispersion of the feudal retainers, a natural consequence of the advance into the country of the production of commodities, and the thirst for gold connected with it. The reigning princes promoted this advance wherever they could do so, in order to lessen the independence of the nobles, which was a danger to them.

But the development of production in commodities gave also a greater value to the land ; on the one side prompting the country communes to be exclusive, and on the other side causing the landowners to lay claim to and appropriate the common property of the commune as their own private possession.

Let us now consider what all this means. The places of refuge for landless people became closed ; at the same time the number of landless people was increased by the natural growth of the population, by the dispersion of the retainers of the nobility, and by the ever-growing burden on the peasantry through State taxation, demands of landlords and the interest of usurers. Hence we cannot wonder that the country proletariat rapidly augmented.

Moreover, it was chiefly the ragged proletariat from which sprang beggars and swindlers, as well as robbers and soldiers.

In the fourteenth century the mercenaries had still been to a large extent the younger sons of peasants, seeking for adventure and booty, who returned to their peasant condition after a few years of military service ; they shared the class-interests of their kin, and were therefore not available for military service against the peasantry—at least in their own country. After their return from war, they augmented the number of peasants capable of bearing arms. In the fifteenth century the ragged proletariat became more and more prominent among the soldiery ; the unclassed, so to speak, who no longer recognised any class-interests, but went through thick and thin for their masters, and were everything to every one—*so long as they were paid.*

The military capacity for resistance on the part of the

peasants must have been diminished by this mercenary spirit and lack of class-feeling, and even to a greater degree by the development which had taken place in the art of war. We have already seen how the Taborites revolutionised this art, and it developed still further in the line adopted by them, for it became increasingly important to exercise the population in the use of weapons, and to train bodies of men in skilful evolutions, in discipline, and in concerted and prompt simultaneous operations of the separate divisions of the army. These new tactics had made democracy invincible in the hands of the Taborites, and now determined the military superiority of the opponents of democracy. The *regular soldier* was alone in a position to practise these tactics, for the peasants and petty townsmen had no time at their disposal during the insurrections occurring in the second half of the fifteenth and in the sixteenth centuries, in which to train a standing army in their midst, at all comparable with that of the Taborites. That side therefore which could *pay* the regular soldier secured the victory.

The application of *gunpowder* to military purposes, which had made rapid strides since the Hussite Wars, operated in a similar way. Gunpowder has been called a democratic invention, because it put an end to knighthood ; but we cannot discover anything " democratic " in the use made of this invention. The influence of gunpowder in breaking the power of the lower nobility is often very much over-estimated, for it must not be forgotten that it helped quite as much to break up the resistance of the *peasant troops* as that of the *knightly armies.* The economic and military bankruptcy of the lower nobility was determined before the use of fire-arms had begun to be of essential importance in the art of war. The development of fire-arms is the last link in that chain, which was forged in the sixteenth century ; after that period the one thing most necessary for carrying on war was money, money—and once again, money ! To purchase fire-arms for the exigencies of war and to employ them for that purpose was the privilege of the wealthy possessors of power—*i.e.*, the great towns and the princes. They helped to cast down knighthood, not in order to favour the peasants and petty townsmen, but to afford advantages to capitalists and to uphold princely dominance.

The cost of the military overthrow of the nobles fell upon the peasantry. In the fourteenth century the noble had been hard pressed from above and from below at the same time ; from above by the princes (in alliance with the middle class); from below by the peasants. Long did he seek to defend himself from both ; but finally he submitted to the princes, who henceforth undertook the task of keeping his peasants down. He sold his independence in order to establish his power over his people more firmly for the future.

This change in affairs was not carried out everywhere in the same way or at the same time. In North Germany, and particularly in the eastern portion of it, it was brought about much later ; but in South and Central Germany the peasant felt its oppressive effects as early as the fifteenth century, and, certainly, the nearer we approach to the sixteenth century the more down-trodden he became. At the beginning of that era his position had become unbearable, according to the apprehension of those times, though it differed in many respects advantageously from that of the working classes of town and country in the present day.

The increase of rents payable in labour, kind, or money, the greater dependence on the lords of the soil, the confiscation of peasant commune property in field and wood in favour of the landlords (the confiscation of the peasant's *private* property took place a little later) could not of course be carried out without violent opposition from the despoiled people. During the fifteenth century one popular insurrection followed another, and they became more frequent and more embittered the further the century advanced.

Then came the Reformation movement, which convulsed the whole nation, and united, at least temporarily, all the local antagonisms into one national class-opposition which extended over almost the whole kingdom. Now also the various peasant agitations joined in one single great movement to throw off the yoke which was crushing them to the ground—the last and most powerful of the great strainings of every nerve among the lower classes on the European continent which had taken place for centuries.

Putting England out of the question, we do not find a similarly grand movement till 1789 in France, where it took place under totally different and more favourable conditions. Irresistible as was the latter revolution, that of 1525 carried the germs of death deep within it from the very first.

With the peasantry other classes rose in arms. Society is much too complicated to make it possible for one class alone to create a great revolutionary disturbance. Nevertheless it is always *one* class to whose share the vanguard falls ; in the present day it is the proletariat ; in 1789 it was the petty citizens ; in 1525 the peasantry.

The allies of the latter we know already ; in 1525 the same classes fought together which had assembled under the banner of the Taborites. Now, as then, a portion of the bankrupt lower nobility took their places by the side of the rebels, chiefly in prominent positions as leaders ; in which position some became heroes through their loyal adherence to their convictions (such as Florian Geyer), while others proved traitors (like Götz von Berlichingen). A large portion also of the town population joined the peasantry, especially in the small towns, the proletariat always being in the front rank. At the beginning of the sixteenth century, the condition of German towns differed from that of the Bohemian in the beginning of the fifteenth. The cities were far more intellectually advanced, but politically they had lost much of their independence, and the proletariat was still the only trusty ally of the peasants. The trade-masters and even the trade-journeymen had been estranged from them. In 1525, therefore, the brunt of the struggle lay more on the peasantry than was the case in the Hussite Wars. The towns interfered but coldly, and the movement found no such support as was offered by Tabor a hundred years before in Bohemia. The cities actively expressed their sympathy for the peasantry, not in military but in intellectual relations by influencing their programme.

On the other hand, the insurgents of 1525 found allies

which the Taborites did not have—namely, the *miners*. These men lived and worked together in great numbers, possessed arms and knew how to make use of them. They were trained in warlike evolutions, and accustomed to be kept under discipline. From a military point of view they stood at a far higher level than all the other ranks of the neighbouring classes of their day, and wherever they entered into any conflict with energy the insurrection remained, in a military sense, invincible.

During the course of the year 1524 every one who was in close touch with the peasants saw clearly that matters must come to a violent crisis, and to a man like Münzer this could not remain a secret. Every peasant had had the same experience as he ; with shouts of joy they had hailed Luther, who had allowed himself to be borne along on the tide of popularity, stirring up the expectation of all classes. But when the common enemy appeared to be vanquished ; when the Pope and his protector, the Emperor, had shown their own impotence in Worms, 1521 ; when the old authority was overturned, and the question was how to bring about the new order of things ; when class-antagonisms showed themselves more strongly ; when it became necessary to decide the question who should appropriate the fruits of Church reform, the lower or the higher classes—then Luther could come to no decision so long as he was not compelled to do so. From the very first the only determined stand he took was against the communistic enthusiasts ; but he resisted every attempt of the lower classes to derive material benefit from the Reformation, by favouring each step taken by the Princes in this direction. *They* were to become the owners of the Church property, not the peasants. " It is not our business to attack the monasteries," he writes, " but to draw hearts away from them. When, then, churches and monasteries are lying deserted, let the reigning princes do with them what they please." [1]

In 1524 it became more and more evident that the lower classes had nothing to expect from Luther's Reformation.

[1] Luther's complete works. Leipzig, 1729. Vol. xix. p. 240. The above was probably written towards the end of July, 1524.

Only through their own power and an armed force would they be able to free themselves from the yoke which was weighing so heavily on their shoulders.

VIII. *Münzer's Preparations for the Insurrection.*

As soon as it became clear that nothing remained to the lower classes but a resort to arms against all exploiters, revolutionary as well as reactionary, no one was more zealous in preparing for the revolt than Münzer, whose circumspection, energy, and intrepidity, made him the central figure in the revolutionary movement of the exploited classes in Thuringia, and gave him an extensive influence far beyond the borders of that province.

The activity of the man can be measured by the accusations against him which poured into the ears of the reigning Princes of Saxony. For example, a certain Friedrich Witzleben complained that his dependents in Wendelstein, Wollmerstadt, and Rosleben had sent delegates to Münzer, asking his permission for the formation of a league against their master, on the ground that he had prevented their attending the Münzer form of Divine worship. Münzer gave his consent, and very probably showed them how to organise themselves. He managed the organisation of the numerous and warlike Mansfeld miners, and sent a letter to the subjects of Duke George of Saxony at Sangershausen, in which he urged them to stand fast to the Gospel (*i.e.*, by the democratic cause), and to resist its enemies.

Münzer also addressed himself to the Orlamünders, with a view to forming an alliance with Karlstadt, who occupied a position similar to his own at Allstätt. But Karlstadt and his followers belonged to a party who deprecated all violent measures. In a reply, written by the people of Orlamünda " to those at Allstätt," stating how " Christians should fight " (printed at Wittenberg, 1524), Karlstadt says: " We will not have recourse to swords and spears ; rather should we be armed against the enemy with the armour of faith. You write that we should join you, and make an alliance with you. Were we to do so, we should no longer be free Christians, but

dependent on men.   Such an act would raise a cry of
' Death to the Gospel ! ' and the tyrants would exult and say,
' These fellows boast of being God's elect, yet form leagues
among themselves, as if God were not strong enough to
defend them ! ' "

While this letter was of no avail to Karlstadt, it really
amounted to a denunciation of Münzer, whom Luther put in
the same category as the Orlamünd agitator.

The most serious incident, however, was the betrayal to the
Princes by Nicol Rugkert of a secret league in Allstätt,
instituted by the agitator.   Melancthon informs us that
" Münzer kept a register of all who had bound themselves to
him, and had sworn to punish unchristian Princes and to
establish a Christian government."   The league had adherents
outside of Allstätt ; for example, in the Mansfeld valley,
Sangerhausen, and even in Zwickau.   In his *Confession*,
Münzer sets forth the aim of the organisation to be : " An
alliance against those who persecute the Gospel."   In regard
to what was to be understood by " the Gospel," he asserts :
" It is an article of our creed, and one which we wish to
realise, that all things are in common [*omnia sunt communia*],
and should be distributed as occasion requires, according to
the several necessities of all.   Any prince, count, or baron
who, after being earnestly reminded of this truth, shall be
unwilling to accept it, is to be beheaded or hanged."

We do not know to what extent the Saxon Princes were
acquainted with the aims of the league at that time ; but
what they did learn was enough, in conjunction with other
indictments, to make them summon the dangerous instigator
to Weimar ; a step to which Luther's animosity to Münzer
was an additional incentive.

Münzer was fearless enough to obey the summons, and go
to Weimar on the 1st of August.   Duke John submitted him
to an examination, from which, however, he was dismissed
unharmed, to await the Duke's final decision.

But Münzer did not remain for this, as his position in
Allstätt had already become untenable.   The Princes were
threatening the little town with chastisement, and now the
Council declared against the agitator, who fled in the night of

the 7th-8th of August. He tells us in his *Apology* that: "When I returned home from the interrogation in Weimar, I intended to preach the earnest Word of God ; but the Councilmen wanted to deliver me over to the arch-enemy of the gospel ; upon perceiving which my longer stay became impossible. I shook the dust from off my feet, for I saw with my own eyes that they esteemed their oath and allegiance far more highly than they did God's Word."

The weak renegade Melancthon endeavours here as elsewhere, to cast the odium of cowardice on Münzer. "Thomas' high spirit," he says, " forsook him at that time ; he ran away and hid himself for six months."

How small a part cowardice had in Münzer's flight from Allstätt, and how little disposed he was to hide himself, are shown by the fact that he went from Allstätt direct to a new theatre of war, Mühlhausen, where we find him as early as the 15th of August. Moreover Melancthon's statement cannot have been merely an error ; for in 1525 he must have had a lively remembrance of the fright which seized Luther and his friends in 1524, when they learned that Münzer had gone to Mühlhausen.

Luther at once wrote to his *confrères* in that town, urging Münzer's banishment, and asking the Council to summon the impostor and force him to declare who had authorised him to preach. " If he says that God and His Spirit have sent him, like the Apostles, *then make him prove it with signs and wonders ;* but forbid his preaching, for when God would change the natural order of things, He signifies it by all manner of miracles." [1]

Luther had good grounds for energetically combating the communistic agitator. Not only were the signs cf the impending insurrection beginning to multiply, but Münzer was more dangerous in Mühlhausen than in Allstätt, as it was a larger town, containing about 6000 inhabitants and controlling a district of nearly 220 square kilomètres.[2] Handicrafts and trade were in a very flourishing condition ; woolweaving and cloth manufacture being in an advanced stage of development. " A very large quantity of cloth was woven in

<hr>

[1] Luther's Complete Works, xix. p. 236.   [2] Merx, p. 48.

Mühlhausen, a profitable trade being carried on with it in Russia, and in other countries in that part of the world" (Galletti, *Geschichte Thuringens*, p. 491). The town was not only rich and powerful, but also independent of the Saxon Princes, as it was one of the few free cities still remaining in Thuringia; and if it were to fall into the hands of the communist enthusiasts, they would have a *point d'appui* which would make them rather dangerous.

Internal affairs were not unfavourable to a popular insurrection in the town, where the great extension of woollen manufacture for export must have produced a fertile soil for rebellious and communistic ideas. In addition to this, Mühlhausen was controlled by " an oppressive, aristocratic government. This free imperial city did not contain more than ninety-six really free burgesses, who formed the Council, and these filled its vacancies exclusively from the patrician class." [1]

Rebellious sentiments in Mühlhausen were not limited to the urban proletarians, the suburban population and the peasants of the surrounding districts dependent on the town: the guild craftsmen were also similarly disposed, although elsewhere they belonged to the privileged classes. It is not surprising, therefore, that the Reformation movement led to a series of violent uprisings among the citizens against the patrician government, in which the populace was led by Heinrich Pfeiffer, a monk who, like so many others of that period, had renounced his vows. Pfeiffer was *par excellence* the leader of the opposition faction among the well-to-do citizens, such as the guild-craftsmen and merchants, so far as the latter did not belong to the patricians; the latter, however, were too strong to allow Pfeiffer to ignore the peasants and proletarians. He therefore addressed himself to these classes, and urged them to unite in a struggle against the town aristocracy.

Moreover Pfeiffer had another ally in the Saxon Princes, who had long craved the possession of the powerful imperial

---

[1] Zimmermann, *Bauernkrieg*, i. p. 191. Zimmermann availed himself of important researches among the State Archives at Mühlhausen.

city, and whose purpose seemed to be served by its internal commotion.[1]

The rebellion was encouraged at its outset by Duke John of Saxony, although he afterwards had Pfeiffer executed as a rebel when he became inconvenient.

In spite of all these opponents, the Council must have had a strong following in the town, for the democrats did not achieve a lasting success. Pfeiffer and his partisans won their first victory in 1523, of which the spoils fell to the well-to-do citizens, who alone received a share in the municipal government, while the proletarians and petty craftsmen in the suburbs, and especially the peasants, came off empty-handed.

We are now led to inquire if this unequal distribution of the fruits of victory gave rise to a change in the disposition of the lower classes. One thing is certain ; the Town Council soon succeeded in banishing Pfeiffer, and Duke John in vain interceded for his return. Nevertheless before long we find him back in Mühlhausen in hot conflict with the Council, fortune smiling first on the one side, then on the other. In the midst of this struggle Münzer arrived in Mühlhausen. The Council was at that time too feeble to comply with Luther's demands for a citation of the agitator, however willing it might have been to do so. " The honourable Council were as little pleased with Münzer as with Pfeiffer, but the populace retained him by force ; for he and his confederate Pfeiffer had just incited and led a rebellion against the others." [2]

Just at this time we find Pfeiffer's party executing a change of front to the left. They raised claims for the peasants and suburban population as well, and carried the day August 27, 1524. It is impossible to determine how far, if at all, Münzer influenced this change.

Another rupture like that of the year 1523, now began to make its appearance among the victors. In 1523 it was the peasants and suburban population who were discontented ; now the burgesses, craftsmen, and tradesmen became alarmed at the peasants and proletarians, who, since Münzer's arrival,

[1] Johann Becherer, *Newe Thuringische Chronica*, Mühlhausen, 1601, p. 473.

[2] Compare Zimmermann, *op. cit.* i. p. 194.

had certainly lost none of their confidence. The burgesses sided with the Council, and as early as September 25th Pfeiffer and Münzer suffered defeat, Münzer being banished, and soon after, Pfeiffer also.

Münzer betook himself to South Germany, like so many others of political prominence in Saxony, *e.g.*, Karlstadt, whom Luther had prevailed upon his sovereign to banish, because he had been very badly received by the Orlamünders in a tour of agitation against that reformer. Münzer's retreat, however, did not imply even a temporary halt in the movement, but merely the search for a new field of activity. He must have been well informed of the events preparing in South Germany ; for Germany (at least South and Central Germany) was at that time covered with a network of secret revolutionary societies, which were in constant intercommunication. The communistic sects in particular supplied a large number of itinerant agitators who kept the different leagues in touch with each other. From the very first establishment of Waldenses, the confidential agents of the communists (" Apostles," " poor priests," or whatever name they might have borne) were as a rule, and with only short interruptions, continually wandering hither and thither. The development of migratory habits among the craftsmen was an additional instrument in bringing about a closer union between these classes of society, as it was for every other class. " All migrating craftsmen belonging to the association, masters as well as journeymen, became ' apostles.' " [1]

Hence, when Münzer repaired to South Germany, he must have been well informed of the condition of things, and have seen that an insurrection was everywhere imminent. At all events, he knew that at the end of August the peasants in Stühlingen had actually revolted, and that the insurrection had rapidly spread to the Swiss frontier. This was sufficient to induce him to go thither as soon as all scope for his activity in Saxony had ceased, beyond all hope of recovery so long as the existing conditions of government continued in that country.

[1] C. A. Cornelius, *Geschichte des Münsterschen Aufruhres.* Leipzig, 1860, p. 41.

He remained but a short time in Nurenberg, not (as many believe) to kindle a revolt (and he would have found partisans enough in that ancient centre of Beghardism), but only to have a tract secretly printed. Affairs in that town did not seem ripe for an insurrection.

His stay in Nurenberg is best explained by Münzer himself in a letter to Christoph N., in Eisleben.[1] The following passage shows the sad state of his circumstances at that time : " If you can," he says, "help me towards my living expenses. But if this angers you, I will not have a farthing." It is evident, therefore, that Münzer had not grown rich in Allstätt and Mühlhausen.

The result of his sojourn in Nurenberg is briefly given by an ancient chronicler named Johann Müllner : " A book-printer of Nurenberg made bold to print a tract by Thomas Münzer ; but the Council seized all the copies, and imprisoned the journeyman, who had acted without the knowledge of his master."

The most high and wise Council, however, by no means succeeded in getting possession of all the copies. Not only was the work circulated before the peasant rebellion, but, in spite of the war to the knife carried on against all insurrectionary writings after that rebellion, copies of this work have been preserved to this day. It is the most vehement and revolutionary of all Münzer's writings, and is entitled : *Hoch verursachte Schutzrede*, or " Apology."[2] With his usual scorn for the prevalent servility of the theologians, he dedicates it to " The Most High First Born Prince and Almighty Lord, Jesus Christ, the gracious King of all kings, the brave Leader of all believers, my most merciful Sovereign and faithful Protector ; and to his afflicted Bride, Suffering Christendom."

After a series of attacks on Luther (*Dr. Ludibrii*), he goes on to say that he has summoned the Princes of Christendom

---

[1] Transcribed in Luther's Complete Works among his writings against Münzer and the rebellious peasants (xix. p. 245).

[2] *Hoch verursachte Schutzrede und antwort wider des Gaistlose Sanfft lebende Fleysch zu Wittemberg, welches mit verklarter weysse durch den Diepstal der heiligen Schrift die erbermdliche Christenheit also guntz jämmerlich besudelt hat.* Thomas Müntzer. Alstedter.

to seize the sword in defence of the Gospel ; appealing at the same time to the Bible in justification of his summons. " Nevertheless there comes an eavesdropping gossip—ah ! the sly fellow !—and says that I wished to raise a rebellion, as he had discovered from my missive to the miners. He accuses me of this, but conceals another most discreet matter ; to wit that I proved to the ruling powers that a whole province had the sword within their grasp, as well as the key for the unlocking, and showed from Daniel vii., Rev. vi., and Rom. xiii. 1–8, that the rulers are not masters, but servants of the sword. They should not act as pleaseth them (Deut. xvii.), but do righteously. It is the greatest abomination on earth that no one will relieve the necessities of the poor. . . . Look ye ! Our sovereign and rulers are at the bottom of all usury, thievery, and robbery ; they take all created things into possession. The fish in the water, birds in the air, the products of the soil—all must be theirs (Isaiah v.). Moreover, they proclaim God's command among the poor, and say : God hath ordained thou shalt not steal ; but themselves do not follow it. Wherefore they oppress the poor husbandmen and craftsmen, and fleece and flay all who are in like condition (Micah iii.). If one of these poor fellows breaks the least jot or tittle of the law, he must hang for it. To all this Dr. Liar (Luther) says : ' Amen.' The rulers themselves make the poor man their enemy by their deeds. If they will not abolish the cause of tumult, how can things be well for any length of time ? Because I say this, it follows that I must be rebellious. Verily !" The remainder of the work consists of an exceedingly bitter polemic against Luther.

After Münzer had delivered this Parthian shot at his opponent, he left Nurenberg, and went to the Swiss frontier, where he passed the winter. The exact place of his sojourn is unknown. According to Cochläus, he extended his journeyings at that time as far as Halle in Tyrol, a mining district which subsequently became the centre of Anabaptism. Many ascribe to his authorship the celebrated Twelve Articles, in which the rebel peasants formulated their demands ; while others even assert that he was the cause of the South German insurrection. The last two statements are certainly without foundation, and that of Cochläus is probably equally so.

The reference in Münzer's *Confession* to his stay on the Swiss frontier is limited to the following passage, which probably contains all the essential particulars of his activity during that period of his career : " At Klettgau and Hegau I proposed certain Articles on the proper form of government ; others presented a modified form of these. They would willingly have received me as one of themselves, but, though grateful to them, I declined. I did not incite the revolt in those places, for it was already in progress. Oekolampadius and Hugowaldus requested me to preach to the people there, and I finally complied."

Münzer, therefore, was not the author of the Twelve Articles, though he had an influence in their production. He looked upon his stay as only temporary ; yet he did not remain inactive but continued to agitate ;—" preached to the people," as he says, or, as Bullinger expresses it : " Sowed his poisonous seed of the peasant insurrection."

While on the Swiss frontier, he had an opportunity of meeting with the leaders of the Swiss Anabaptists ; but though his relations with these men are important to that sect, they afford but little insight into the character of the Thuringian communist and his work. An account of these relations would demand an inquiry into the beginnings of the Anabaptist order. In order, therefore, to avoid undue interruption in the course of this description, we will not pursue this point further at present, but will return to it in the next chapter.

IX. *The Peasant War.*

In the beginning of the year 1525, perhaps as early as January, Münzer left Swabia to return to Thuringia. He had a motive for doing so, for he knew that the outbreak of the movement was imminent.

Like the uprising of the peasants in England in 1381, which broke out simultaneously at all points, the insurrection in Germany was arranged to take place in all parts on the same day, the 2nd of April ; but it occurred at an earlier date in some localities, owing either to the impatience of the participants, or to force of circumstances. Hence we cannot doubt that the revolt was organised and directed by a widely ramified conspiracy.

The age in which guild secrets could be kept for centuries was also peculiarly favourable to hidden leagues. Not only were sectarian doctrines propagated by means of secret associations, but political deeds were often effected in like manner both in town and country. Many of these associations acquired great importance, such as the *Bundschuh* (peasants of the shoe) and the *Arme Konrad* (poor comrade), which were the inaugurators of the Peasant War.

Hence in spite of portents in various places as early as the autumn of 1524, and the zealous preparations for an insurrection during the winter, the ruling classes were taken by surprise ; so that at the outset the insurgents almost everywhere gained the advantage.

On his way from Swabia, Münzer fell in with bodies of rebels, and on one occasion was within a hair's-breadth of coming utterly to grief, being taken prisoner in the Fulda district with a mob of malcontents. On the 22nd of February the receiver of taxes in Allstätt, Hans Jeyss, who was always well informed of Münzer's movements, wrote to Spalatin : " I add for your information that Thomas Münzer has been at Fulda, where he was thrown into prison. The Abbot said to the innkeeper at Schwartzburg, that had he known it was Thomas Münzer, he would not have let him go free."

Shortly after this (March 12th) we again find Münzer in Mühlhausen, where Pfeiffer had previously made his appearance (December). On March 17th, a successful revolt made them masters of the town ; being nearly the same day and month in which, more than three hundred years afterwards, the populace in 1848 seized Berlin, and the proletariat gained possession of Paris. Hans Jeyss wrote about the affair to Spalatin, giving remarkable prominence to the part played by Pfeiffer, and ignoring Münzer, but showing an accurate appreciation of the elements by which the fight was won. I must tell you," he says, " of the dreadful discord and tumult caused for a whole day in Mühlhausen by a preacher named Pfeiffer. To sum up, Lord *Omnes*" (the populace) "wrested the government from the Council, which can neither rule, punish, write, nor act in any way against the popular will.

"After Pfeiffer and Münzer had been banished, and the latter had visited and left Nurenberg, Pfeiffer returned to Mühlhausen, where he busied himself in the neighbouring villages by propagating his views. He complained to the peasants that he had been driven from the town only because he had preached the truth and had wished to deliver the people from the yoke of the Council and ruling authorities, and from all oppression. At his behest the peasants of these villages armed themselves and advanced in a body to the suburb of the town, where he delivered a revolutionary address. As soon as it came to the ears of the Council that Pfeiffer was trying to force his way into Mühlhausen, they made ready for resistance, called their forces together, and marched out against him. Just as the fight was about to begin, the burgesses, who should have remained true to the Council, turned against it, and played a villainously treacherous part. Seeing that the populace had fallen away from the Council, the leader of the municipal forces endeavoured to put a stop to the uproar, and, after great labour and trouble, succeeded in doing so; not, however, until the Council had been forced to allow Pfeiffer and Münzer to continue their preaching, and a promise had been exacted that nothing should be done without the consent and knowledge of the commune. Thus all power was taken from the Council, and very strange things went on in Mühlhausen."

Very strange things in truth : *A communistic community was established in the town.*

"This was the beginning of the new Christian government," writes Melancthon. "They afterwards drove out the monks, and appropriated all the property of the Church. The Knights of St. John possessed a manor at that place, with a large rental ; Thomas seized this manor . . . He taught that all things should be in common, as is written in the Acts of the Apostles, and by this means made the people so wanton

that they would no longer work. When one of them wanted
corn or cloth, he went to some rich man (to whomsoever it
pleased him) and demanded it as a Christian right, on the
ground that Christ had proclaimed that all things should
be shared with the needy. If any wealthy person proved
unwilling to give what was demanded of him, it was taken
by force ; and this happened in many cases. Moreover, those
who lived with Thomas in the manor house of the Hospitallers acted in like manner."

Becherer tells us that : " In the government Münzer was
dictator, and managed everything as it pleased him. . . . In
particular, he made the community of goods compulsory ;
from which it resulted that people left their craft-work and
daily labour, believing that before they had consumed the
possessions of the princes and barons, the churches and
monasteries, God would further provide. This mode of life
was carried on by Münzer for some months." [1]

We need not inquire into the bad effects said to have been
produced by the communistic regimen on trade and production, as they have no basis in fact. This indeed is shown
by the circumstance that the government of the revolutionary
commune at Mühlhausen did not last more than two months;
almost exactly the duration of the Paris Commune of 1871,
which began March 18th and ended May 28th, while that
of Mühlhausen continued from March 17th to May 25th.
Indeed Münzer left Mühlhausen before May 12th. And in
these few weeks communism is supposed to have exercised a
sensible influence on production, in the midst of the most
dreadful exigencies of a war which enlisted the services of
every labourer capable of bearing arms !

Melancthon, it is true, tells us that communism lasted a
year in Mühlhausen ! Let it be imagined that in the autumn
of 1871, a modern author should have written a history of
the Paris Commune, in which he stated that it lasted a year !
It is difficult to say which is the more surprising, the cool
audacity of the " mild and timid " Melancthon, or the cre-
dulity of his public.

And it is from such " contemporaneous sources " that most

[1] Becherer, *op. cit.*, p. 479.

of the histories of communistic movements have been compiled !

Meanwhile the falsifications can easily be discovered with the exercise of a little caution. Much more confusion, however, has been created by the completely inaccurate accounts of the part played by Münzer in Mühlhausen. Becherer and Melancthon represent him as a dictator whose will was law, and Luther occasionally expresses himself in a similar way. The latter writes in one of his letters : "*Müntzer Mulhusi Rex et Imperator est.*"

As a matter of fact Münzer's position was an extremely disagreeable one. He had conquered not by the strength of his adherents, but by a compromise with Pfeiffer's party, who were not communistic, but outspokenly bourgeois in feeling. Moreover, he did not mount to the head of the government, but remained simply a preacher, and even as such acquired no decisive influence. The policy of the town was entirely out of harmony with his own, and in all important matters he met with opposition from Pfeiffer, who was backed up by the majority.

Mühlhausen was no Tabor ; the latter may be designated as a communistic colony and a new institution, to which communists flocked for the purpose of building up an " exclusive people." Circumstances were quite different in the ancient imperial town of Mühlhausen, where the communists found their chief supporters in the proletariat, together with some circles of the petty, independent, suburban craftsmen and the peasants of the neighbourhood. These strata of the population were at that time far too weak to force their will upon the middle class. Through a fortuitous combination of favourable circumstances, and a clever and energetic use of them for their own ends, the communists succeeded in playing a decisive part between the two contending parties, much resembling that of the needle on the balance ; but toleration was all that they were able to obtain from those who, by their help, had been placed in power. We must not imagine that the whole town of Mühlhausen was organised on the communistic basis. At all events, the only gain to the Brethren was the permission to transform their secret organisation into an open one, and to establish a "commune" within the town's domain, of which the seat was probably the manor of the Hospitallers.

We may judge of the small number of Münzer's adherents in Mühlhausen from the fact that when he marched away to help the peasants, he was accompanied by only three hundred men.

It is easy to believe Melancthon's statement that the Münzer commune, "occupying the manor of the Hospitallers," derived its revenues during the few weeks of its existence, not merely from the labour of its members, but also, and chiefly, from the spoils obtained from churches, monasteries, and castles ; for we know that the Taborites maintained themselves in a similar way. In those days the goods of the Church were *res nullius*—no one's property— which he might seize "who had the power," chief among such being the princes, while here and there, perhaps, a few poor devils might share in the plunder.

We have already pointed out that Münzer and Pfeiffer were opposed on fundamental principles. But from this antagonism others arose which were of a tactical nature.

As a petty townsman of pre-capitalistic times, Pfeiffer considered himself the representative of local interests only ; Münzer, like the communists of his time in general, was, on the contrary, cosmopolitan in feeling. Pfeiffer looked upon the insurrection in Mühlhausen as a purely local event, while for Münzer it was a link in the great chain of revolutionary uprisings, which, by co-operating, were to give the finishing stroke to tyranny and spoliation. That which Tabor had previously been for Bohemia, the fortified town of Mühlhausen was now to become for Thuringia, namely, the *point d'appui* of the whole rebellion, and in closest touch with the revolts in Franconia and Swabia.

Pfeiffer (and when we speak of Pfeiffer and Münzer we do not refer to the two individuals alone, but to the parties as well, of which they were the most prominent representatives) was, it is true, present in a few predatory expeditions into the neighbouring purely Catholic districts, but he did not contemplate anything beyond a petty town quarrel. Münzer, on the other hand, was well aware that victory in Mühlhausen did not signify the close of the revolutionary struggle, but was only a preliminary to the decisive battle. It behoved him, therefore, to prepare and organise the masses, train them in the use of arms, and combine the revolts in different districts into a common movement.

Perhaps nowhere in Germany were the peasants so unused to arms, so lacking in military capacity, and so wholly unprepared for war as in Thuringia. Time therefore was needed to supply them with weapons and to train them in their use.

Münzer did all he could. He was specially solicitous with regard to heavy artillery, and had cannon cast in the monastery of the Barefooted Friars. The value he placed upon these guns—perhaps more as instruments of moral suasion than as weapons of war—is seen from the fact that he sent information concerning them as far as Swabia ; and this fact alone shows how eager he was for an alliance with the South German insurgents.

He devoted himself with still greater energy to stirring up and combining the revolutionists in Thuringia ; displaying a feverish anxiety in speech and writing, and sending letters of exhortation and encouragement in all directions.

The mine-labourers seemed of more importance to him than the untrustworthy Mühlhauseners and badly armed peasants. These miners formed the most warlike and defiant part of Saxony's population, and in consequence Münzer directed his attention to them. He formed an alliance with those of the Erzgebirge Mountains, after striving first of all to rouse an insurrection among his nearest mining neighbours, the Mansfelders ; his friendliness with them ever since his Allstätt days giving him good cause to hope for their aid.

A letter written by him at that time to his confederates in Mansfeld, Balthasar, Barthel, &c., for the purpose of starting the agitation among the miners, is reproduced in Luther's works as one of " three abominable, revolutionary writings by Thomas Münzer " (xix. p. 289 *sqq.*). It reads : " Before all things, the pure fear of God. Dear brethren, how long will you sleep ? How long will it be ere you confess why God of His good will has to all appearance abandoned you ? It is high time. Hold back your brethren from mocking at godly testimony, else must you all perish. Germany, France, Italy, are all aroused. Our masters wish to make a game of it ; but the villains cannot escape their fate. During Easter week three churches were destroyed in Fulda. In Kletgau, Hegau, and Schwatzwald the peasants are up, three thousand strong, and their numbers are growing daily. I am anxious lest the foolish fellows should agree to a treacherous compact, for they do not yet perceive the mischief. Where there are only two of you who trust in God and seek His name and honour, they shall not be afraid of a hundred thousand. But forward, forward, forward ! It is high time. Let this letter be given to the mine-associates. My printer will come in a few days. I have received the missive, but cannot do more at present. I had wished to instruct the brothers myself, that their hearts might grow much larger than the castles and armour of all the godless rascals on earth. Forward, forward, forward while the fire is hot ! Let your swords be ever warm with blood ; forge the hammer on the anvil of Nimrod ; raze his tower to the ground ! "

Münzer's letter was well received ; a large number of miners assembled in the Mansfeld district, disturbances began to arise, and the impetus given to the Mansfelders extended to the mining population near Meissen. "Even before the foolish rioters rushed on to the bloody day at Frankenhausen," says Hering, "many miners from the revolutionary domain of Count Mansfeld had taken flight to our mountains, either because they saw no promise of good in remaining at home, or because they hoped, by the aid of the 'new wisdom,' to play an important part in other places." [1]

The rioters succeeded in gaining influence, and in assisting an attempt at revolution in the neighbourhood of Zwickau, where the enthusiasts, under Storch and Münzer, had previously acquired power and paved the way for an uprising.

In April there was, in fact, a revolt among the peasants and miners in the Erzgebirge Mountains, which, like similar

[1] *Geschichte des sächsischen Hochlandes*, p. 203.

movements elsewhere in Germany, was not wholly suppressed till after the fight at Frankenhausen.

Münzer was, as a rule, unsuccessful in his efforts to bring about a co-operation of the revolutionary movements in the various districts of Saxony.

He found the separatism of the petty townsmen and peasants too powerful for him. The equality of economic pressure in all places, the stirring up of the whole nation by the Reformation movement, and, last but not least, the indefatigable interlocal activity of the communistic "apostles" had been just sufficient at its commencement to make the insurrection of the peasants and their allies an affair which embraced the largest part of the nation ; so that the revolt broke out almost simultaneously in all parts. In its progress, however, and when it became a question of securing the fruits of the early victories and taking advantage of them, the local separatism became more conspicuous than ever ; for it was too deeply rooted in circumstances to be suppressed for more than a very short time, and then only to a very small extent.

With this separatism there was associated the fatal childishness of the peasants. That inexperienced folk believed that the word of a prince was, if not better, at least not worse than that of any other honourable man. They had no inkling of the new State craft, which promoted dishonesty and mendacity to the rank of highly estimable princely virtues.

Instead of co-operating, each district and each town which had made cause with the insurgents depended on its own strong arm ; and a few empty promises on the part of their rulers (in which they held up the prospect of granting the demands of the insurgents) were sufficient as a rule to scatter the rebels, and induce them to lay down their arms. In this way the princes found time to collect troops, combine, and easily overcome one after another of the isolated peasant masses which, if united, could have made a good stand. Moreover, while on the side of the peasants the absence of any definite plans became more and more conspicuous, the growing danger increased the cohesion and systematic co-operation of the princes.

The rulers rose everywhere in their might to stifle the insurrection in the blood of the rebels. In the last week of April, Truchsess von Waldburg, then leader of the Swabian league's army, had almost suppressed the revolt in Swabia, Landgrave Philip having done the same in Hesse, while large bodies of veteran troops had been despatched against the insurgents of Franconia and Thuringia.

In the beginning of May the good "evangelical" Landgrave Philip of Hesse united his forces with those of the arch Catholic George of Saxony and a few petty princes, who were afterwards joined by the new Elector of Saxony, John,[1] for the purpose of putting an end to the Thuringian revolt. The headquarters of the rebellion were at the town of Frankenhausen, a few miles distant from the Mansfeld mines, and celebrated for its salt deposits, which employed a large number of workmen.[2]   Most of the military forces of the rebels had been concentrated at this place and not, as would have been more natural, at Mühlhausen, a well-fortified town provided with artillery, or at a more southern point, *e.g.*, Erfurt or Eisenach, both of which were in the hands of the insurrectionists, and from which it would have been easier to keep in touch with the revolt in Franconia.

The encampment before Frankenhausen seemed of the greatest importance both to the princes and rebels, and, to reach it, Philip of Hesse executed a very singular movement. He pushed on past Eisenach and Langensalza, leaving Mühlhausen on his right and Erfurt on his left, and marched straight to Frankenhausen.   While this evidences the importance of that town, the fact that Philip could perform this movement, without being in the least threatened or even molested by the Mühlhauseners or Erfurters, proves the total lack of cohesion, co-operation, and plan among the insurgents.

The importance of Frankenhausen can be explained by its proximity to the Mansfeld mines, with their numerous war-

---

[1] John's brother, the peace-loving Frederick, had died on the 5th May.

[2] G. Sartorius, *Versuch einer Geschichte des deutschen Bauernkriegs.* Berlin, 1795, p. 319.

like workmen; for if the insurrection had spread thither the princes would have had a severe task before them.

Münzer too was fully alive to the value of Frankenhausen, and did his utmost to direct all his available forces to that place. He also wrote to the Erfurters, but they did not move. Nor could he induce even the Mühlhauseners to go to the help of the men before Frankenhausen. How did the affairs of the peasants of that place concern the petty townsmen of the imperial city? Even the usually energetic Pfeiffer remained inactive, thus obliging Münzer to march out in sole command of his three hundred men after the Mühlhauseners had grudgingly lent him eight mounted cannon.

Münzer fared no better with the Mansfeld miners. There is, unfortunately, a total lack of minute information concerning his negotiations with these people. In Spangenberg's *Mansfeldischer Chronik* (chapter 362) we find only the following notice, still more briefly reproduced by Bieringen in his *Beschreibung des Mansfeldischen Bergwerks*: "The peasants of Mansfeld were also in revolt. Count Albrecht exerted himself most diligently, and promised the miners all manner of things, in order to keep them at home and prevent their joining the rebellious peasants in the field."

Albrecht seems to have succeeded. Münzer had good grounds for the fear expressed in the above-quoted letter to the miners that "the foolish fellows would agree to a treacherous compact;" for as soon as their demands had been granted most of them quieted down and troubled themselves no further about the rebellious peasants. They sent out a few reinforcing parties, only to be surprised, however, by Count Albrecht's cavalry, which held all the roads.

One possibility still remained, namely, to carry the insurrection into Mansfeld itself, and in that way involve the miners in the struggle. But this chance also was not taken advantage of. The peasants before Frankenhausen were foolish enough to engage in negotiations with Albrecht, which he carefully managed to prolong from day to day until the armies of the princes arrived.

The Count had agreed with the peasants for a conference

on the 12th of May; but he did not make his appearance, pleading important affairs as an excuse, and, instead, summoned the peasants to a meeting on the next Sunday, May 14th. "In the meantime," Luther tells us, "God so ordered that Thomas Münzer came from Mühlhausen to Frankenhausen."[1]

Münzer, who detected the Count's artifice, caused the immediate breaking off of these negotiations, and made every effort to provoke a battle between Albrecht and the peasants before the arrival of the princes. The outrageously rude letters written by Münzer to Mansfeld at that time are incomprehensible except as deliberate provocations to that end. Zimmermann looks upon them as evidences of a state of self deception on the part of Münzer, arising from his frenzy and despair; but his arrangement of affairs indicates the possession of a clear intellect.

Meanwhile the Mansfelders did not grant Münzer the boon of allowing themselves to be provoked; and either the consciousness of the weakness of his forces, or perhaps their unwillingness, prevented him from making the attack.

It was soon too late. Münzer had reached Frankenhausen May 12th; on the 14th Landgrave Philip of Hesse and Duke George Henry of Brunswick arrived, to be followed on the 15th by Duke George of Saxony with his army.

The fate of the men before Frankenhausen was now sealed, and with it that of the Thuringian insurrection. On one side stood 8,000 badly armed, undisciplined peasants, almost without artillery; on the other, about the same number of well-equipped, veteran soldiers with numerous cannon.

Descriptions of the fight at Frankenhausen have generally been based on Melancthon's account. According to this, Münzer first of all delivered an eloquent speech to the peasants, which was followed by a still more eloquent one by Landgrave Philip to his troops; whereupon the latter advanced to the attack. "The poor folk, however, stood still and sang '*Nun bitten wir den heiligen Geist*' ('Now

---

[1] *Erschreckliche Geschichte und Gerichte Gotts über Thomas Münzer.* Luther's Works, xix. p. 288.

pray we to the Holy Ghost') as if they were demented. They neither defended themselves nor fled, many of them trusting to the great promise made by Thomas, that God would show help from heaven ; for Thomas had said that he would hold all the balls in his sleeves." As the miracle did not take place, and as the soldiers continued cutting their way into the ranks of the peasants, these creatures at last took to flight and were butchered in heaps. A strange *fight* indeed !

Is it possible that Münzer and the peasants could have been such utter fools as they are here depicted ?

Let us first of all consider the speeches. That of Münzer is in a style altogether different from his own, and has an empty bathos about it in no way characteristic of him. But on closer inspection the speech of the Landgrave seems a still stranger production. It is a categorical answer to Münzer's—as if Philip of Hesse had stood by and refuted the former's complaint point by point ! Let us, for example, compare the following passages :—

Münzer :	Landgrave :
"But what are our princes doing? They take no interest in the government, turn a deaf ear to the poor people, do not administer justice, nor combat murder and robbery, and visit no criminal nor wanton with punishment."	"Whereas it is invented and fabricated that we do not care for the general peace of the land, and that we do not execute judgment nor combat murder and robbery : we now declare ourselves to be, with all our abilities, assiduous in the maintenance of a peaceable government."

And more to the same effect. The more closely these two speeches are examined, the clearer it becomes that they were not actually delivered, but were devised by the learned schoolmaster on the pattern of the speeches of statesmen and army leaders handed down to us by Thucydides and Livy. They are rhetorical exercises, written for definite purposes. The dissolute mercenaries, gathered from all countries, could not have been impressed in the smallest degree by the prelection of the Landgrave on morals and justice, and the necessity and utility of imposts, and so forth, with the affecting peroration that it was a question of fighting for the safety of wife and child. This hypothetical speech, however, must have raised the Landgrave in the estimation of the educated philistines for whom Melancthon wrote. It was to these that the speech was delivered, and not to the soldiers.

On the other hand, Münzer's speech is composed with the sole purpose of making him ridiculous. Melancthon makes him say at the close of his address : " Let not the weak flesh terrify you, but go boldly to the attack of the enemy. You need not fear the shot, for you shall see that I will hold in my sleeves all the cannon balls fired at you," &c.

Nowhere in Münzer's writings has he expressed himself so absurdly about practical things, his mysticism consisting solely in believing that God held direct intercourse with him and that his doctrines proceeded from the Holy Spirit. He never asserted that he could perform miracles. Hence we have no hesitation in pronouncing this speech an impudent invention.

It is, moreover, a clumsy invention ; so clumsy, indeed, that a hundred years ago Strobel became convinced that not Münzer but " Melancthon was certainly the author " of the speech (p. 112). In spite of this, however, it is still used by writers in forming their judgment of Münzer, *e.g.*, by Janssen.

There was little time for speech-making, if the battle is correctly described in the pamphlet entitled, *Ain nützlicher Dialogus odder gesprechbuchlein zwischen einem Müntzerischen-schwermer zu Frankenhausen geschlagen belangende.* Wittenberg, 1525." The enthusiast says : " How now ! Is it honourable for princes and barons to give us three hours for deliberation and yet not keep faith a quarter of an hour, but, as soon as they have won over Count von Stolberg with some of the nobility from our side, to begin firing at us with cannon and then immediately attack us ? "

All of which means that the princes parleyed with the peasants, demanding their surrender, and gave them three hours' grace. In the meantime they induced the nobles on the side of the populace to come over to them, and, long before the truce had expired, threw themselves upon the unsuspicious peasants and butchered them.

This certainly was not very honourable, and we can well understand Melancthon's pains to devise another account of the affair. While, however, his version is wholly nonsensical, the description given in the *Dialogus* is in exact accordance with the mode of procedure universally adopted by the princes at that time in their dealing with the peasantry. In spite of their superior strength, they resorted to treachery and breach of faith to gain the mastery over their opponents. By this means, and not by any imbecile expectation among Münzer's followers, that he would actually catch the cannon-balls in his coat-sleeves, by far the greater number of the insurgents were slaughtered—from 5,000 to 6,000 out of 8,000!—while the princely forces suffered hardly any loss worth mentioning.

After the victory was won the troops pushed on into Frankenhausen, and, as Landgrave Philip himself wrote on the following day, " All males found there were slain and the town given over to pillage."

Münzer, with a part of the vanquished forces, fled into the town, and as the enemy's cavalry was at his heels, rushed headlong into one of the first houses near the gate, disguised himself by wrapping up his head, threw himself on a bed, and feigned illness. But his artifice failed. A soldier who entered the room recognised him by the contents of his satchel. He was immediately seized, and brought before the Landgrave of Hesse and Duke George. " When he came before the princes they asked him why he had thus led the poor folk astray. He answered defiantly that he had acted rightly and had purposed punishing the princes "—a truly bold reply! Melancthon, who tells us this, momentarily forgets that he always represents Münzer as being exceptionally pusillanimous.

The princes at once had him put to the rack and feasted on his agonies, after which he was sent as a " booty-farthing " to Count Ernest von Mansfeld. " If he had before ' been cruelly tortured,' he was now, after a few days, ' barbarously dealt with' in the tower of Heldrungen " (Zimmermann).

It was here that he was tortured into making the confession, from the protocol of which we have so repeatedly quoted.

He revoked nothing, and, concerning his secret league, revealed only such things as could not injure anybody. Not one of the confederates named by him is mentioned among those who were executed ; hence he probably inculpated only such as had already perished. As the fight of Frankenhausen had broken the force of the movement in Thuringia, nothing further remained to the princes but to take bloody revenge —a task which they carefully accomplished.

It being a sufficient cause of congratulation that the Mansfeld miners remained peaceable, they were left for a time unmolested. Spangenberg tells us that it was not until the next year that "the miners began to be somewhat harshly dealt with, by the imposition of additional labour, from which, in spite of energetic remonstrances, they could obtain. no relief." On the contrary, troops were sent to "quiet" them, and they were deprived of all freedom of speech and of meeting.

Worse still was Mühlhausen's expiation for its desertion of the insurgents' cause at the critical moment. From Frankenhausen the allied princes at once pushed on to the imperial city. In vain did the town appeal for assistance to the Franconian insurrectionists. These now treated the Mühlhauseners as they themselves had treated the defenders of Frankenhausen. As soon as the siege began (May 19th) despondency spread rapidly among the rebellious citizens. Seeing that all was lost, Pfeiffer escaped on the 24th, with four hundred men, to gain the uplands of Franconia ; but the cavalry of the princes overtook him, and made him prisoner, together with ninety-two of his men.

On a written promise of mercy from the princes, Mühlhausen capitulated May 25th. In practice this mercy consisted in the execution of several citizens and the pillage of the town. The city, moreover, lost its independence, and fell into the power of the Saxon princes, who thus gained what they had hoped for from the insurrection ; while the rebels, who had helped them to gain their ends, were executed, including Pfeiffer and Münzer, who had been brought to Mühlhausen.

Pfeiffer died defiant and unrepentant. With regard to Münzer, Melancthon naturally asserts that he was "very faint-hearted in the last extremity." As evidence of this he relates, that, from downright terror, Münzer was unable to utter a single word, and consequently could not repeat the Creed. Duke Henry of Brunswick had therefore to recite it for him. Immediately afterwards, however, our authority makes the man who was speechless from terror deliver one of those eloquent addresses so much beloved by the classical and rhetorically-educated schoolmaster.

The other chroniclers of the time make no mention of Münzer's "faint-heartedness" (compare Zimmermann, ii. p. 444). In addition to the utterly worthless testimony of Melancthon, there is only one piece of evidence from which it is possible to draw conclusions as to the agitator's despair in his last days, viz., his letter to the Council and commune of Mühlhausen, written in his prison at Heldrungen, and dated May 17th. In this he exhorts his friends not to exasperate the higher authorities, as his death was deserved, and was well calculated to open the eyes of the "foolish." He implores them to look after his poor wife. Once more he beseeches them not to provoke the authorities for purposes of self-interest, as they had already done, but to abandon the rebellion and beg the pardon of the princes.

Without doubt this letter betrays faint-heartedness. We cannot agree with Zimmermann, who puts a more favourable construction upon it.

But is the letter genuine? It did not proceed from Münzer's own hand. He himself says that he dictated it to a certain Christoph Lau. Why did he dictate it? Why did he not write it himself? For whose interest was it that such a letter from Münzer should come to Mühlhausen? We answer, for the interest of the princes alone. It was composed on May 17th, and on May 19th the siege began. It was calculated to make this siege easier, and to produce despondency among the besieged. Is not the assumption probable that Münzer's name was made use of by the princes for carrying out one of those tricks of war so common at the period?

The least that can be said, is that the document is highly suspicious and is not sufficient to corroborate Melancthon's statement.

Hence we can truly say that nothing certain is known

regarding Münzer's last moments, and that the accusations of pusillanimity on his part are unsubstantiated.

It does not in the least affect our judgment of the man whether his nerves were or were not completely under his control to the very last. We have dealt with this question only because the great stress laid on Münzer's alleged cowardice, without any tangible basis, is of significance, not for him, but for his opponents.

But the furious attacks on Münzer made by the advocates of reaction have themselves proved the most powerful means of keeping his memory green among the populace of Germany, and of preserving their undiminished sympathy for him.

In the eyes of the German working-classes Münzer was and is the most brilliant embodiment of heretical communism.

CHAPTER V

THE ANABAPTISTS

I. *The Anabaptists before the Peasant War.*

A T the period of the German Reformation one centre of the communist movement lay in Saxony. Another existed in Switzerland—that peculiar conglomeration of peasant and urban republics, which had concentrated themselves round the central mass of the Alps for united defence against their common enemies.

They had completely freed themselves from the German Empire, and had succeeded in setting limits to Papal spoliation.

This new and independent commonwealth, however, had not at that time become a unified state. Almost the only bond of union between its constituent parts was the knowledge that each, by itself, was powerless against its princely neighbours. But with this common interest, there existed others of an antagonistic nature between the rustic, primitive cantons, where economics were behind the age, and the rich cities which were far advanced in that respect.

This antagonism was manifested clearly during the Reformation, in which movement the primitive cantons had no interest. Papal exploitation, already materially diminished in the confederation, pressed lightly, as a rule, on these poor districts. On the other hand, they had every reason for remaining on a good footing with the Catholic Powers (France, Milan, Venice, the Pope, and the Hapsburgs), as these were the chief consumers of the only valuable commodity which the peasants and petty nobility of Switzerland could at that time bring into the market, namely, their warlike sons. *Reislaufen*, or mercenary service, was the chief source of revenue for the country folk, especially in the mountain cantons. A union with the Reformation movement boded a breach with the Catholic Powers, and threatened this source of wealth with exhaustion. Hence the honest country folk had held fast to the faith of their fathers.

The towns were differently situated. Their middle-class citizens had no interest in mercenary war service ; on the contrary, they disliked it, as it strengthened the power of their enemies, the nobility, and increased the warlike capacities of the lower classes from whom they derived their wealth. For the Swiss mercenaries were not homeless tatterdemalians, but sons of peasants, who, after the completion of their war service, returned to their native land.

The towns, indeed, had every reason for animosity against the Catholic Powers. Moreover, though Papal exploitation was more restricted in Switzerland than in Germany, that covetous Power held more tenaciously to its rights in the towns than in the poor mountain districts. The antagonism to the Catholic princes (*par excellence*, the Hapsburgs) was every whit as great as the enmity to the Papacy. The German Reformation was a revolt, not only against the Pope, but in like manner against the Emperor, *i.e.*, the House of Hapsburg, and it was so regarded in Switzerland also.

The House of Hapsburg had long ceased to be the "hereditary enemy" of the primitive Swiss cantons, which were already too firmly established to be threatened by that dynasty ; and while having nothing to gain by opposition to it, they had nothing to lose in the way of war-pay and bribe-money. Quite otherwise was it with the cities of North Switzerland bordering on the territories of the Hapsburgs, which, menaced and coveted by that House, were in constant enmity to it. Zurich, in particular, had the liveliest interest in the struggle with that line of monarchs, and was the pioneer of the Reformation in Switzerland; while the primitive cantons made cause with Catholicism, the successors of Tell allying themselves with the Hapsburg Ferdinand.

In Switzerland, as in Germany, the Reformation brought
a communistic movement to the surface; but as the circumstances of the confederation were quite different from those
of Saxony, the character of the communism in the two
countries also differed greatly.

While in Saxony the movement was materially influenced
by Taborite tradition, in Switzerland these exercised hardly
appreciable power. The movement, however, had for a long
time been considerably exposed to the influences of the
Waldenses and Beghards; the former coming from Southern
France and Northern Italy, and the latter from the Netherlands along the Rhine valley, finally reaching Bâle by way of
Cologne and Strassburg.

In contrast to the Taborites, who favoured violent measures,
the Waldenses were peacefully inclined. This contrast alone
must have resulted in producing other sentiments among the
communists of Switzerland than those prevalent in Saxony,
as well as different ideas and actions. But the character of
a social movement in any country is determined much less by
imported doctrines, than by its peculiar social and political
circumstances. Saxony was distinguished by its mining
industry, especially by its silver mines. While this industry
was favourable to the growth of the power of its princes, it
also created a strong and defiant proletariat among the
miners, living together, as they did, in large masses. It
encouraged production for the markets in the agricultural
districts, but, at the same time, engendered a thirst for land
among the landlords, and intensified to the highest degree
all the social antagonisms of that epoch.

It was quite otherwise with Switzerland, where there was
no mining industry and hence no warlike proletariat. Agriculture to a large extent was still at a very primitive stage.
Land communism was very strong, and there was not the
least vestige of absolute princely power. We find rather a
collection of peasant and town republics, with a peasant and
urban democracy, which, so long as it felt itself weak and
menaced, was in sympathy with communism, whose nearest
enemy was its enemy also.

All this must have tended to strengthen the peaceable

tendencies of the Waldenses and Beghards in Switzerland and to make class antagonisms less acute than in Saxony, where the movement acquired more of a proletarian character. In Münzer's time there were very few communists in Saxony belonging to the upper classes. This is one of the reasons why Münzer towered to such a height above the nameless masses who supported him and made him feared, but among whom there were no prominent combatants able, by their writings, to hand down their memory and personality to posterity.

It was quite otherwise with the Swiss communists and those influenced by them, who counted numerous men of social prominence and culture in their ranks. It is impossible to keep our glance long fixed on any individual, for we are confused by the brilliant constellation of their interesting and characteristic men of talent. Though the Swiss movement is feebler than the Saxon, and from an historical point of view less important, it is more valuable to literature, and stands on a higher intellectual plane.

We have perhaps said enough as to the generic character of the movement.

Numerous traces of the Waldenses and Beghards are to be found in Switzerland during the fourteenth and fifteenth centuries ; but they are only blood traces ; in other words, executions. The sects were chiefly composed of people from the lower classes, such as craftsmen, proletarians, and peasants, who preached communism secretly in hidden confederacies. Together with this proletarian movement however, a sort of *salon*-communism seems to have been instituted at the beginning of the sixteenth century.

While Zurich was the Wittenberg of the confederation, Bâle played the same *rôle* in Switzerland that Erfurt did in Saxony, as it was the headquarters of Swiss Humanism. A circle of free-thinking savants and artists was formed in the town, of which the central figure, after 1513, was Erasmus, the bosom friend of Thomas More. All sorts of novel ideas were discussed in this coterie, including probably many peculiar to the later order of Anabaptists ; for among the " erudite men " gathered at that time in Bâle, we find several who subsequently became leaders of that sect. Conrad Grebel, the son of a Zurich patrician, and already "a distinguished defender of the Gospel," was there in 1521 and 1522 ; Dr. Balthasar Hubneir, from Waldshut, was in frequent communication with the circle ; and among its members were the Swabian Wilhelm Reublin, pastor of St. Albans, Bâle, and Ulrich Hugwald, a Bâle professor, who, as we have seen, had joined Oekolampadius in requesting Münzer to agitate. We also find Ludwig Hätzer, the bookbinder Andreas auf der Stülzen, Simon Stumpf, and others, all of whom were subsequently zealous agitators among the Anabaptists.

We may also mention the significant fact that Thomas More's *Utopia* had at that time aroused marked attention in Bâle.

The first edition of this work (which was written in Latin) appeared in Louvain, in the year 1516, under the supervision of More's friend Erasmus, who was then staying in that town. In 1518 it became necessary to issue a new edition, which came out in Bâle and was produced by the celebrated printer, Froben. We can see from a letter written by Beatus Rhenanus to Pirkheimer [1] how eagerly *Utopia* was discussed in Bâle.

In 1524, the German translation by Claudius Canticula was also published in Bâle : this was the first translation of the book into any language.

Nothing positive, however, is known about the communistic movement in Bâle ; and it has hitherto been impossible to remove the veil of obscurity covering the infancy of the Anabaptist order, or rather its connection with the earlier communistic movements. The first clear indication of the new sect appeared in Zurich at the time of Zwingli's Reformation.

The Lutheran Reformation began with the resistance to one of the most active means of taking money from Germany to Italy—the sale of indulgences. Zwingli's activity in the direction of reform (first as pastor in Glarus from 1506 to 1516, then as parish-priest in Einsiedeln from 1516 to 1519, and lastly as pastor in Zurich) began with a struggle against the means by which the money of the Papacy was brought

[1] Given in my *Thomas More und seine Utopie.*

into Switzerland, viz., mercenary war service. Luther began as a theologian, Zwingli as a politician, his first attacks being directed, not against Catholic dogmas, but against the neighbouring Valois and Hapsburg dynasties. In 1519, he was still so high in favour with the Vatican, that when he fell ill with the plague, the Papal legate hastened to send him his body-physician. Not until the waves of the German Reformation reached Switzerland, did the conflict in that country with the temporal power of the Pope become one against Catholicism (1522). As soon, however, as the Zurichers had entered this path, they went rapidly forward without encountering any serious obstacles.

Though Zwingli surpassed Luther in perspicuity and consistency, the Zwinglian Reformation movement none the less followed, in one respect, the same direction as the Lutheran. Like the latter, it exerted itself at the beginning to bring about the co-operation of all the classes who were dissatisfied with existing ecclesiastical conditions. In Zwingli's case, however, as in Luther's, the united struggle was followed by a rupture. Each of the allied parties and classes sought to profit by the victory in the furtherance of its own interests, and in accordance with its own views. The leader of the movement, the reformer, who had hitherto been supported by all classes, was now forced to decide in favour of one of these in opposition to the others, and thus to turn against a part of his former co-workers. This is a peculiarity of all revolutionary movements which are accomplished by the co-operation of different classes having opposing interests. When the conflict with the ruling Church began in Zurich, the communistic sectarians of that place no longer deemed it necessary to maintain strict secrecy. As early as the spring of 1522, it came to the knowledge of the authorities that an "heretical school" existed in the town ; an association in which the bookseller, Andreas auf der Stülzen (who had belonged to the Bâle circle) acted as teacher. This association had not yet been proscribed ; on the contrary, we find its members in friendly intercourse with Zwingli.

Late in the autumn of 1522, Conrad Grebel returned from Bâle to Zurich, and immediately joined the   heretical school." Independent and wealthy from his earliest years, he had studied in Vienna and Paris, acquiring some fame as a savant, but also seriously impairing his health by the excesses of his student life.

On his return to his home in Zurich, he devoted himself with enthusiasm to the cause of the Church movement, and became one of the " Brethren," though continuing to be on the best of terms with Zwingli.

He was followed by many of his associates in the Bâle circle, to whom Zurich seemed a freer field for their activity. Wilhelm Reublin left his living in Bâle and received one in Wietikon ; Simon Stumpf became pastor in Höngg, near Zurich ; and Ludwig Hätzer, an erudite young priest from Thurgau, who had also been in Bâle, was to be found in Zurich in 1523.

The associates who thus flocked in from abroad were joined by numerous proselytes from the town itself. Among these the most prominent was Felix Manz, a philologian, who with Grebel was soon in the front rank of the " Spirituals," as the Zurich Brethren were first called.

The community continued to grow, and at length began to feel its strength. Zwingli cast loving glances at it. The chief concern of the association was now to urge him onward along the path of social reform ; the effort, however, resulting in a quarrel, which became more and more bitter.

The Brethren demanded the abolition of Church imposts— tributes and tithes ; a step which Zwingli himself had openly advocated. But he now grew apprehensive of the league. On the 22nd of June, 1523, the Great Council of the town pronounced emphatically against the idea of attacking the Church tithes; a hint which was apparently not lost on Zwingli, for three days latter he delivered a sermon in the cathedral, in which he sided with the Council. This showed that he intended to sever his connection with the Brethren.

Meanwhile this did not make the Brethren yield. They invited Zwingli to organise the Church in such a way as to make it independent of the State. The answer was the introduction of the State Church in the autumn, and the decision that all Church affairs should in future be referred to the Great Council, *i.e.*, to the governing classes.

This arrangement was a great blow to the " Spirituals," who had not begun the struggle with the Papal Church merely to place a compliant instrument of power in the hands of the wealthy. The conflict between them and Zwingli now became a bitter one ; but while the " Spirituals " fought with words only, Zwingli had the whole power of the State at his disposal, and made abundant use of it. As early as the end of 1523, the Brethren began to be arrested and banished, Simon Stumpf being among the first victims, in December.

The persecution, however, did not overawe the Brethren ; it rather increased their zeal, and bound them more closely together. The sect grew rapidly both in the town and country, as the exiles carried their doctrines into the neighbouring cantons, where they soon gained a following. At the same time the Brethren began to dissociate themselves more and more from the mass of the population, and the condemnation of infant baptism gradually came to the fore, as their distinguishing tenet.

Such was the state of affairs in the beginning of the year 1525.

II. *The Doctrines of the Anabaptists.*

Up to the year 1525 the theorists of the Anabaptists had not spoken, their deductions dealing chiefly with the theological confirmation and amplification of their doctrines. The fundamental features of these doctrines were sufficiently evident at the beginning of the Peasant War. This seems the fittest place for explaining them, before proceeding with the account of the external affairs of the sect.

That which most strikes the observer concerning the Anabaptists is the great diversity of opinion prevailing among them. In his *Chronica*, which appeared in 1531, Franck (who knew and understood them thoroughly and sympathised with them on many points, although sceptically and timorously) says in regard to them : " Although dissensions exist in all sects, yet are the Baptists peculiarly disunited and split up ; in so much that I know not what certainly and finally to write about· them." [1]

Bullinger writes in the same strain in his work against the Anabaptists. " Many hold," he says, " that it is impossible to give an accurate account of all the distinctions and antagonistic opinions, and pernicious, horrible sects or factions existing among the Anabaptists.   In truth, few communities will be found which are unanimous in their views, and have not each its own mystery, *i.e.*, its own fantasy."   For that reason he refrains from attempting to describe all the sects, and limits himself to a recapitulation of their most important tendencies.[2]

Dissensions and divergences of views were not peculiar to the Anabaptists.   They are in part due to the same tolerance in matters of faith which had enabled the most diverse sects to dwell together peaceably in Tabor, and in part to the circumstance that the various sects only rarely acquired a stable, recognised organisation.   Hence the conception of what an Anabaptist really was remained, perhaps, quite as uncertain as that of a " Nihilist " of to-day in Russia.   Contemporary historians include among them partisans of the most varied modes of thought.   On the other hand, it is natural that every revolutionary—and hence critical—movement should maintain a critical attitude, not only towards its opponents, but also towards its adherents. This makes it liable to disruption in its very infancy, and so long as it is feeling its way without firm foothold.   The Anabaptists (at least in Germany) never passed beyond this stage.

Bullinger is more minute than Franck in his account of the different factions among the Anabaptists, but also more bitter.   We shall confine ourselves to Franck's narrative, and give a few of its details.

Many of the distinctions given by this author are of a

---

[1] *Chronica, Zeytbuch und bibel von anbegyn biss inn diss gegenwarlig, MDCXXXI. jar.* Strassburg, 1531. Fol. 445.

[2] *Der Widertäuffer nursprung, furgang, Secten, wäsen frömemen und gemeine vier leer Artickcl,* etc. Zurich, 1531, p. 17.

subordinate character, and relate to differences of natural temperament or idiosyncrasy ; in which category we may place the various views held in regard to revelations and dreams.   Other points deal with certain tactical matters of little import.

But even on weighty questions and first principles there was no perfect unanimity among the Anabaptists.

Foremost of all stood the fundamental question of private proprietorship.

" Some," says Franck, " regard themselves alone as holy and pure.   Holding themselves aloof from others, they have all things in common ; no one calls anything his own, and the possession of any property is a sin.

" Others have all things so far in common that they allow no one among them to suffer want.   Not that one can seize another's goods, but that in case of necessity the goods of each belong in common to the sufferer ; and no one is allowed to hide anything from another, but must keep open house.   While, however, the giver should be ready and willing, the receiver should be unwilling, and, as far as possible, spare his brother, and avoid being a burden to him. But herein there is much hypocrisy, deceit, and lying, as they themselves well know.

" In some places, *e.g.*, at Austerlitz in Moravia, they have *Oeconomos*, or stewards, and a common kitchen-sack, from which each one is given what he is in want of ; but whether this is really so, and the distribution just, I do not inquire. These anathematise other Brethren who do not walk in what they consider the right way ; and this often happens, since each community puts a ban upon other brotherhoods who do not subscribe in all things to its tenets. . . .

" Other Baptists lay no stress on the brotherly feeling and community of goods just mentioned, and esteem it unnecessary and arrogant on the part of the Fraternities which call themselves perfect Christians and despise all else. In this sect each works for himself, and the members help, question each other, and shake hands in a way quite hypocritical (to my thinking), although I lay no blame on those who do these things in sincerity."

Hence among the Anabaptists, as among the Taborites and Bohemian Brethren, we find two parties : one strict, taking communism seriously, abolishing all private rights in property, and supporting the Brethren from the common "kitchen-sack" ; and, at the same time, the more moderate faction which recognised private proprietorship, and only demanded that each should so possess " as if he possessed nothing." The appearance of these two parties nearly simultaneously is not an accidental, but a typical phenomenon, consequent, by the very nature of things, on the communistic movement, so long as it adhered to the basis of communism in the means of consumption.

The question of marriage is intimately connected with that of private proprietorship.

According to Franck, some taught that no one should live in family life with those of another faith ; and many wedlocks were broken up in this way. Others held opposite views.

Some thought it a duty to forsake house and family after the example of the apostles (St. Luke xviii. 28-30), while many preached the contrary.

" There was also a sect among them the members of which wished, together with all things else, to have their wives in common ; but they were soon suppressed by the other Brethren of the community, and driven out. Many inculpated Hut and Hätzer as leaders of this sect. If this be true, these men at all events atoned for their sin."

Ludwig Hätzer of Thurgau is already known to us. Not only was he opposed to the bolder thinkers of his party on questions of marriage, but he was one of those Baptists who denied the divinity of Christ, and maintained that He was only a teacher and example, not an " idol." We do not know how far his views were shared by others. In 1529 he was put to death at Constance, for adultery.

Hans Hut, of Franconia, was a bookbinder, and a zealous partisan of Münzer (who was himself far from advocating the community of wives). After the suppression of the Peasant Insurrection in Thuringia, he joined the South German Anabaptists.

The tendencies for which he and Hätzer were condemned call to mind those of the Adamites in Bohemia and the Brothers and Sisters of the Free-Spirit ; and it is noteworthy that Bullinger speaks of a sect of " Free-Brothers " among the Baptists, who not only in name but in their opinions showed a close kinship with the Brothers of the Free-Spirit. We cannot decisively say whether this similarity rests upon tradition, or whether under the same conditions, but without any connection with their forerunners, like events led to like consequences.

"The Free Brethren," says Bullinger "(whom nearly all other Baptists call the rude, wild Brothers, and curse and scorn) make the eighth sect of this people. From the very origin of the order they were rather numerous in various localities, especially in the Zurich highlands. The Baptists interpreted Christian freedom in a fleshly sense, wishing to be above all laws, because Christ had made them free. They also imagined themselves exempt from the payment of rents and tithes, and furthermore from the duties of labour. Some of the more discreet, however, teach that although these things are not incumbent as between the Brethren, yet should the heathen be paid, that they may have no cause for complaint, and may not revile the doctrines. Nevertheless serfdom should cease among Christians. Some of these Free Brothers (abandoned, dissolute knaves) convinced wanton women that unless these hazarded their honour, it would be impossible for them to be saved. To this end they blasphemously abused the Word of God, which says that he cannot be saved who is not willing to forfeit and lose all that he holds dear. In like manner all ignominy and disgrace must be suffered for Christ's sake. Because Christ said that publicans and harlots should enter the kingdom of heaven before the righteous, therefore women are to turn harlots, yielding up their honour, and thus be greater in heaven than virtuous wives. Others are more subtle ; for they teach that as all things are held in common, so should the wives be also. Some affirm that after they have been rebaptized they are born again, and cannot sin ; the flesh alone can and may sin. In this way great scandal and wantonness were caused by many

false pretences and lies, since they dared to say concerning
all these things, that they were in accordance with God's
will. Certain wanton knaves among them instituted what
they called spiritual marriage ; wives were told that they
committed heinous sin with their husbands if these had not
been rebaptized, since in that case they were no better than
heathens ; but that with Baptists they did not sin, there
being a spiritual marriage between them." [1]

We have, unfortunately, been unable to discover any further
contemporaneous information concerning the Free Brethren.
Bullinger's polemical treatise is by no means an unprejudiced
source ; but in all essential points we may rely upon the
accuracy of its representations of the sect, particularly on
points in which their doctrines touch upon those of the
Brothers and Sisters of the Free-Spirit ; namely, their " free-
love," " communistic anarchism," and their sinlessness based
on the assumption that what they did was God's will.

Though the Anabaptists were no more unanimous in
their opinions about government or public authority than
in those concerning private property and marriage, they all
agreed that they would have as little as possible to do with
the Government. They wished to know nothing of it ; at the
same time they deprecated violent resistance, and preached
the duty of suffering obedience.

Franck informs us that they taught the duty of unresisting
submission to violence. A Christian should fill no office ;
" he may not have any kind of servant ; neither may he go to
war, or clench his fist." Let vengeance be of God.

Some among them proclaimed that no one should take an
oath. " Furthermore no Christian may take an official position
in which his duty would oblige him to sit in a criminal court
and judge matters of life and death, or concern himself with
war." Others at least tolerated necessary self-defence. "Nevertheless they all with one voice teach obedience to the authorities
in things that be not contrary to God's will ; and the giving
not only of rent and taxes, but of the cloak with the coat, and
all that is not absolutely needful. They also say that they
are ready to suffer violence, and even to obey tyrants. . . .

[1] *Wiedertäufer*, fol. 32.

So far as I have discoursed with the latter, they have replied
to me that they are here to suffer with patience for Christ's
sake, not to fight with impatience ; because the precepts and
demands of the gospel were defended and established by
suffering and martyrdom, not by violence ; as the peasants
had it in mind to do."

Much as they agreed with the Zurich Brethren in other
matters, their views on the subject of violence were the main
cause of their separation from Münzer and the majority of
German communists before the Peasant War.

A letter is still extant which was addressed to Münzer on
the 5th of September, 1524, by Grebel, Manz Andreas von
der Stülzen, Hans Okenfuss, Heinrich Aberli, and others.
They affirm that they are at one with him in many things,
and that "you and Karlstadt are esteemed among us as the
purest proclaimers and preachers of the purest Word of God."
They rejoice that "we have found one who is of the same
Christian understanding as ourselves. We who are poor in
spirit have been taught and strengthened beyond measure by
your tracts." But he is not radical enough in his doctrines,
and they exhort him "seriously to bestir himself, and preach
without fear godly words only ; to set up godly usages . . .
and to reject, hate, and curse all human designs, words, usages,
and opinions, and even your own." They attack his German
Mass, which they consider too far removed from apostolic
simplicity, and also inveigh against his advocacy of violence.
Whosoever will not believe, and struggles against God's Word
"should not be put to death, but be esteemed a heathen and
a publican. The gospel and its believers are not to be protected with the sword, nor should the latter so protect themselves ; yet this, from what we have gathered from our Brethren,
is your opinion. True, believing Christians are sheep among
wolves, sheep for the slaughter ; they must be baptized in
anguish and want, in tribulation and persecution, in suffering
and death ; by these must they be proved, and obtain the
home of everlasting rest, not by physical, but by spiritual
strangling. Moreover, they must not make use of the sword
of the world, nor of war, as killing is an entirely bygone thing
with them."

We do not know whether Münzer received this letter, nor what reply he gave to it ; but soon after its composition we find him on the Swiss frontier in communication with the Swiss Anabaptists. We are limited to conjecture respecting the nature of this intercourse, though the events which transpired after Münzer's return to Thuringia, lead us to infer that no agreement was arrived at concerning the employment of violent measures.

The question of such measures was a crucial one with the Anabaptists, as it had previously been with the Bohemian Brethren. This is seen from the fact that in spite of their tolerance in other matters, and the existence among them of the most diverse tendencies, they always protested against Münzer's being considered one of them. Moreover, that reformer's partisans held aloof from the Baptists. Franck tells us : " It is said that Münzer still has (1531) a large number of secret followers in Thuringia, *who are not Baptists*. Furthermore, as far as I have been informed on trustworthy authority, he has not even rebaptized."

This last circumstance is not in itself any proof that Münzer did not belong to the Baptists. Like these, Münzer publicly declared against infant baptism. In his *Protestation* he writes : " In the days of the apostles care was taken that the adversary should not mix the tares with the wheat. For that reason adults only were admitted as members of the Church, after long instruction. . . . Ah ! What shall I say ? In all the books of the Fathers of the Church from the earliest extant, there is not one single word which discloses or indicates the true mode of baptism. I ask all who are learned in letters to point out to me the place in Holy Writ in which it is asserted that a single child under age was baptized by Christ and His messengers, or which may be adduced in support of infant baptism."

At the end of January, or beginning of February, 1525, the Zurich Brethren had begun to introduce the practice of rebaptism ; at a time when Münzer had probably left to take part in the great revolutionary war, and when that sort of sectarian controversy must have seemed to him trivial and of absolutely no importance.

The idea of rebaptism (or rather late baptism) was not new. It sprang up at a very early date among the Waldenses, and was afterwards especially prominent in the early days of the Bohemian Brethren. Peter Chelcicky was of the opinion that " it were better to baptize adults only, after the manner of the ancient Church, *i.e.*, those who could confirm their faith by their works." While not wholly repudiating infant baptism, he preferred that the rite should be limited to adults only. When the community of Bohemian Brethren was formed at Lhota in 1407, their first act was rebaptism, which was performed on all who were present ; and late baptism maintained itself among the fraternity until the rise of the Anabaptists. At that time the Bohemian Brethren had acquired the character of middle-class people, and did not wish to be confounded with the Anabaptists, who bore the same features as the original followers of Chelcicky. Adult baptism now became a dangerous symbol, and for that reason the dislike to it in the Bohemian sects continued to increase until a synod held at Jungbunzlau in 1534 (the year of the Munster uprising) put a final end to the practice.[1] Hence it was no new principle, the acceptance of which gave the Zurich Brethren their name. In fact the opposition to infant baptism was a logical consequence of the opposition to the State Church.

So long as the Catholic Church in Occidental Christendom was truly Catholic, baptism implied the reception into general society. At that time there was nothing contrary to common sense in infant baptism. It was quite otherwise after the formation of opposing heretical parties, who contested the claim of the Catholic Church, that it comprised the whole of society. When other ecclesiastical organisations had been instituted, the demand was naturally advanced that each individual should not be involuntarily apportioned to a designated Church through the accident of birth, but remain free to decide until he was able to think for himself.

This conclusion, however, was not arrived at by all the Protestant sects. The Protestantism of the ruling classes consisted merely in the effort to get possession of the Church

---

[1] Gindely, *Geschichte der Böhmischen Brüder*, i. pp. 36 and 224.

as a means of government, and to incorporate it in the State. The Church became a part of the State—the State Church; and the Government in those countries to which the Reformation spread determined to what Church—to what " faith "— the citizens of the State should belong. This was afterwards displayed in the most marked manner in monarchical Germany, where the principle was formulated : *cujus regio, ejus religio ;* and where the subjects of a prince were obliged forthwith and uncomplainingly to change their faith, if their sovereign for any reason changed his, or bequeathed, gave, sold, or ceded them to another monarch of a different belief.

In democratic Protestant commonwealths the power of the State Church did not lead to such absurd consequences as in monarchies ; but the consequences became apparent sooner, and first of all in Zurich, where, as we have seen, Zwingli had introduced the State Church in 1523. The baptism of adults was incompatible, however, with the inauguration of a National Church. As every individual belonged by birth to a particular country, so in those countries having a State Church, he belonged by birth to a particular confession. Adult baptism implied a denial of State authority ; the denial of its right to fix the belief of its native-born citizens. As administrator of the State of Zurich, Zwingli could not recognise late baptism, although earlier, and as long as he was in the opposition he avowed himself to be in favour of the practice.

On the other hand, the Brethren were made to adhere more firmly to the right of adult baptism by the increasing severity of the persecution, and the growing consciousness that they were in the minority and must renounce all hope of getting the government into their hands. They saw that they could vindicate their claims only by separating from the mass of the people and organising themselves into a peculiar community of " saints " and " elect "—two appellations which sound very arrogant, and only show that the Brethren had abandoned the hope of ever constituting the mass of the population.

Thus the question of adult baptism (or as its opponents said, *re*-baptism) came more and more to the front. It was just as far from being the objective cause of the struggle as was the question of Communion in both kinds among the Hussites.[1] But as was the case with the lay chalice, circumstances caused rebaptism to be the standard round which the Brethren gathered—a token by which they recognised each other, and from which they received the name they have borne in history.[2]

III. *The Fortune and Fate of the Anabaptists in Switzerland.*

The first decisive blow received by the Anabaptists fell upon them before the outbreak of the Peasant War.

Inflamed by their preachers, and especially by Reublin, many parents refused to have their children baptized. In vain did pastors and Councilmen exert themselves to persuade the recalcitrants to yield. On the 18th of January, therefore, the Council issued an order for the compulsory baptism of children, at the same time enacting the punishment of exile to any one transgressing the decree. The execution of the order began three days later, by the banishment of Reublin, Hätzer, Andreas von der Stulzen, together with Brödli, from Graubünden, who acted as preacher in Zollikon, but supported himself by manual labour.

The answer to this blow was fit and bold. An assembly was convened of the Brothers remaining in Zurich, at which Jürg Blaurock, at one time a monk in Chur, rose and asked Conrad Grebel to baptize him with the true Christian baptism. After the ceremony had been performed, Jürg baptized all others present at the meeting. From that time

---

[1] Zwingli himself says this in a letter to Vadian of May 28, 1525, in which he designates the conflict with the Baptists as one of the severest he had ever carried on. All previous struggles had been comparatively child's play. But resistance was necessary, *as it was not merely a question concerning baptism*, but of insurrection, destruction, and contempt of authority. (Egli, *Züricher Wiedertäufer*, p. 34.)

[2] "Rebaptists" or "Anabaptists"; from the Greek *Ana*, a particle containing the idea of repetition. The members of the sect protested against this appellation. They did not baptize twice, but maintained that infant baptism was no real baptism; being, as Hubmeir calls it, only a child-bath. (In a work entitled, *Vom Christenlichen Tauff der Glaubieen*, 1525.)

rebaptism, or late baptism, was the recognised symbol of admission to the league of Brethren. An attempt was made to arrive, at the same time, at a practical realisation of communism.[1]

When the Zurich Brethren espoused the doctrine of rebaptism, they did so with the full consciousness of what awaited them.

"The Council caused many to be thrown into prison, among whom were Manz and Blaurock. Interdictions, trials, and punishments followed; then more imprisonments, conferences, and severer punishments. But this people had a spirit which mocked at the theology of Zwingli, and as wind spreads the fire, so did violence spread the name of their Church far and wide."[2]

In fact the exiles from Zurich soon sowed the seed of their doctrines throughout all German Switzerland, their greatest success being achieved on the German frontier, in Waldshut, Schaffhausen, and St. Galle.

In these and other towns of Switzerland and South Germany, the Zurich Reformation movement met with an active response; and, as in Zurich, there also appeared a radical Anabaptist party, who wished to go beyond the reform of Zwingli, and who were more successful than their coadjutors had been in the capital, where the population was less plebeian in character.

The wholesale expulsions from Zurich at the beginning of the year 1525 helped to stir up the above-mentioned towns. Grebel repaired to Schaffhausen; Brodli began to preach at Hallau, in the vicinity of the same town; and Reublin finally went to Waldshut. In Schaffhausen the new doctrines made but slow progress; but Hallau was soon won over, as well as Waldshut, where the leader of the movement was Dr.

---

[1] We have it on the evidence of an eye-witness, Heini Frei (called Gigli), that: "It was thought that all things should be in common and be heaped together; and that what any one lacked and asked for, he should take from the heap, as far as his actual needs demanded. It was also thought that persons of wealth and high family should be gladly admitted, and be induced to join" (Egli, *Züricher Wiedertäufer*, pp. 24, 97).

[2] Cornelius, *Geschichte des Münsterischen Aufruhrs*, ii. pp. 29, 30.

Balthasar Hubmeier, who, as we know, had had dealings with the Bâle circle.

This man merits a somewhat closer view. Born in Friedberg, near Augsburg, in 1480, he had devoted himself to a scholastic career, and had been made professor in the University of Ingolstadt, of which he was appointed Pro-Rector in 1515. He passed the following year at Regensburg, where he was preacher in the cathedral, and became conspicuous chiefly for his agitation against the Jews, whom the handicraftsmen accused of causing the decay of the town and the crafts. In 1519 the Jews were banished, and soon after Hubmeier also left. What drove him away we do not know; perhaps his participation in the Reformation movement. He betook himself to Waldshut, which was at that time in the possession of the Hapsburgs, and there he soon acquired an important influence as a preacher, especially among the common people. This influence was increased when, owing to the impulse given to the movement in Waldshut by the Zurich Reformation, a democratic agitation began against the ruling dynasty. This agitation, which finally led to the insurrection of the town against the Hapsburgs on the eve of the Peasant War, was headed by Hubmeier, whose *rôle* was the same as that played in Zurich by Zwingli, with whom he was in constant communication.

As we have already remarked, the success of this movement was coincident with the prosperity of the Anabaptists in Waldshut.

When Zwingli took up the cudgels against the Brethren, Hubmeier was forced to a decision. In Waldshut the common people had more power than in Zurich, and were in closer proximity to the rebellious peasants of South Germany. Hubmeier separated himself from Zwingli, and with his community went over to the Baptists, with whom he had previously been in sympathy, and was on many points in accord. When Reublin came to Waldshut, Hubmeier was baptized by him (Easter, 1525). More than three hundred citizens followed his example, and with Hubmeier the town was soon won over to the cause. This rebellious city became " a rock of the Baptist Church ; a centre whence

revival preachers and missions were dispatched in all directions" (Cornelius).

A rapid increase took place simultaneously in the St. Galle
community, and all Appenzell was soon roused to excitement.

Manz carried the Baptist doctrines to Graubünden; others
spread them in Bâle and Berne; while in the canton of
Zurich itself the agitation did not stagnate, in spite of all
the measures taken by the authorities. For a long time
it was particularly successful in the highlands of the
Grüningen.

These great successes would have been impossible without
the Peasant War, which stirred up the people of Switzerland
and Southern Germany. But when this great war was at an
end; when the rebellious German peasantry lay in the dust,
bleeding from a thousand wounds, the position of things in
the confederacy was altered for the Baptists. The lower
classes now grew faint-hearted and despairing, while the
rulers became more arrogant, their thirst for blood fired by
the famous example of their German neighbours. In the
second half of the year 1525 the persecution of the
Anabaptists became general throughout Switzerland, and
all the more bitter and cruel in proportion to the increase
of danger threatening from the communistic sectarians, under
the ægis of the Peasant War.

As early as the beginning of June the Council of St. Galle
was roused from its lethargy and decreed the prohibition of
rebaptism. Burgesses were forced to swear unconditional
obedience to the authorities, under penalty of banishment
from the town. In July Manz was arrested by the Council
of Chur and handed over to Zurich, while in August the
Council of Schaffhausen gained the mastery over the Anabaptists. October saw the arrest of Grebel and Blaurock,
and in November Berne enacted the penalty of banishment
on the advocates of Anabaptism. Finally Waldshut, the
rock of the Anabaptists, fell into the hands of the Austrian
Government without resort to arms, and Hubmeier, to whom
all other loopholes of escape were closed, fled to Zurich, where
he was seized and imprisoned.

This year, which during its first half had been so full of

brilliant success for the Anabaptists, ended in the complete overthrow and dispersion of the entire league.

Most of them fled to Germany, *e.g.*, Rueblin, Hätzer, and Blaurock.

Others repented and renounced their errors, among whom the best known was Hubmeier. After he had recanted and sworn never again to enter the canton of Zurich, he was mercifully set free (April, 1526). "Nevertheless," mourns Bullinger, "however reasonable and right-minded the simple erring folk were made by this act of Dr. Balthasar, there were many Baptists who neither by this nor by any other means could be induced to better themselves." [1]

The authorities pursued them with corporal punishments of increased severity. As early as March 7, 1526, the Council of Zurich had decreed that all who obstinately adhered to the Anabaptist cause "should be laid in the tower, kept on bread and water, and left to die and rot," women and maidens as well. Moreover, it threatened with rigorous punishment all who might shelter an Anabaptist or supply him with food and drink. Finally, the death penalty was ordained for those who should relapse, the first to suffer being Felix Manz. He was drowned on the 5th of January, and his property confiscated.

Persecution however did not succeed in suppressing the doctrine of Anabaptism in Switzerland; and indeed no communistic sect has hitherto being annihilated by violent measures. But circumstances no longer favoured the sect, and hence, after the overthrow of the German peasants, the communistic movement in the Swiss confederacy was soon forced back to the level at which it stood before the beginning of the Reformation, viz., that of a secret league, boding no danger to the governing classes but in the highest degree dangerous to its members—a league whose existence was made known only by occasional law proceedings and executions. As far as publicity was concerned, the movement had vanished.

[1] *Der Widerläuffer Ursprung*, p. 13.

IV. *The Anabaptists in South Germany.*

It would be natural to presume that the suppression of the Peasant insurrection, producing, as it did, so violent a reaction against the Baptists in neighbouring countries, must have made any success of that order in Germany itself quite impossible. But while this view would accord with the circumstances of a modern, centralised government, it does not take into account the feudal, local separatism so strong in the German Empire at that time. If this separatism increased the difficulty of combining all the revolutionary or rebellious parties into one common movement, it also diminished the energy of the reactionary blow, which did not fall on all these classes simultaneously or with equal force.

The majority of the large free cities of the Empire had confronted the Peasant insurrection with great coolness. Not only did the higher classes of burgesses—the patricians—stand in a position of enmity to the peasants, but the middle and lower classes of the urban population—the town democracy—entertained only a lukewarm sympathy for the rural population ; a lukewarmness which was often not far removed from aversion.

But as the democracy of the large towns had refrained from strengthening with their power the insurrection of the peasantry, they were not affected—or at least directly affected —by the overthrow of that insurrection. The democracy of most of the imperial cities of South Germany was unbroken after the Peasant War. But at that period an acute character was given to the conflicts between this democracy and the urban aristocracy on the one hand, and, on the other, between the whole body of the urban population and the princely powers who were aspiring to the rule and exploitation of the towns—conflicts which indeed never wholly ceased in those centuries.

The mass of the population in the Imperial cities had welcomed Luther's resistance to the Pope with joy, and given it their support ; their enthusiasm, however, diminished in proportion to Luther's increasing lukewarmness towards the democracy.

At the same time that Luther began to sever himself from the democracy, there arose in Zurich a form of Church Reformation which quite coincided with the interests of the urban guild-democracy. It soon excited the attention of the Imperial towns of South Germany, where it gained a footing ; without, however, at the outset, placing itself in opposition to Lutheranism. But the two parties were bound to come into antagonism as soon as Luther and his followers declared themselves against the democracy. And thus the epoch of the Peasant War precisely indicates the period of the beginning of the great struggle between Luther and Zwingli ; seemingly only a conflict over a word ; a battle to decide whether Christ said : " This " (the bread) "*is* my body," or " This *signifies* my body " ; but in reality a battle between middle-class democratic reformation and princely reformation, fought out with theological arguments, but concerning very mundane matters.

All Germany had been full of the struggle since 1525, but it was carried on most eagerly in the South German Imperial cities of Strassburg, Ulm, Constance, Lindau, Meinningen, Augsburg, &c. As had already been the case under similar conditions, the communists were the *tertius gaudens*. By their conflict with the Wittenberg pope, they now acquired room and light for a freer development, just as they had previously done, by their struggle with the Roman Pope. The adherents of Zwingli in South Germany were in a position to use the Anabaptists as a tool against the Lutherans ; hence they tolerated that sect during the years immediately following 1525, Zwingli himself, now their persecutor in Zurich, having, indeed, very recently favoured them.

South Germany became the asylum of political refugees from the free republic, who went there in large numbers and rapidly gained many adherents. Their peaceable intentions, which repudiated all resort to violence, exactly harmonised with the universal frame of mind among the lower classes after the suppression of the Peasant rebellion. Some who had previously been partisans of Münzer, went over to them ; *e.g.*, Hans Hut, the bookbinder, and Melchoir Rinck. Rinck was at one time schoolmaster at Hersfeld, and afterwards pastor at Eckartshaufen in the jurisdiction of Eisenach. He had, moreover, fought at Frankenhausen, but, more fortunate than Münzer, escaped with his life.

The subsequent increase among the order of the Anabaptists in Germany was so rapid that it was thought by many in that country that the order had, generally speaking, come into existence either during or after the Peasant War. The Baptists themselves encouraged this view, hoping thereby to refute the accusation that they had plotted that insurrection, as was firmly asserted by their opponents. In support of their denial they could appeal to the fact that the adoption of rebaptism as a symbol of the Brotherhood, their outspoken severance from the Zwinglian Church, and their constitution as a separate religious community took place no earlier than the beginning of the year 1525.

Sebastian Franck accepts this representation, exerting himself most zealously to prove that they were in nowise rebelliously inclined.

At all events, Franck's view is nearer the truth than the one still more widely disseminated and adopted by Bullinger—that Münzer was the founder of the Baptist sect. Bullinger had, it is true, seen the beginnings of Anabaptism in Zurich, but the Zurich pastor must have been desirous of shifting the birthplace of the inconvenient order from the home of Zwinglianism to that of Lutheranism.

The headquarters of the Baptist order in South Germany were Augsburg and Strassburg, two weaver towns in which Beghardism was very strong.

Another centre was Nurenberg, where we know Münzer found many congenial spirits, although the patrician element was too strong to admit of a successful popular movement at that time.

At the end of the year 1524 (perhaps immediately after Münzer's arrival in the town) a number of " heretics " were thrown into prison at Nurenberg, among whom were Dürer's pupil, Jörg Penz, and Hans Denck, who had been appointed Rector of the school at Sebald, on the recommendation of Oekolampadius at Bâle.

The chief personages among the accused were exiled,

including Denck, who went to Switzerland, where the cause of the Brethren was beginning to be highly prosperous. At the commencement of the year 1525 we find him as proof-reader in a printing establishment at St. Galle; but the autumn of the same year saw him once more at Augsburg in Germany. In this town the enmity between Lutheranism and Zwinglianism was beginning to show itself in its acutest form; there the battle fought at that time between the two parties raged at its fiercest, and consequently the Baptists came under conditions which were most favourable to them.

The community grew rapidly. According to Urbanus Rhegius it already numbered 1,100 members in 1527. This increase is chiefly ascribed to the agency of Denck, " who, with his vagabonds (wandering agitators), wished to establish his new Baptist order, and hid himself in a corner, where he secretly poured out his poison," over this Urbanus Rhegius laments in a pamphlet against Denck.[1]

Denck was certainly much favoured by circumstances in Augsburg; but a large part of the success he attained must be attributed to his zeal and intelligence. He and Hubmeier stood in the front rank of the vanguard of the Brethren. Peter Gynoräus, who lived in Augsburg in 1526, speaks of him as the " head of the Anabaptists." Bucer calls him the "pope"; and in a letter to Zwingli of December 2, 1527, Haller calls him the " Apollo of the Anabaptists."

As an able man of erudition and a philosopher, Denck directed his activity above all to divesting the Baptist doctrines of all that was material or " fleshly," and to making them more " spiritual." He was one of the foremost representatives of the more moderate (or perhaps more practical and placable) party among the Anabaptists, who chafed under the burden not only of the strict enforcement of the principle of community in goods, but of complete passivity towards the Government. It is true that the antagonism between the two parties did not attain to its full development in Germany; it first reached its climax in Moravia, where the community found more elbow-room, and could better allow itself the

---

[1] *Wider den newen Taufforden. Notwendige Warnung an alle christ-glaubigen durch die Diener des Evangelii zu Augsburg.* 1527.

luxury of internal quarrels. But a new practical party in opposition to the old Zurich faction was beginning already to be conspicuous in Germany and especially in Augsburg, where the Brotherhood was exceedingly prosperous, and where also it included among its members representatives of the higher classes; of whom we may mention Eitelhans Langenmantel, "a burgess belonging to one of the first families in Augsburg." [1]

As was the case with the Bohemian Brethren, the larger part of the educated members of the Anabaptist community belonged to the moderate party. Next to Denck, the most prominent of these was Hubmeier, who, it is true, deserted the sect in Zurich, but again joined it as soon as he knew that the walls of Zurich were behind him.

Meanwhile there were men of education on the other side, *e.g.*, Eitelhans Langenmantel, who, if the *Short Discourse* on *the True Community* is justly ascribed to him, made cause with the stricter form of communism.

The most determined advocate of the rigorous party was the bookbinder and accountant, Hans Hut, who, as we have seen, had been through the Münzer school, and was accused of being a member of the "Community of Wives in Common."

Denck and Hut had already encountered each other at the second Augsburg Congress of the Brethren.

Augsburg was so important a place that the two primary synods of the Baptists were held there. Among those who took part in the first of these, convened in the spring of 1526, were Hans Denck, Hans Hut, Ludwig Hätzer, and Balthasar Hubmeier. This Congress sanctioned the introduction of late Baptism into Germany, the practice having hitherto been confined to Switzerland.

Greater importance, however, attaches to the second Congress in August, 1527, which was attended by more than sixty delegates from Germany, Austria, and Switzerland. Its chief task was the organisation of the propaganda work, the sending of " apostles " into different districts, and perhaps also the settling of the programme, or " Confession."

[1] Beck, *Die Geschichtsbücher der Wiedertäufer in Oesterreich Ungarn.* Vienna, 1883, p. 36.

" Unfortunately," says Keller, who is our authority with regard to these two Congresses, " we are not in possession of the protocols of the resolutions passed by this assembly. It is certain, however, that after long debate (in which a difference arose between Denck and Hut) the delegates unanimously embodied their resolutions ; and it was Denck's propositions which carried the day."[1]

Together with the delegates to these two Congresses from the South Germany of that period, we meet with some from Austria, to which country Anabaptism had also penetrated ; first of all to the parts of Tyrol bordering on Switzerland and the neighbouring mountain regions.

Tyrol at that time played a much more important part in economics and politics than she does to-day. In that province and in the district bordering on its eastern frontier, the mining industry was more highly developed than in any other land with the exception of Saxony and Bohemia. It could boast not only of rich iron and copper ores and salt deposits, but also of numerous veins of gold and silver. The large output of these mines must have contributed to the intensification of indigenous social antagonisms, though this effect was less evident in its mountainous regions than in those of Saxony. The chief cause of this difference lay in the inaccessibility of the country and the isolation and sterility of its lonely valleys. The inhabitants of the side valleys were untouched by the influence of the few commercial routes traversing the lofty mountain passes. Their wants remained those of olden times, and the ways and means of satisfying them had not changed. No prospect of gained allured the merchant into their pathless wilds, and the peasant produced no surplus for barter.

The wealth produced by the mining population, especially in the gold and silver mines, contributed but slightly to the encouragement of manufacture, for the chief shareholders of the mines of Tyrol were non-Tyrolese, the most important being the Fuggers and Hochstetters of Augsburg. Moreover, Spaniards also were among those who worked the Tyrolese mines. Even the share that fell to the sovereigns of the

[1] *Die Reformation*, p. 429.

land, the Hapsburgs, did not remain in the country, but was scattered abroad in support of their foreign policy, going into the pockets of mercenaries from Switzerland, the Netherlands, and Spain, and enriching the ministers of various Courts whom it was necessary to bribe, as well as the German Electors and their officials.

Hence in Tyrol, though some districts were highly developed in economics, we find others which were very backward. The old constitution of the Markgenossenschaft still prevailed to a very great extent, and there was but little exploitation of peasants—at least north of the Brenner. The climax of class-antagonism was reached only in the towns and mining localities and their environs.

Hence when the waves of the Peasant War of 1525 beat upon the Tyrol and Salzburg Alps and created a stir among the population of those districts, it was not the peasants but the miners who stood at the head of the insurrection.[1]

The military strength of the miners then became evident, and proved how dangerous the uprising in Thuringia might have been if the miners of that province had thrown themselves heartily into it. The rebellions of 1525 in Northern Tyrol and the Salzburg district were the only ones which were not suppressed by military force. They were conquered by moral means, *i.e.*, by broken promises and by utilising the narrow spirit of local separatism, exhibited quite as plainly among the Salzburg miners as among the Mansfelders. A few of the more dangerous uprisings were subdued by the reform of some all too flagrant abuses, and a free hand was thus obtained for dealing with the other insurgents. After these had been defeated and time gained for the massing of troops, it became possible to subdue those districts which had remained unconquered.

Subjugated and depressed, yet without having suffered military defeat, the lower classes of Tyrol were every whit as discontented and ill-disposed after the Peasant War as those of South Germany, though not so disheartened.

This was the frame of mind in which they were found by

[1] This is fully dealt with in my treatise *Die Bergarbeiter und der Bauernkrieg.* Neue Zeit, 1889, p. 508, *sqq.*

the Anabaptist preachers from Switzerland and Bavaria, to whom it soon became clear that Tyrol offered a fertile soil for the growth of their doctrines.

The Baptist sect achieved its greatest success in the mining districts. Before the Peasant War these localities had gladly embraced Lutheranism, which in the countries of the Catholic Hapsburgs had borne the character of direct enmity to the ruling powers. " In addition to the clergy, laymen, and even miners, clerks of Court, students and others had the audacity to preach the new Gospels. . . . Enthusiasm for the new doctrines sprang up in all directions, the nucleus of the adversaries of the ancient Church being the Brotherhood at Schwaz, with its numerous adherents from the mining population." [1]

The year 1525 saw the beginning of the alienation of the democratic classes from Luther's doctrine, which had emerged from its chrysalis as an enemy to their order ; and, as soon as the doctrines of the Baptists became known to them, these classes eagerly went over to that sect.

As early as 1526 there were reports of certain " Brethren " in the valley of the Inn, among whom was Pilgrim Marbeck, a judge in the Court of Mines in the mining district of Rattenburg. In 1527, other centres of Anabaptism had been formed in Schwaz, Kitzbichel, Sterzing, Klauzen, &c., where the miners were the most zealous partisans of the Fraternity.[2]

It may be incidentally mentioned that the number of weavers among the Tyrolese Baptists was surprisingly large ; but there was no lack of members from other labouring classes, and they even had a few adherents belonging to the nobility.

The number of Baptists in Tyrol increased with extraordinary rapidity in the years immediately following the Peasant War, as it also did in the towns of South Germany.

But the period of unrestricted propagation in all these districts was extremely short ; for hardly had the sect begun

---

[1] Loserth, Der Anabaptismus in Tyrol von seinem Anfängen bis zum Tode Jakob Hutters. Vienna, 1892, p. 21.

[2] Loserth, op. cit. p. 37, and many other passages. Compare also Beck, Die Geschichtsbücher der Wiederläufer, pp. 80, 81.

to get a noticeable following when the municipal and State authorities united in instituting a persecution against it. It was of no avail to the Baptists that (even on the admission of their enemies) they led a submissive and peaceable life, and repudiated all tumults; these doctrines would, it was asserted, inevitably lead to a revolution. We find this argument used in a pamphlet against them written in the year 1528. (*Ein kurzer Unterricht.*[1]) " It is true," the writer says, " that the Anabaptists enjoin obedience to the authorities; but this is only an artifice. They have devised their devilish doctrines for the sole purpose of making themselves great and powerful, and as soon as this object is attained they will set themselves up against the authorities and pursue their vile wantonness. He who teaches that all things are in common, has naught else in his mind than to excite the subjects against the rulers ordained by God, the poor against the rich, and to cause discontent and tumult."

This argument must have met with cordial support from the ruling classes at the end of the third decade of the sixteenth century, when the remembrance of the Peasant War was still fresh. An additional cause for opposition to the Anabaptists lay in the fact that they threatened danger, not to the small villages, but to the rich and powerful cities; and finally it must not be overlooked that, in spite of their peaceableness a large contingent of the Anabaptists, and especially the proletarian adherents of Hut, could not conceal a vein of strongly rebellious sentiment. It is true that they all denounced every attempt at an armed insurrection as foolish and sinful; nevertheless many of them were convinced that the fall of the governing class was at hand, though they no longer relied on an internal uprising for the realisation of their wishes, but put their trust in a foreign war.

Even Hut built his hopes on the impending invasion of the

---

[1] The full title runs *Ein kurzer vnterricht den Pfarherrn vnd Predigern Inn meïner gnedïgen Herrn der Marggrafen zu Brandenburg,* &c. *Fürstent-humben und Landen hientben in Franken vnd auf dem Gebïrg verordnet, wes sie das volck wider etliche verfürische lere der widertauffer an den Feyertägen auff der Cantzel zum getreulichsten und besten aus Gotlicher schrifft vermanen und vnterrichten sollen.*

Turks, which he proclaimed would result in the destruction of the Empire. While this was in progress the associates were to keep hidden, but show themselves as soon as the Turks had done their part in the work to be accomplished. He even went so far as to give an exact date for the beginning of the millennium, viz., Whitsuntide, 1528.

This was no chimera. The Turks really were approaching. The Sultan Suleiman came in 1529 instead of 1528 ; but though he succeeded in seizing Hungary he did not penetrate so far as Germany. He was driven back before the walls of Vienna, to the affliction not only of the zealous Anabaptists, but also of the more energetic among the Emperor's princely opponents, especially Landgrave Philip of Hesse, so much extolled by patriotic historians.

The communists, therefore, were not the only " traitors to their country."

The sympathy for the Turks shown by a section of the Anabaptists did not make public sentiment more favourable to them, above all in countries under the sway of the Emperor.

Persecution of the Anabaptists was the chief after-effect of the Peasant War ; for it had aroused the thirst for blood and revenge among the ruling classes quite as much as it had terrorised them, and after its close they looked upon every sympathiser with the lower classes, however submissive and peaceable he might be, as a deadly enemy, who could not be too bitterly resisted or too cruelly punished.

Protestants and Catholics emulated each other in their persecution of the unfortunate sect. "The greatest amount of blood flowed in Catholic countries," writes Cornelius (*Münsterischen Aufruhr*, ii. p. 57). " In Germany the Protestants surpassed even the Catholics in rigorous and bloody persecution," says Beck (*Die Geschichtsbücher der Wiedertäufer*, xviii.). Neither of the two parties, indeed, could boast of gaining the advantage in this respect.

Though in the year 1526 the persecution of the Baptists was limited to a few isolated cases, it increased in rigour with the accession of adherents to the sect. The year 1527 saw many executions of the. Brethren, but the universal, cruel chase really began in the following year, with an Imperial mandate of the 4th of January, which imposed the death penalty on all who espoused Anabaptism. This mandate was ratified by the Reichstag of Speir in 1529—the one at which the evangelical party protested against every act of intolerance directed against them, and thus led to their being called " Protestants."

In pursuance of the sixth clause in the decree of this Reichstag, the Baptists were to be killed like wild beasts as soon as captured, without the sentence of a judge, and even without judicial inquiry!

This decree did not remain a dead letter; indeed certain States added to its severity while carrying it out.

" Some," writes one of the chroniclers of the Anabaptists, "were racked and drawn asunder; others burnt to ashes and dust; some roasted on pillars, torn with red-hot pincers or locked in together and burnt. Others were hanged on trees, beheaded with the sword, or thrown into the water. Many were gagged so that they could not speak, and in this manner led to their death.

" They were led to the slaughter and the shambles like sheep and lambs. Some either starved or rotted in darksome prisons; very many, before they were killed, being tormented with all sorts of torture. Some who were deemed too young for execution were whipped with rods, and many lay for years in dungeons and prisons. Numbers had holes burnt in their cheeks, and were then sent away. The remainder, who had escaped from all these things, were hunted from one country and place to another. Like owls and ravens, which dare not fly by day, they were often compelled to dwell in, and hide among rocks and clefts, in wild forests, or in caves and pits. In some places their Scriptural books were interdicted, and in many burnt."

We may judge of the fury of the persecution from the fact that, with the exception of those who escaped by a natural death, nearly all the prominent Baptists came to a violent end. Among those who avoided this fate were the invalid Conrad Grebel, who died in Graubünden, in the summer of 1526, and Denck, who was carried off by the plague in Bâle at the end of the year 1527.

As has already been mentioned, the first martyr to the cause was Felix Manz ; to be followed on May 21, 1527, by the erudite Michel Sattler of Staufen, in Breisgau, who had been a monk, but had joined the Brethren in 1524. He was taken prisoner at Rothenburg on the Neckar, "torn with red-hot pincers and afterwards burnt, steadfast in God." Hans Hut met his fate in Augsburg while attempting to escape from prison ; and in 1528 Brödli and Hubmeier suffered a martyr's death. In 1529 Langenmantel was executed, Blaurock burnt at the stake at Klausen in Tyrol, and Hätzer beheaded at Constance.

All who were sentenced to death met their end steadfastly and courageously ; even Hubmeier, who, it is true, had previously exhibited considerable weakness. He was seized at Nikolsburg, in Moravia, in the summer of 1527, and dragged to Vienna, at the instance of Ferdinand (brother to the Emperor Charles), who had been in possession of the power of the Hapsburg House in Germany since 1521, and King of Hungary and Bohemia since 1526. In imitation of his conduct at Zurich in 1525 Hubmeier now sought to save himself by a recantation of his errors ; even declaring his willingness to submit to the judgment of a Church Council as regards Baptism and the Lord's Supper, and simultaneously offering his good services to Ferdinand, the persecutor of heretics. In a memorial—his "account"—to the King, of January 3, 1528, after lauding Ferdinand's well-known clemency, he prays that " Your Majesty would graciously and compassionately pardon me, an imprisoned and afflicted man now lying in a dungeon, in great sickness, cold, and tribulation ; for with God's help I will so conduct, dispose, and restrain myself that it shall meet with your Royal Majesty's approval. I promise with exceeding earnestness and diligence to direct the people to devotion, godly fear and obedience, as I have always prevailed upon myself to do." [1]

But all petitions and promises were in vain. As leader of the Waldshut opposition, Hubmeier had been a rebel to the

[1] Quoted by Loserth in *Dr. Balthasar Hubmeier und die Anfänge der Wiedertäufer in Mähren*, Brunn, 1893, p. 180.

Hapsburgs, and this was a crime never forgiven by that House.

When Hubmeier saw that his doom was sealed, he took courage, inspired by his brave wife Elizabeth, daughter of a burgess of Reichenau, on Lake Constance, whom he had married at Waldshut in 1524. She exhorted him to be brave, and he perished at the stake in Vienna, steadfast in his faith (1528). Three days afterwards his faithful wife was thrown into the Danube and drowned.

The weakness displayed by Hubmeier was very rare among the Baptists. One is astonished at the firmness and joy with which as a rule they went to their death. The Baptists glory in their heroes quite as much as Christian writers, who point to the noble deaths of the martyrs of primitive Christianity in proof of the sanctity and sublimity of their cause.

All this steadfastness and heroism, however, had but *one* consequence—viz., the enormous increase of Anabaptist martyrs, who, according to Sebastian Franck, already numbered 2000, in 1530.

It is commonly asserted that ideas cannot be stamped out by violence. There are many proofs of the truth of this dictum, and it is comforting to all who are persecuted ; but in this unqualified form it is not true. Admittedly, an idea itself cannot be annihilated by violence ; but by itself alone an idea is a mere shadow, without any effective force. The strength to which a social ideal attains—and it is only this kind of ideal which is under consideration—is dependent upon the individuals who uphold it—*i.e.*, upon their power in society. If it is possible to annihilate a class which upholds a given idea, then that idea will perish with its advocates.

The sixteenth century belonged to governmental abso-lutism. Even in the few free cities, the power of the executive authority amongst the lower classes became continuously more unlimited. If absolutism had succeeded in mastering the opposition of the knights, peasants, and petty burgesses, it could easily have crushed the communistic agitations of a few proletarians and powerless idealists. Anabaptism vanished in South Germany quite as suddenly as it had arisen. Relentless persecution was one of the causes, and indeed the most active cause of its rapid disappearance; but this was aided in no small degree by the circumstance that at the very moment the persecution began the Baptists found, outside of Germany, an asylum to which they flocked in large numbers. This asylum was Moravia—the America of the sixteenth century.

V. *The Anabaptists in Moravia.*

Moravia offered very favourable conditions for the development of the Baptist power. Being under the same rulers as Bohemia, the Margravate had shared the fate of that country during and after the Hussite Wars. The conflicts which rent Germany asunder in the first decade of the sixteenth century had long ago been fought out in the countries under the Bohemian Crown, and had led to a compromise between the old and new faiths, and to the consequent prevalence of religious toleration. Side by side with the Catholics and Utraquists the sect of the Bohemian Brethren had arisen, without in the slightest degree endangering the State or society, and to the great economic advantage of the barons in whose districts they dwelt.

In Bohemia and Moravia a new sect did not need the protection of government to secure its toleration. Since the Hussite Wars the sovereigns had been powerless, while the higher nobility enjoyed almost complete independence. If a sect had gained the good graces of a baron, it might settle quietly in his domain, let the sovereign think what he might. This condition of things was not changed until Bohemia and Moravia fell into the hands of the Catholic Hapsburgs (1526).

In spite of these favourable circumstances, the Anabaptists never gained a firm foothold in Bohemia. This is explained by the relations between the nationalities composing the population of that country. In the sixteenth century the national antagonism which had attained to such a height in the previous century was still very strong, and Germans could have hardly felt quite at ease among the Czech population. In Moravia, on the contrary, national antagonisms had never been so intense, and Germans could more easily find a home there.

Early in the autumn of 1526 Hubmeier, with a large following, went from Augsburg to Moravia, and was hospitably received at Nikolsburg, in the domain of Baron Leonhard von Lichtenstein, who himself received baptism. A community was there organised, and—this is particularly significant—a printing house immediately established, in which Hubmeier's works were printed.

The fame of the new "Emmaus" soon spread on all sides among the Brethren, and led many a one to escape persecution by a flight to the promised land. Freedom and prosperity however tended only to increase the already existing schism. The antagonism between the strict and moderate parties, which had previously appeared in Germany, but had been forced into the background by the persecution, came to its full development in Moravia. The respective leaders of the two parties were Hubmeier and Hut, both refugees from Germany.

The impending war with Turkey made the rupture wider. A war-tax was levied to carry on the war with the unbelievers. Should the Baptists pay this? They deprecated war, and the strengthening of the Imperial power against the Turks accorded ill with Hut's plans, as he expected to derive benefit for his sect from the invasion of the infidels. A series of discussions on this subject took place at Nikolsburg.

The chronicles of the Anabaptists inform us that : " After the cry went forth in 1527 that the Turks intended laying siege to Vienna, the Brethren and elders of the community assembled in the courtyard of the parsonage at Pergen, near Nikolsburg . . . to hold a conference on the above-mentioned matters, but did not arrive at a unanimous decision." And in another place : " Hans Hut and others met in the castle of Lichtenstein at Nikolsburg, to take counsel concerning the sword ; whether or not they were to use or to wear it, and whether the war-tax should be paid, besides other mandates ; but they could not come to an agreement, and consequently separated.

" As Hut could not and would not agree with Baron

Leonhard von Lichtenstein that the sword was necessary, he was detained against his will in the castle. Some well-wisher, however, who had his interests at heart, managed to lower him from his prison window in a net. The following day great murmuring and complaint arose among the townfolk against Baron Leonhard and his adherents, because he had violently detained Hut in his castle. This induced Balthasar Hubmeier and his colleagues to deliver a public discourse in the hospital, explaining why they had been unable to come to an agreement touching the sword and tax." [1]

Thus it appears that affairs among the peaceable Brethren had at that time reached a very critical stage.

Hans Hut did not remain in Moravia. In the autumn of 1527 we find him once more at Augsburg, where he was seized, and, as already related, put to death. Hubmeier, however, continued his campaign against the more severe tendencies. His publication, *Concerning the Sword*, is devoted exclusively to polemics against his opponents among the Brethren.

At the same time he published controversial treatises against Zwingli and his followers, and one of these shows that his communism was of a mild type. In his *Discourse upon Master Ulrich Zwingli's Pamphlet concerning Infant Baptism* he says, in reply to the reproach that he advocated "the community of goods," [2]—*i.e.*, communism : "I have always, and in every way, taught that community of property means that one man should have compassion on another ; that he should feed the hungry, give drink to the thirsty, and clothe the naked ; for in truth, we are not masters of our possessions, but stewards or dispensers only. Certainly none could think that we ought to take from another what belongs to him, and make it common property, but rather give the cloak in addition to the coat." It is not very satisfactory, however, that Hubmeier, when he was arrested, sought in his *Account* to recommend himself

---

[1] Beck, *Die Geschichtsbücher*, &c. pp. 49, 51.

[2] *Ein Gesprech Balthasar Huebmörs von Friedberg, Doktors. auff Mayster Ulrich Zwinglens zu Zurich Taufbuechlein von dem Kindertauf.* Nikolsburg, 1526.

to the favour of King Ferdinand by particularising his sharp opposition to Hans Hut. He there speaks of "the Day of Judgment," which in the language of that age meant nothing less than revolution. "Although Christ has given us many signs by which to recognise how near at hand is the day of His coming, still no one knows this day but God alone. I have been almost severe against Johannes Hut and his adherents, because they have fixed a definite time for the last day—viz., next Whitsuntide ; because they have preached to the people, and induced them to sell houses and property, to forsake wife and child ; and have prevailed upon the foolish to leave their work and run after him—an error which has arisen from a great want of right comprehension of the Bible." Out of the three and a half years spoken of in Daniel, Hut had made four ordinary years, which was a great mistake. According to Hubmeier's calculation, one day of Daniel's year equals one of our ordinary years ; therefore these three and a half years would amount to 1277 ordinary years. "What I laid before him plainly and earnestly was that he had persuaded and misled the poor people, and for this I reproved him." The revolutionary who awaited a revolution only after 1277 years was, at any rate, not a dangerous member of society.

The strife between the two opinions was in no way ended by the death of both the great adversaries, even though it died down for a time—*i.e.*, when the transitory persecution of the Baptists extended to Moravia itself, and public attention was at the time drawn to the Turkish invasion.

Many Brethren set forth from Germany for Moravia during these troubles, and a "people" settled down at Rossitz under Gabriel Ascherham, after whom they were called the *Gabrielists*. Finding themselves too circumscribed there, a portion, chiefly inhabitants of the Palatinate, withdrew to Auspitz under the leadership of Philip Flener, and were in consequence called *Philippists*. Being opposed to the more severe views, both communities had joined the milder sect, but they could not agree among themselves. Among the Nikolsburg townsmen, the dispute between the two parties continued to be carried on, and the stricter faction now received the nickname of *Communists* (*Gemeinschaftler*) or *Staffists* (*Stübler*), and their opponents that of *Swordists* (*Schwertler*).

On the side of the latter was Leonhard von Lichtenstein ; but when the quarrel became too bitter even for him, he compelled the strict communists, now risen to two hundred strong, to quit the district (1524). ˙ The moment the latter turned their backs on the old community, they gave free play to their communism. " At that time these men spread out a mantle before the people, and every one laid down his possessions on it for the support of the needy, under no compulsion or pressure, but with hearty willingness, according to the teaching of the Prophets and Apostles." [1]

They withdrew to Austerlitz, where the Picards had settled themselves as early as 1511. Here they were received with open arms by the lords of Kaunitz, in whose territories Austerlitz lay, and were soon followed by numerous partisans, this town becoming the capital of the Baptists in Moravia.

Disputes, however, could not be avoided even among the people of Austerlitz. Wilhelm Reublin of Auspitz gives us a graphic description of this in a letter to his friend, Pilgram Marbeck (the above mentioned mine-magistrate), written January 26, 1531 ; wherein he relates how and why he and his adherents were driven out of Austerlitz (January 8th). Among other things, he reproaches those who remained behind with " managing the community of temporal and personal property dishonestly and fraudulently. . . . They were respecters of persons, permitting the rich to have their own little houses, so that Franz and his wife led a life like the nobles. At meals the ordinary Brethren had been content with peas and cabbages, but the elders and their wives had roast meat, fish, fowls, and good wine ; many of their wives I have never seen at the common table. While some might be in want of shoes and shirts, they themselves must have good breeches, coats, and furs, in abundance." [2]

Reublin and his adherents withdrew to Auspitz, and there

---

[1] Beck, *Geschichtsbücher*, p. 75.

[2] The letter has been printed in full as Supplement V. to Cornelius, *Münsterischer Aufruhr*, vol. ii. p. 235.

formed a community of their own; but having kept back forty gulden which he had brought with him from Germany, instead of paying them into the common fund, Reublin was soon declared to be a "lying, unfaithful, malignant Ananias," and was accordingly expelled. In 1531, the disturbances in Baptist localities in Moravia reached their culminating point. Franck, who published his *Chronik* at that time, characterises the position of the Moravian Brethren very exactly in the passage already quoted (p. 164), in which he points out that a great many in their community were anathematised, and expresses his doubts as to whether there was "just distribution" in Austerlitz.

"The Fraternity have proceeded from one carnal license to another," relates the Baptists' historian in Moravia of those times: "They have become exactly like the world." [1]

But what appeared to be a process of dissolution was in reality one of fermentation, which produced clear and lasting results.

The effect of all these contests was a communistic organisation which maintained itself for nearly a whole century, and which was only ultimately crushed by superior force. The chief merit of the definitive Baptist organisation is due to the Tyrolese immigrants, who flocked by hundreds into Moravia in 1529, and impressed their stamp on the movement there. Prominent among their leaders was the hatter Jakob, called after his trade Huter (frequently confounded with Hans Hut). His influence upon the organisation was so great that a community in Moravia was called after him, being known as the Huter Fraternity. How far Huter's genius alone impressed itself upon the new organisation, or how far he was the executor of the will of the numbers who stood behind him and lent him their strength, it is very difficult in these days to determine.

In the autumn of 1529 Jakob Huter and Schützinger with their adherents came from the Tyrol to Austerlitz, and entered into close connection with the community there. Perceiving that circumstances were favourable to their party in Moravia, Jakob returned to the Tyrol in order to despatch "one small

---

[1] Beck, *Geschichtsbücher*, p. 99.

community after another" to the land of his adoption. These new-comers brought enthusiasm, self-sacrifice, and discipline with them, and formed the kernel of the communistic communities which fused the other internal elements into a peaceful and steady harmony.

In August, 1533, Huter himself returned with numerous followers, for in Tyrol "tyranny had reached to such a height that it was impossible for the faithful to remain any longer." Such was the opinion of the Brothers who were assembled at the Congress in the district of Gufidaun (Tyrol) in the July of that year. The real work of the organisation now began, and must have been carried on with the greatest energy and with the fullest consciousness of the aim for which they were working. We may judge so at least from the fact that the peculiar characteristics of the Baptist community remained unchanged up to the time of their rising in Munster. This insurrection spurred on the sharpest persecution of the Anabaptists, which horrified for a time even a portion of the Moravian nobility, so that they withdrew their protection from the Baptists. The first great persecution began in Moravia, the result of which was that the Baptist community was obliged to dissolve itself, and its members were banished. We learn through this circumstance how large the Fraternity had grown at that time, its numbers amounting, as it was estimated, to from three thousand to four thousand.

Huter also was forced to take refuge in flight. The protest against the persecution of the Brethren which he sent on May 1, 1535, to the Governor-General of Moravia, shows the exceeding boldness of the man. "Alas and woe!" he exclaimed, among other things, "and again eternal woe to you, ye Moravian lords, that you should have promised and agreed to the demands of the tyrant and enemy of divine truth, Ferdinand, to drive the pious and god-fearing out of the country, and that you should dread mortal, vain man more than the Almighty and the Lord." [1]

This protest could produce but one result, that of making the pursuit after Huter more keen. "The authorities have

---

[1] The protest is printed as Supplement XVII. to Loserth's *Anabaptismus in Tyrol bis zum Tode Huters*, pp. 171–175.

hunted down Brother Jakob in a most determined manner, often exclaiming, 'If we only had Jakob Huter!' as though they wished to imply that if he could be got rid of, everything would return to the old condition."[1]

Huter managed, however, to escape to the Tyrol, though he was no safer there than he had been in Moravia, being finally taken prisoner in Klausen, November, 1535. Of his treatment the Brethren relate: "They made him sit in ice-cold water, and afterwards led him into a hot room and beat him with rods. They also wounded him in the body, and after pouring brandy into his wounds, set him alight and let him burn," &c., &c. He was burnt early on a morning of March, 1536, with great secrecy, for fear of the people.

Though their leader had fallen, the community possessed sufficient internal strength to enable it to surmount this and many another blow. In 1536 the Baptists were again allowed to assemble in Moravia, as the lords upon whose properties they had settled had recognised the economic importance of these industrious and skilful workmen during the persecution, and were glad to summon them back. Forth they came, therefore, out of all their hiding-places, and before long were able not only to repair the old injuries, but to take measures for the founding of fresh communities.

Far from doing the Baptists any harm, the persecution seemed on the contrary to have strengthened them, as it had eliminated all doubtful elements from among them. Their unanimity was much greater after the year 1536 than it had been before that date, and they thenceforth made great strides, all the other branches being finally absorbed into the Huter community.

The strictest communism was now the basis of the organisations of Moravian Baptists. To possess even the most trifling things as personal property was considered a sin. "On being condemned to death, Hans Schmidt sent his ear-pick to his Magdalena as a remembrance, provided *the Brothers had no objection.* This same Hans Schmidt paid for his faith in the community of property with his head.

"Whosoever joins himself to the Baptists is obliged to

[1] Beck, *Geschichtsbücher,* p. 117.

relinquish all his possessions, and give them over to the appointed directors. The communities consist chiefly of poor people, work-people, and trades-people ; but we learn from the public records in the Tyrol that, quite apart from a few isolated members of the nobility, some really opulent peasants turned towards the new teaching." [1]

Whatever a member might present to the community belonged to it absolutely, and was not merely capital advanced. Even should the donor retire or be expelled, he could not receive the contribution back.

In State and military affairs the stricter doctrines remained triumphant; the regulation being that in all equitable things the authorities were to be submitted to, but that God was to be obeyed rather than man, *i.e.*, the Baptists reserved to themselves the right to decide the cases in which obedience was justifiable. They continued, therefore, to repudiate any share in the executive power, such as the carrying on of war, or even the payment of a war tax.

"If any man require of us something which God has not commanded, such as a *tax for war*, or an *executioner's wages*, or other things which are not becoming to a Christian, and which are not authorised by Scripture, we must in no wise consent." Such was the declaration of the Baptists in 1545, in a memorial to the Moravian Diet.

The development among the Baptists was different from that among the Bohemian Brethren. Among the latter the moderate side triumphed in the battle between the two conflicting opinions, while among the former the strict faction gained the mastery.

The causes for these differences must be sought in the circumstances in the midst of which the two sects lived.

The Bohemian Brethren worked among their own nation, and as soon as their community began to thrive and spread, the possibility naturally occurred to them (accompanied by the desire) of gaining the whole nation to their cause. Every attempt of practical efficacy in this direction led, however, in

---

[1] Loserth, *Der Kommunismus der Mährischen Wiedertäufer im 16 und 17 Jahrhundert*, pp. 102, 106. Wien 18.

those days of rising commercialism, to a modification of their communistic tendencies and their abstention from politics.

The Baptists in Moravia, on the contrary, were Germans in the midst of a Czech population, and chose to remain so. They felt themselves strangers in a foreign land and could reconcile themselves without effort to remaining a small sect ; a tiny circle of the "elect" and "godly" in the midst of the heathen. They had but few points of sympathy with their surroundings, and even these had no attractions for them, but drew them closer to each other.

It is a familiar phenomenon that even without communistic organisation, people of similar origin or similar language, living in the midst of a foreign population, experience a greater sense of solidarity than they feel while in their own homes.

Hence still another condition of things arose. Among the Bohemian Brethren, the advance of moderate views went hand in hand with the admission of men of letters into the Brotherhood. The learned men thus admitted within the community formed the most determined champions of the moderate opinions, perhaps because their views were broader, perhaps because they felt most keenly the loss of social status which the sect had suffered.

The learned men among the Anabaptists also were, in the majority of cases, holders of the moderate opinions. But the first persecution in Germany, which began in 1527 and lasted till the commencement of the Thirty Years' War, swept away nearly all of them, and they have had no followers. From that time no men of letters are to be found among the Baptists, nearly all the persons of consequence being thenceforth simply working people. The hatred of learning, which had always been perceptible in most of the communistic sects during the Middle Ages and the period of the Reformation, could now display itself among them unhindered.

" The profound contempt of the Anabaptists for all literary subjects," says Loserth, " for universities and learned individuals, has astonished their contemporaries." Fischer, a Catholic priest, and a bigoted enemy of the Anabaptists, exclaims : " Are not these Anabaptists then chiefly winedressers, peasants, tradesmen ; uncouth, coarse, ignorant,

illiterate people, scarcely distinguishable from the common
rabble ?   Do they not despise all the liberal arts as well
as the Holy Scriptures, *i.e.*, when the latter are of no use
to them?   Do they not contemn all the universities?   Do
they not hinder the influence of all the learned ?   Do they
not repudiate all history ? "   There is much truth in what
Fischer asserts.   In the numerous judicial trials, and in the
epistles to the communities in Moravia, they expressed unhesitatingly their contempt for the learned professions ; nay,
they even treated their learned judges and the missionary
priests of the different Confessions somewhat disrespectfully
for the same reason.[1]

The fact that after the first persecution no more learned
men joined the Baptists is chiefly attributable to the circumstances which this persecution called into existence.
From 1527 every one who professed the faith of the
Baptists was outlawed from respectable society.   If he
could not make up his mind to become a peasant among
peasants, a workman with workman, or to banish himself
to the limits of the civilised world, then it was wiser for
him, however strong his convictions of the truth of the
Baptist faith, to keep them closely concealed within his
own breast.

Next to these circumstances another point comes into
consideration which explains the triumph of the stricter
opinions among the Baptists.

The same persecution which exterminated literary men
in the Baptist movement drove the great mass of the
Tyrolean Brethren into Moravia ; amongst them were
numerous miners, who had passed through the school of
capitalistic exactions, and had learnt systematic discipline
and co-operation in that industry.   About the same time
the weavers appeared, among whom communistic enthusiasm had always been particularly strong.   Thus it is
chiefly due to the pressure of these circumstances that
the stricter communism of the Moravian Fraternities
gained the upper hand.

Like all the various kinds of Fraternities hitherto con-

[1] Loserth, *Kommunismus der Wiedertäufer*, p. 144.

sidered, the fundamental principle of this sect was the association of the consumers and the community of the means of consumption. With this was necessarily combined the abolition of the private family ; but the Moravian Baptists certainly never arrived· at the abolition of individual marriages. One form of this abolition—celibacy—was forbidden to them in consequence of the practice being a tenet of the Romish Church, which they opposed on the ground that it would have placed them on a level with the monks, the most detested of all the defenders of the Papacy, and the champions of the worst sort of exactions and corruptions of those times. The free intercourse of the sexes was even more opposed than celibacy to the convictions of the petty citizens, and that small peasant world, in whose sphere of thought the proletariat of that time also moved.

Greater freedom in love or marriage was more appreciated by the upper revolutionary classes—the princes, merchants, and humanist savants of the sixteenth century —than by the elements from which the Baptists were recruited. Happiness and the consciousness of their position in life were possible among the upper classes, and all the conditions of society only engendered self-satisfaction more strongly and actively, encouraging individualism and a hatred of every kind of restraint. The communists among the ill-used and downtrodden classes, on the other hand, could only hold their ground in the conflicts of their times (to some extent, at all events) by sinking their personality in a great association. These communists, with their gloomy asceticism, looked upon sexual pleasure, as upon every other sort of pleasure, as something unworthy a thought ; and they considered the self-assertion of individualism to be also sinful, rejecting it the more carefully in that it appeared to them to be united with wantonness and arrogance among the upper classes. The modern conception of individual sexual affection was at that time in its infancy, and its preliminary conditions were to be found rather among some of the upper classes than among the lower.

Thus in the Reformation the courtiers of the princes were the very ones who urged the easier dissolution of marriage. Luther and Melancthon even held that plurality of wives was permissible, and Luther himself declared that illicit sexual intercourse was more deserving than chastity. " All nuns and monks, who are without faith, and trust in their purity and their order, are not worthy to rock a baptized child, or to make pap for it, even if it be a bastard. Why ? Because they have not God's Word for their Orders or their life ; neither may they boast that God is pleased with what they do, a boast which a woman may make even if she bear an illegitimate child."

Amidst the communists of that time, on the contrary, the greatest strictness with regard to marriage prevailed, with few exceptions. Adultery was a serious crime, and marriage was held to be indissoluble. " What God has joined together let no man put asunder," said the Baptists. In a case of adultery, not only was the guilty party punished with temporary exclusion, but the guiltless husband also came in for his share of condemnation. He might no longer have anything to do with the guilty party, at all events as long as the latter was not completely absolved. Any lapse with regard to this regulation drew down upon him a relentless sentence of expulsion. Thus, for example, we are told in the *Chronicle* of the year 1530, of one Jörg Zaunring, the successor of Wilhelm Reublin in the headship of the Auspitz community : " When one, to wit Thomas Lindl, had committed adultery with the wife of Jörg Zaunring, they [perhaps the elders] only banished these two secretly ; and Jörg, during the time of his wife's punishment, renounced and withheld himself from her. But as soon as the two were again admitted and had received the pardon of their sins, Zaunring took his wife back again as before ; and this being publicly known, *the community could not suffer this disgrace of adultery and harlotry to be so lightly punished.* . . . Linhard Schmerbacher, a server of the secular needs, pointed out to the community that Jörg Zaunring had by this transaction participated in the debauch, and the members at once passed sentence unanimously ; because the ' members of Christ cannot be the members of a harlot,' these two transgressors were justly expelled from the community." [1]

Expulsion was the severest punishment inflicted by the Baptists.

There is no trace of any community of wives. They were, on the contrary, much stricter on marriage questions than the " heathen." But there was little of marriage left among the Baptists except the pairing. In consequence of the gloomy, joyless asceticism which interdicted dancing and courtship, individual sexual affection was more strange to them than to the mass of the population of their times : marriages, therefore, were mostly arranged by the elders (the heads of the community) similar to the pairing in Plato's Republic, and among the *Perfectionists* of Oneida.

Apart from the pairing, the essential features of individual marriages were done away with by the community of house-keeping and the education of the children in common.

The community was made up of households (*Haushaben*) scattered over the whole of Moravia. At the time of greatest prosperity there were seventy of these, in each of which from 400 to 600 persons or more lived together, and in the largest of them even 2,000. " They all had but one kitchen, one bakehouse, one brewhouse, one school, one room for women in child-bed, one room in which the mothers and the children were with each other, and so on.

" In such a household there was one who was host and householder, who purchased all the wheat, wine, wool, hemp, salt, cattle and every necessary, out of the money of all the trades and all the incomes, and divided it according to the several needs of all in the house ; food for the children, the lying-in women and all other people being brought into one room, the eating-room. Sisters were appointed for the sick, who carried them their food and waited upon them.

" The very old were placed apart ; and to them some-

[1] Beck, *Geschichtsbücher*, p. 101.

what more was allowed than to the young and healthy, but to all a sufficiency was granted according to their several wants and the wealth of the community." [1]

A letter, written to the "Elder Brothers at Wintz," gives us some details in regard to the food served at these general meals. It was indited at the time of the decline of the communities, when, driven out of Moravia, they dragged on a miserable existence in Hungary (1642). "How we keep our table with food and drink : we have meat at supper every day, and in the mornings once, twice, thrice, or four times during the week, according as the seasons serve. At the other meals we are content with vegetables.

"Twice every day at meals a luscious drink of wine ; otherwise nothing at midday, nor in the afternoon (*Marend*), nor in the evening ; but when we go to evening prayers we receive a drink, and sometimes even have beer.

"With the bread, which is generally to be had in the house, we are quite content, even if we are not permitted to bake anything special during the whole year ; this, how-ever, we are permitted to do when there is any peculiar reason, such as for the Day of the Lord's Remembrance, or the festivals of Easter, Whitsuntide, and Christmas." [2]

The fare of the *Geschwistriget* (Brothers and Sisters), as the Baptists called themselves amongst each other, was simple but abundant. There was no fixed rule for it, but, as has been already observed, "every one received according to his needs and the common wealth." How this was managed is shown us in a food regulation of 1509 (made for a time of famine), which portioned out the food according to age, sex, business, condition of health, &c., &c. Even this rough and primitive community stands far above the "State-kitchens" with their similarity of food and equally large portions for everybody, which

[1] Andreas Ehrenpreis, *A Circular Letter . . . concerning brotherly Com-munion, which is the highest precept of Love.* 1650. Quoted by Loserth, *Der Kommunismus der Mährischen Wiedertäufer*, p. 115 sqq. Ehrenpreis, a miller who was head of the united Fraternity from 1639 to 1662.

[2] Beck, *Geschichtsbücher*, pp. 406, 407.

Eugène Richter's fancy has pictured in the democratic *State of the Future* of the twentieth century.

After the community in housekeeping, the joint training of the Baptist children is specially worthy of remark. Beck speaks of the " Spartan education of the children, who went into the general room from their mother's breasts, and grew up strangers to their parents and to all feelings of childhood" (Beck's history, p. 17). It would have been more accurate if he had called it the Platonic instead of the Spartan education of the children. Many points put us in mind of Plato's Republic, and others of More's Utopia, and it is not impossible that these were borrowed from them, Plato not being unknown to the communists of that time. Münzer refers to him (compare p. 121) as well as the Sebastian Franck who was so closely allied to the Baptists. The men of letters who were connected with the Baptist movement at its commencement certainly knew Plato. More's Utopia was also pondered and discussed in the Humanist circle at Bâle, which gathered round Erasmus of Rotterdam, and influenced so many of the early learned Baptists. It is not impossible—perhaps even very probable—that suggestions from these writings were conveyed even to the uneducated Brethren by the scholars. This fact has not been proved, however, and it is not absolutely necessary to accept it in order to explain the similarity between some of Huter's institutions and those of Plato and More ; as this may have for its basis the fact that the logic of events led the uncultivated proletariat in Moravia to adopt the same course which the Greek philosopher and the English humanist have described as the outcome of their conceptions.

The followers of Huter did not go so far as Plato in taking the child from the mother immediately after its birth, and making it impossible for her to recognise it again. There was a special room for the lying-in women, another of the same kind for women nursing their infants, and the child remained with its mother in the latter. Nevertheless, at eighteen months or two years of age, we find it already at school, in the general institution for education.

This was one of the points which gave the enemies of the Baptists the greatest cause for animadversion. "The perverted Anabaptists act against nature," wrote Fischer, the priest, in 1607. "They are less intelligent than the little birds, and more unmerciful towards their young than are the wild beasts; for, as soon as the child is weaned, it is taken from its mother and given over to the appointed Sisters. After that, schoolmasters and cross, ill-tempered governesses, who are strangers to it, strike it at times passionately and mercilessly, without love, decency, or pity. Children are thus brought up with the greatest strictness, so that many a mother, after five or six years, neither recognises nor knows her offspring, and much incest springs up from this cause." The children brought up under such a system are miserably sickly and "swollen."

Facts proved this not to be the case. Fischer even contradicts himself; for, in other passages, he laments over the circumstance that the well-to-do classes in Moravia preferred to take women from the Anabaptist schools as wet-nurses and children's maids, which they certainly would not have done if the results of these schools had been so disastrous as he has implied. "God-'a-mercy! It has come to such a pitch that nearly all the women in Moravia must have none but the Anabaptist women as *mid-wives*, *wet-nurses*, and *children's maids*, as if they alone were the most experienced in these things." Nothing could testify more highly to the superiority of the communistic education than this admission of a most hostile enemy of communism.

Not only were their women in demand as instructresses for the young, but their schools also enjoyed such an excellent reputation that *persons of other faiths gladly sent their children to them.*

Like other communists, since the time of the Waldenses, the Huterites laid the greatest stress upon a sound popular education. Their school regulations and their rules for the masters are worthy of notice even in the present day, but they were magnificent performances for the sixteenth century, a period which, probably, represented the lowest level of pedagogism, and exhibited its cruelty and roughness in its schools.

The Baptists declare : " *Hard blows will not effect much ;* children should be worked upon through teaching ; if men possessed the fear of God, so that they could control themselves, they would require no schoolmaster."

The Baptist schools possessed a numerous staff of schoolmasters and " school-sisters," as well as " children's maids " under a " school-mother." These had charge not only of the spiritual, but also of the bodily welfare of the young.

Both training and tuition were regulated by " old customs " which were formulated in 1568, and this school system lays great stress upon the physical well-being of youth. It says, for example : " If a child be brought to school, its state of health must be carefully investigated. Should it have any bad illness, such as putrid fever, syphilis, or the like, it must be separated from the other children during sleep, and while eating and washing."

" If a school-mother has cleansed the mouth of a sick child, she must not examine the mouth of a healthy one with unwashed fingers, but before doing so must always cleanse her fingers with a clean towel and water." She is also to instruct the school-sisters how to clean a child's mouth.

Great importance was universally attached to the maintenance of a most scrupulous degree of cleanliness.

The Sisters had to keep watch over the slumber of the little ones, and to refrain from striking them if they cried out somewhat in their sleep. Should one throw off its coverings, it was to be recovered, lest it should take cold. During the night nothing was to be given to a child to eat, unless it was ill. Without real necessity, no sleeping child was to be roused by force, &c., &c.

Children were not to be treated with unnecessary severity. Should it be necessary to blame a child a little at spinning, instructresses were to refrain from impulsive blows. A notice to the schoolmaster was sufficient. The schoolmaster punished the big boys ; the school-mother the girls. For such offences as thieving, lying, and other sins, the degree of the penalty was always to be determined with the advice of a Brother, and too severe punishments, like blows on the head or the mouth, were strictly forbidden.

The training of children was to be individual : " In the bringing up of a child, great watchfulness is required, and a fine power of discrimination ; for one is best drawn by kindness, another by gifts, while a third requires strict discipline."

These extracts from the school regulations should be enough to prove that Loserth is correct when he says they contain maxims which would do honour even to schools of modern days.

It is not known what subjects were taught by the instructors beyond reading and writing—in which all the Baptists were fairly skilled. But mental culture appears to have gone hand in hand with productive work, the girls at least being kept at the spinning-wheel from an early age.

To what age the school regulations extended is almost unknown ; but on leaving school the children were sent into the various industries, or agriculture, or into the household. The primary duty in all industrial and agricultural work was to provide for the necessities of the community. Before these were supplied, no work could be undertaken for outsiders.

The Baptists, however, were excellent and diligent workmen, and their labour supplied an important surplus. Their achievements were specially prominent in the departments of horse-breeding, mills, brewing, and later on in cutlery and cloth-making as well, which became their most important trade. Here again we find wool-weaving in intimate connection with communism. The great proportion of their produce was sold, thus affording them the opportunity of steadily extending the production of certain commodities far beyond their own needs, and thereby attaining to production on a large scale in some branches of industry.

The household system and that of production had at all times been in close connection, and in earlier ages was even more conspicuous than at the period under consideration, the extent of the industrial or rural establishment determining that of the family. The capitalistic form of production altered all this by separating the workshop from the household, so that there was no longer any interdependence between the two.

The extent of the family, however, did not remain without influence upon that of the industrial establishment.

Communal housekeeping—*e.g.*, that of the monasteries and the Beghard houses—always encouraged the tendency towards the establishment of industries and farms on a large scale. If about twenty weavers shared in a common household, they always bought the raw material in common, and manufactured it together in one place. This tendency, however, had but little opportunity for developing itself. In one of these institutions—the monastery—it was checked, because, sooner or later, these organisations invariably ceased to be associations of workmen, and became communities of idlers. And in the others—Beghard houses and similar institutions—the development was hindered by persecutions. Both of these flourished as associations for work, in an age when, socially and technically, the conditions of wholesale business were not in existence.

This was not the case with the Anabaptists in Moravia. Their institutions were more secure than most of the Beghard houses had been ; nevertheless, as strangers who were only tolerated and who had suffered from the constant enmity of the rulers, they were unable to develop their households into communities of idlers, as the monasteries had done. Finally, they began at a period when numerous provisions for co-operative production were already in existence. The mining and smelting houses were already regulated and worked by capitalists on a wholesale scale. At that time the crafts also were striving in many ways to extend themselves into manufactories, and to burst the barriers raised by the guilds. If from one thousand to two thousand persons formed themselves into a common household, that household's inherent tendency towards the establishment and development of industry and farming on a large scale must have found ample scope.

In the case of the Anabaptists " everything was carried on upon a wholesale basis, and the individual artisans worked into each other's hands." It was strictly forbidden to take the raw material elsewhere than from the Anabaptists themselves, always supposing that they possessed what they wanted. Thus with the butchers, the hides of the animals were delivered to the tanners, and by them prepared and handed over

to the saddlers, harness-makers, and shoemakers.   It was the
same with the cotton department, the weavers, cloth-makers,
tailors, &c., &c.   Only a few raw materials like iron, refined
oil, and others were bought from the outside world, and thus
connection with people not included in the community was
largely due to the fact that some manufactures such as knives,
scythes, bolting cloths, cloth, shoes, &c., &c., found eager purchasers, not only among their own Brethren, but also among
surrounding neighbours.

One of the raw materials which they bought, and which
Loserth (to whom we owe these details) ought to have mentioned, was wool, as it was one of their most important commodities.   Their cloth manufacture flourished to such a high
degree that the Moravian wool was not sufficient to supply
the demand, and they were obliged to import it, probably
from Hungary.

Every trade possessed its purveyors, its distributors (or
cutters-out) and foremen.   The first-mentioned bought the
necessary raw material wholesale ; the others distributed it to
the individual workmen, and supervised their systematic co-
operation in its manufacture.   The regulations for these
offices and for production in general occupied the Brethren
very much.   This is proved by the numerous labour-ordinances
which they have left ; but, unfortunately, none of those re-
ferring to the crafts have been preserved.   We have, therefore,
no detailed evidence as to the height to which Baptists' production on a large scale reached ; neither do we know to
what extent the division of labour and systematic co-operative
work was carried in particular industries.

It is certain that they had made a great stride in advance
of the guild-crafts of that day towards the manufacture system.
They were always careful to stand abreast with their times in
technical matters, and for this reason millers, for example,
were from time to time sent to Switzerland, in order to study
the business methods of that country.

Successful as they were in the handicrafts technically, they
were even more so commercially, particularly as they either
bought the raw material wholesale, or drew upon their own
resources.   It was also to their advantage that they were able

to surmount the crises of trade more easily than was possible for private producers ; but they could not entirely avoid occasional overproduction, since they worked wholesale for the market. Yet the results of overproduction were not very disastrous. It was only necessary for a time to employ the overplus of labour in agriculture instead of the industries, and there work never failed.

To all these advantages of the communistic wholesale trade as compared with the " individualism " of the isolated trader there was naturally joined the fact that the maintenance of each individual in large co-operative households cost much less than in the small private households of the trade-masters. And thus it cannot surprise us that from the time of the organisation of the Huter communities of Moravia, the complaints on the subject of ruinous competition made by the guild-masters against the communists were never silenced.

As early as 1545 the Fraternity declared in their memorial to the Moravian Diet : " Half of the towns, as we hear, complain and lament about us, as if we took the bread out of the mouths of the agriculturalists ; but we know only this—that we apply ourselves diligently in everything to honourable work, to pay each one his penny, so that our integrity is well known in nearly all nations. Therefore, if any one unjustly complain of us, we cannot on that account deteriorate our work."

In the year 1600 the *Chronik* relates : " During this year a great outcry from our adversaries has gone abroad in Moravia, that the Fraternity increases beyond measure in that country, and by their trade do no small damage and hurt to the commercial interests of the towns and boroughs. For this reason the reigning princes have resolved to forbid us to erect new households, and yet they permit the territorial lords to make use of the Brothers as workmen." [1]

As in the system of their schools, so in their methods of production, the superiority of the Baptists over their opponents was brought most forcibly to light by the complaints of the latter. We recommend this fact to the consideration of all those who maintain that, under no

[1] Beck, *Geschichtsbücher*, pp. 171, 331.

circumstances, can communism be a sound economic principle.

The same cause which made the town journeymen the enemies of the Huterites, won for them the favour of the great landed proprietors upon whose estates they lived and to whom they paid rent. As it was by and through the Anabaptists that the nobility came to wealth and power, they became economically indispensable to them. Thus the Anabaptists gained economic importance, not only by their own produce, but also by their workmen who were hired by numerous employers. No small number of Sisters were engaged in private service also, as nurses and governesses, as we have already seen. At the same time, the Brothers were active in private agricultural and industrial establishments, such as mills. But they were especially popular as managers ; which may probably be explained by the fact that the administration of the large households had highly developed the talent for organisation and management among them. One of their fiercest enemies, Christopher Fischer, wrathfully writes : " You have so far captivated the nobles in Moravia, that they follow your advice and lead in everything, and have given you appointments in all their establishments as cashiers, butlers, borough-stewards, millers, shepherds, masters of fisheries, gardeners, foresters, and bailiffs ; you are high in consideration and repute among them, so that you eat and drink with them, and get favours of all kinds from them. Is not this what is meant by ' to rule and to reign?' "

The staunch Fischer of course exaggerates, but it is true that the Baptists were very much sought after as stewards. Strictly speaking, however, it was not isolated individuals who were in private service, but the whole community. Individuals were employed in private service merely as the deputies of the commune. Not only were they under the discipline of the community, but they were obliged to yield up to it all their earnings ; not merely their salaries and wages, but even their *gratuities* and *presents*, whether these consisted of money or anything else.

Generally speaking the enforcement of this regulation

seems to have given no trouble, except in the case of the doctors. With all their contempt for learning, the Baptists greatly esteemed pharmacology and the use of mineral waters. Their surgeons had not apparently much to do with science ; but they must have been very clever practitioners, for they were sought after throughout the whole country ; indeed one was sometimes summoned to the Imperial Court, in spite of the horror of communism which prevailed there.

The constitution of the Fraternity was democratic. At its head stood clerical and secular officials ; the former, " the Servants of the Word," were either "apostles," who wandered about the world to enlist new disciples, or were preachers at home ; the secular functionaries, "the Servants of Need," were the purchasers, foremen, householders and stewards. The chief authority lay with the community itself, but in order that it should not be consulted on every occasion, there was a Council of Elders, with whom the servants of the Fraternity despatched business of minor importance. At the head of the general community was a Bishop. That functionary, however, was not elected ; but from among those who appeared to be suitable for the post, one was selected by the casting of lots, and was called "Chosen of the Lord." He could not, however, enter on his office before the community had sanctioned the "Will of God," and ratified the choice.

The singular commune here delineated maintained its communal existence in full strength for nearly a century, and finally fell, *not from internal deterioration but through external force.*

Ever since Bohemia and Moravia had come under the sway of the House of Hapsburg it had been in continual, though sometimes bloodless, war with the independent nobles of these countries. At length there came that decisive struggle which ushered in the Thirty Years' War, and ended in the complete destruction of the nobles in the Battle of Weiss Berg, near Prague (1620). The nobility were almost annihilated, and with them fell their *protégés*, the Bohemian Brethren, and the other Huter communities of Moravia.

On the 22nd of February, 1622, Cardinal Dietrichstein

issued letters patent by order of Ferdinand, decreeing that "all such as are attached to the Huter Fraternity, be they men or women, are not to be found, or suffered to set foot, in Moravia after the expiration of four weeks from the date notified, under pain of extreme penalty to body and life."

On this occasion the decree of banishment did not remain on paper only. The organised Baptist community in Moravia came to an end. Many of the Baptists became Catholics, although most of them in their hearts remained true to the old teachings. and sometimes even transmitted them to the younger generation ; others perished through fugitive wanderings in winter ; but a portion at length succeeded, after losing nearly all their possessions, in reaching Hungary, where, as early as 1546, a branch of the Brotherhood had already established several households. The Hungarian chiefs required colonists, and received them gladly. They organised themselves in their new homes after the old methods, but were never again of any importance. The association never recovered from the frightful blow which had struck it down and robbed it of all its possessions. The state of affairs at that time in Hungary, where Turkish inroads and civil wars alternated with each other, was not such as to allow a poor community to rise to opulence. It therefore declined and perished, and with it perished its communism.

Whether the community would have stood its ground if it had been allowed to develop progressively and unmolested, can neither be positively affirmed nor denied. It is not very probable, however, that it would have succeeded in maintaining its communism permanently uninjured in the midst of the capitalist society with which it was in the closest economic relation by reason of its production of commodities and the hiring out of its labour.

In any case, however, the community of the Huterites in Moravia has the greatest significance in the history of socialism. It is the ripest fruit of heretical communism, and most clearly demonstrates to us the tendencies of the Anabaptists. Its original lines are still the same as those of the monastic system ; the household is only a sort of cloister. But it makes some steps beyond this in the direction of modern socialism, because it introduces marriage into monastic communism and develops industrial production on a large scale in such a way that the latter is no longer merely an accessory to communism, but begins to form its basis.

In spite of their importance and singularity, the Anabaptist organisations in Moravia have been lost to remembrance for a long time. " It is an extraordinary thing that even the recollection of the Anabaptists in Moravia should have disappeared so universally from the popular mind, and that their memory should have been revived but a short time ago, and then only by learned historians." [1] Thus writes a Bohemian historian in 1858. Since then learned investigations have shed a searching light upon them, thanks chiefly to the zeal of Dr. Joseph Beck, who collected extraordinarily_ extensive material on the subject, and himself partly published the *Chronicle* of the Anabaptists, which has been so often quoted here, and which appeared in 1883. After the publication, however, his bequest still offered great treasures, which Loserth has admirably brought to light. But beyond this particular history, the Moravian Anabaptists have not yet met with due consideration, while historians of the old communism have almost completely ignored them.

This need not surprise us. These writers were not actuated by a desire to comprehend socialism, but to collect materials which seemed useful for its condemnation. For such a purpose the Moravian Anabaptists were but poorly qualified. The Anabaptist insurrection in Münster appeared much more suited to this design. Hence it is this insurrection which is set forth in the usual books of history as the embodiment of the Anabaptist character. It was referred to by preference when historians wished to point out what horrors communism of necessity involved.

As a rule when one hears of the Anabaptists, he at once thinks of the outbreak in Münster ; and whoever mentions them, speaks with bated breath, as of some wild Walpurgis Night.

We will see whether this is justified, and how far it is so.

[1] Gindely, *Geschichte der Böhmischen Brüder*, vol. ii. p. 19.

VI. *The Disturbances in Münster.*

The Reformation movement began to develop itself and to let loose the class antagonisms of that era later in North, than in South Germany. In a great measure this is attributable to the economic backwardness of the North Germans. In those districts of the North-West which were more highly developed, the Reformation agitation was checked by the proximity of the Hapsburg Netherlands, from which Charles V. could exercise far more adverse influence upon the border districts than he could upon the other parts of the Empire.

The peasants in the North did not join in the universal movement, as the events of the year 1525 in South and Central Germany found no echo among them, partly on account of their being in a better position than their brothers in Upper Germany, and partly because single districts were more separated from each other, and intercourse between them was consequently less frequent than in the more thickly settled North.

Only two aspects of the Reformation were prominent in South Germany; the *princely* and the *municipal;* but the municipal Reformation in the North was marked by severer and keener contests between the municipal and the princely authorities on the one side, and on the other between the guilds and the municipal patricians. The analogy with South Germany goes still further; for the struggle between these conflicting classes could not be fought out without the lowest stratum of the urban population taking part in the movement.

The most celebrated and powerful of the North German cities which played a part in the Reformation was the Hanse town Lübeck.

The aristocratic Town Council sided with the existing authority, *i.e.*, the Catholic Church, while the democrats made the cause of the " Gospel " their own. In 1530 an insurrection gained the victory over the nobles and Church; the constitution was changed to suit democratic ideas, and the Church property confiscated by the town. But this victory had been won only by the guilds combining with the masses of the "common" people. The leader in the conflict, and the most prominent representative of the union was Jürg Wullenweber, Burgomaster of Lübeck, in the year 1533. The fact that he had been obliged to rely on the common people makes it comprehensible why he should have manifested sympathy with the Anabaptists. So notorious was this sympathy, that when he was Burgomaster of the town, the report went through Germany that Lübeck had been won over to the cause of the Anabaptists. Whether Wullenweber really did favour the opinion of the Baptists, and if so, to what extent, cannot now be ascertained. Certain it is, however, that the Anabaptists in Lübeck gained no advantage from his sympathy, nor did any of the other North German cities in which they were numerously represented.

In one town only were they temporarily successful, thanks to a singular conjunction of circumstances—in Münster.

North-Western Germany was particularly rich in ecclesiastical principalities; Cologne, Münster, Paderborn, Osnabrück, Minden, &c. Of these, the Archbishopric of Cologne and the Bishopric of Münster were by far the most important.

The social and political contests in the ecclesiastical principalities took a special colour. There the reigning prince united in his person the ruling powers of both Church and State; though he was by no means an absolute prince in consequence. Much more dependent on the Emperor and the Pope than a secular lord, he was at the same time more of a puppet than a ruler among the nobility and clergy in his dominions. The election of Bishops had everywhere been monopolised by the Chapter for themselves, and these, like the higher and more lucrative places in the Church generally, had become a privilege of the nobility (in Münster since 1392). Nobility and clergy were in consequence bound together in a close association of mutual interests, and they presented a far more formidable phalanx against their elected ruler than was the case in the secular principalities. The constitutional States had, in consequence, more to say in the ecclesiastical provinces than in the others; but in the constitutional States, again, the nobility and the Church were in the majority, when united. The cities were always out-voted; the lesser among them were oppressed, while the greater were driven to help themselves in whatever way they could.

Under these circumstances the nobility and the higher Church dignitaries had the most to lose, and therefore held fast to the old faith. They preferred sharing with the Vatican the huge amount of wealth which the Church had amassed in the ecclesiastical principalities, to losing it altogether.

The Bishops, on the other hand, were not to be depended on. Only too easily did they give way to the temptation which the example of their temporal neighbours offered them. Conversion to the Lutheran doctrines promised them not only independence of the Pope, who taxed them heavily, but a free right over Church property and great power over the nobles. It is, therefore, not at all surprising that the Bishops of Münster, like many of their colleagues, opposed the Evangelical doctrines in a very lukewarm and half-hearted manner; and, indeed, not seldom secretly favoured them.

When Bernt Rothmann, in 1531, began to preach Lutheran doctrines in the suburb of Münster (St. Moritz) the Chapter appealed in vain to Bishop Frederick, petitioning him to restrain the mischief which was being done. He certainly forbade Rothmann to preach, but did not do the smallest thing to enforce his mandate, thus enabling Rothmann to continue his ministry undisturbed. Only an Imperial command at last induced the Bishop to stop him (in January, 1532). Rothmann quitted St. Moritz; not to turn his back on the country, however, but to be the better able to assail the Church in Münster at its centre; that is, he transferred his preaching to Münster itself.

Münster was a large city, rich and well fortified, the chief town, not only of the bishopric, but of the whole of West-phalia. Democracy had proved itself particularly strong there. Originally, as was the case in every mediæval town, the Council had been exclusively in the hands of the patricians, the "hereditary race" (*Erbmänner*), as they were called in Münster. But when the trades and handicrafts began to flourish, and the guilds attained to power and importance, they also were admitted into the Council, which was thenceforward selected annually by ten electors (*Korgensten*), who were nominated by the assembled citizens. Only half of the four-and-twenty members of the Council were to be drawn from the aristocratic class ; but as the management of municipal affairs had already become an occupation which demanded more time and knowledge than was, as a rule, attainable for a man of the lower classes, the twelve seats in the Council which appertained to the citizens again and again fell to the members of a few wealthy families, from among whom, little by little, a second aristocracy was developed, less eminent than the Erbmänner, but united to them by association of interests.

Thus the Council gradually became once more exclusively representative of the municipal aristocracy ; men who lived partly on their rents from the leasing of their landed property, and partly by commercial enterprise. But, next to the Council, the power of the companies or guilds held its ground. There were seventeen guilds in Münster, each of which possessed its own Guildhall, and made bye-laws for its own guidance. The " Schohaus" Guildhall was the central point of the assembled civic guilds. In Lent, shortly after the election of the Council, the four-and-twenty guildmasters met there, and elected two aldermen. " These," says a Münster historian of those times, " are the heads and representatives of the whole community of burgesses, and their authority is so great that they, together with the guildmasters, could reverse the decisions of the Council if they wished. Hence the magistrates can hardly decide anything of importance in matters concerning the welfare of the community, without the consent of the above-mentioned principals." [1]

In peaceful times, certainly, the Council was at liberty to act very much according to its own sweet will ; but if it came to a conflict between the community and the Council, or between the clergy and community, the authority of the Council vanished very quickly.

[1] H. v. Kerssenbroick, *Geschichte der Wiedertäufer zu Münster. nebst einer Beschreibung der Haubtstadt dieses Landes.* 1771, vol. i. p. 98.

This had been practically demonstrated more than once, especially in 1525. The mighty struggle in Upper Germany did not pass over Lower Germany without leaving its traces. In the towns the "common man" everywhere arose; the result of this, in Cologne as in Münster, was an agitation against the clergy, which increased into violent rebellion when the Council endeavoured to oppose the movement. The people resisted, and nominated a committee of forty men, who formulated the demands of the community in thirty-six articles; not concerning religious subjects, but on *economic* questions; thus proving that the guilds were the instigators of the movement.

But though the articles were accepted by the Council (the Chapter even signing some of them), they were not carried in their entirety. The overthrow of the North German uprising brought the South German agitation also to a standstill, while, at the same time, it set free the power of the victorious princes, and enabled them to help their friends in the South. It came to a compromise between the clergy and the town, by which the rights of the clergy were restored; and, in return, the latter relinquished all their original claims to compensation and security against any contingent future injury.

Peace was thereby restored, though the opposition of the civic elements (particularly the town democracy) to the rich, privileged, and tax-imposing clergy continued. The mighty catastrophe of 1525 had set the masses in motion, though they had taken but little interest in the Reformation up to that time. This was the case, not only with Münster, but with the whole of Lower Germany, where the "cause of the Gospel" now found a joyful reception. The clergy were at the head of the movement, which had originally been purely economic, but now began to make use of religious arguments, and to assume an apparently purely religious character.

This is a phenomenon which often meets us in the period of the Reformation, and finds its analogy in modern middle-class and proletarian movements.

The cause of this is not difficult to discover. As long as a social movement is merely a question of the special demands of the moment, its economic character is clearly evident. But the deeper its penetration and the greater its expansion, the more it seeks to transform the whole of society—*i.e.*, the whole of the commonwealth—the greater becomes the necessity for establishing a rational connection between its separate claims. Thoughtful men will feel impelled to be clear as to the ultimate aims of a movement whose first efforts represent only passing demands, and will endeavour to explain these on lofty general principles. In proportion to the limit of economic knowledge in any age, and the generally subversive aims of the movement, the arguments and theories of the agitators appear as a rule more and more mystical, and the malcontents more easily lose a right comprehension of the economic basis of their agitation. When, for example, the cause of a movement happens to be only a question of free-trade, or some trifling tax ; or when it concerns shorter hours of labour and higher wages, the economic principle is clear enough to the most shortsighted. But if the movement has to do with the general class-antagonism of the middle class or proletariat against existing society, then, to a superficial observer, the economic basis is almost wholly lost sight of, and it becomes a question of the everlasting principles of natural right, reason, justice, &c., &c. At the time of the Reformation, the general tone of thought was not legal, but theological, and, in consequence, the more radical a social movement, the more theological were its party words ; such as the " Will of God," the " Word of Christ," and others of a similar nature.

In the year 1529 the democratic Protestant movement in Lower Germany received a special stimulus. At that time a terrible famine broke out, which lasted till 1531, as Sebastian Franck tells us in his Chronicles, published in this year. At some places a bushel of rye cost three shillings and sixpence, and in the following summer nine shillings. In 1531 the price went up still more. In Dortmund in 1530, a bushel of rye cost five shillings and sixpence ; in 1531 the price had gone up to fourteen shillings. A devastating plague, the so-called " English sweating sickness," ravaged the country, at the same time as the famine.

Then came the Turkish invasion, which was felt in Lower Germany, in consequence of the war-tax, *i.e.*, the "Turkish tax," which was at once levied. But in those parts of the country which had nothing to fear from the Turks, this tax must have been most exasperating, in the midst of so much distress, especially as the rate of assessment was not low. For instance, in the Duke of Cleves' Principality it was 10 per cent. on the income.

This must have intensified the social antagonism immensely, adding bitterness to the contests of the democracy against the wealthy clergy, who knew only too well how to avoid taxation themselves, and to whom, in their short-sighted avarice, it did not occur to subscribe voluntarily to the war expenses.

In this state of affairs the preaching of Bernhard Rothmann found a favourable hearing ; and when he withdrew in 1532 from St. Moritz to Münster, he was received with open arms by the democracy, and protected from all attempts at violence. The most prominent of the democratic party was a rich cloth-merchant, named Bernhard Knipperdollinck ; "a stately man, still young in years, with beautiful hair and beard ; brave, frank, and strong in appearance, gestures, and movements ; full of plans, clever in speech, and swift in deed" (Cornelius) ; stubborn, active, and with a propensity for the romantic.

It was very fortunate for the struggling, aspiring democracy at a time when they had to put forth all their strength in defence of Rothmann, that the clerical authorities were taken up with internal affairs which were characteristic of the Church at that period.

Bishop Frederick was an ease-loving noble, whom the office of Bishop pleased so long as it occasioned little trouble and brought in plenty of money. Now, when the difficulties of the Church multiplied, when Pope, Emperor, and Chapter urged him to a more energetic policy in defence of the Church, the Bishop's chair grew odious to him. He therefore looked about for a successor who should take the episcopal commission off his hands for a good round price ; and such a person he at last found in Bishop Eric of Paderborn and

Osnabrück, a noble as greedy of land as he was capable of paying for it, and who gladly seized the opportunity to add yet a third episcopal commission to the two he already possessed. The Catholic Archbishop of Cologne and the Lutheran Elector of Saxony were the intermediaries in this clerical traffic (whether they received commission fees is not known). The purchase-money was fixed at 40,000 gulden. By a gross fraud, these nobles, as pious as they were powerful, gained the consent of the Chapter : a counterfeit agreement was laid before the latter, instead of the real one, in which only half of the true amount was stated as the purchase-money. And it was a person of this class who took upon himself to defend religion, morals, and property against the Anabaptists !

After he had received his price, Eric was provisionally elected Bishop in 1531, and Frederick laid down his episcopal dignity in March, 1532.

During this interim the heretics throve gaily in Münster. The entrance of the new Bishop upon his office did not affect them much, however, as he looked upon himself in the light of a ruler rather than a Bishop, and the spread of the Lutheran teaching was even less distasteful to him than it had been to his predecessor. Moreover, he was the close friend of the Elector John of Saxony (one of the intermediaries in the purchase of the Bishop's chair) and of Landgrave Philip of Hesse, both leaders of the Evangelical movement in Germany. In fact, so little did he hesitate to manifest his Protestant sympathies, that he acted as a witness to the marriage of Graf von Tecklenburg with a nun who had quitted the cloister.

The election of the Bishop strengthened the Protestant cause in Münster enormously, but also led to a division of the movement into two parties. Much as Eric inclined towards the Reformation, it was not the Reformation of the lower classes, but of the higher, that he favoured ; a reformation which increased the power of the rulers, but not that of the democracy, at the expense of the Church.

Against the clerical party and the knighthood, Eric sought for the support of the town patricians and the Council, with its adherents ; the two together forming a " moderate party " which coquetted with the Lutherans.

So long as all their adversaries were Catholics, the urban democracy were willing to make the Lutheran doctrines serve as the foundation of their faith ; but now that Lutheranism threatened to be turned from a weapon of defence into one in the hands of their most dangerous enemies, viz., the Bishop and the patricians, they began to lose their sympathy with Luther's teachings, and to turn towards Zwinglianism, which was better suited to their wants.

Eric and the Council considered it most important that they should get the upper hand of the municipal democracy ; and by beginning in this way they were sure of the assistance of the clergy. On the 17th of April, 1532, the Bishop issued a mandate, in which he offered a prospect of speedy reform in the Church ; but asked, first of all, that the preacher whom the community had so arbitrarily protected should be removed.

The Council, thereupon, gave orders to Rothmann to discontinue his sermons ; but the community would not consent, declaring that they would retain their preacher under all circumstances (April 28th).

Again the democracy were in luck. " In fact," writes the good episcopalian, Kerssenbroick, " this upright Bishop would have effected much in this matter by means of his own authority and the support of his friends, if he had not been prevented by a premature death. Making more merry than usual at his castle of Fürstenau, situated in the Diocese of Osnabrück, he suddenly became ill ; though some assert that he died suddenly, on May 14th, after having emptied a large beaker of wine." [1]

This event was the signal for an insurrection in all the three bishoprics which had been harassed and oppressed during the lifetime of him who had expired in so holy a manner. In Osnabrück, Paderborn, and Münster the people rose, drove away the Catholic priests, and appointed Protestant pastors of their own way of thinking ; the Council being nowhere in a position to check them. In Osnabrück

[1] Kerssenbroick, *op. cit.* vol. i. p. 204.

a compromise was effected between the clerical party and the town by the interposition of the knights. Paderborn was utterly crushed by force in October, 1532, by the Archbishop Hermann of Cologne; but in Münster, on the contrary, the rebels understood better how to carry out their plans.

The Chapter had immediately elected Franz v. Waldeck to succeed Eric; and on June 28th a letter from him arrived in Münster, summoning the town to return to its allegiance. The assembly of the hereditary aristocrats declared itself ready to submit; but that of the guilds decreed (July 1st) the formation of a confederacy for the defence of the gospel. The appointment of the committee of thirty-six men so frightened the Town Council that they joined it, and granted the demands of the community. The committee of thirty-six immediately urged the reorganisation of the Church on Evangelical principles, and sought for help from abroad, finally concluding an alliance with Philip of Hesse; and when, in October, Bishop Franz, supported by the clerical and secular aristocracy, made preparations to overcome Münster by force, the community compelled the Council to make counter preparations; three hundred soldiers were enrolled and the fortifications repaired.

There were unimportant collisions between the parties; but the Bishop shrank from a decisive advance upon the strong city, which threatened him either with defeat or with foreign intervention and the loss of his independence. Moreover, his coffers were empty, and the greedy clergy refused to make sacrifices for him. The Emperor, the most powerful protector of Catholicism in that region, was himself financially embarrassed at that time, in consequence of the Turkish war. Bishop Franz therefore endeavoured to return to the policy of his predecessor, and to make peace with the Council, entering into negotiations for this purpose.

Self-interest inclined the Council to make concessions, but the people would hear nothing of the kind. "Not a step backwards! rather let us kill and eat our children!" cried Knipperdollinck; and the masses supported him.

In order to manage the negotiations with more chance of success, the Bishop had betaken himself to the little town of Telgt, in the neighbourhood of Münster. But the proximity of the Bishop incited the warlike community to anything but peace. A sudden attack on Telgt was secretly planned and successfully carried out on the night of December 26th ; but the Bishop himself was not captured, as he had accidentally left Telgt the day before. A great number, however, of the most illustrious representatives of the Catholic cause—ecclesiastical and secular aristocrats and fugitive hereditary patricians from Münster—were taken prisoners.

This victory had important results. By the interposition of Philip of Hesse a treaty was concluded (February 14, 1533), of which the chief stipulation was that the Bishop, Council, and knights should permit the democratic party such advantages as they had gained in the insurrection. *Münster was thenceforth recognised as an Evangelical town.*

VII. *The Anabaptists in Strassburg and the Netherlands.*

The democratic guilds had been victorious in Münster, but having won all their successes solely through the help of the lower masses of the population, they could not, as had often happened before in similar cases, throw aside the tools which had been used as soon as they had attained their object. The victory had been won by a lucky stroke of fortune, not by a decisive defeat of the adversary in open fight. Peace, therefore, merely meant a temporary cessation of hostilities, while the prospect of more severe battles loomed up before the middle-class democracy, making them afraid to drop their connection with the proletarian democrats. The convictions of the latter found their most congenial expression in Anabaptism. The prominent position which the proletariat had attained in Münster made that town the centre of the Baptist faith in Lower Germany.

Zwinglians having made their appearance in Münster during the year 1532, in addition to Catholics and Lutherans, the Baptists joined them. The two centres from which Anabaptist doctrines spread into Lower Germany were Strassburg and the Netherlands.

In Strassburg, which was in close economic and political

intercourse with the great towns of North Switzerland, the Zwinglian State Church triumphed in 1525. The struggle of Zwinglianism against Catholicism and Lutheranism assisted the Baptists in Strassburg, as in other South German towns. After Augsburg, as we have already seen, Strassburg became the most important centre of the South German Baptist community. It there held its ground longer than in other places, thanks to the power possessed by the " common man," and to the fear of an insurrection, which prevented the Council from taking decisive measures against the Baptists. So strong were these people in this powerful capital, that the most important of the Church leaders there, especially Capito, continued the policy at first followed by Zwingli, and for a long time showed a great inclination towards Baptist opinions.

During the great persecution Strassburg was a city of refuge for those " Brothers " who did not emigrate to Moravia, and after the Baptist community in Augsburg had been cruelly suppressed, it became the metropolis of the movement in South Germany, so long as such a movement could be said to exist.

Nearly all the prominent men among the South German Baptists passed through the new metropolis at various times ; but the most important of them all was the journeyman furrier, Melchoir Hofmann, from Hall in Swabia, a man who had travelled a great deal. In 1523 he had preached the Evangelical doctrines in Livland, and had become a preacher in the German community at Stockholm. Driven from there, he took refuge in Holstein, where King Frederick of Denmark granted him the means of livelihood and freedom to preach. But when he changed from Lutheranism to Zwinglianism, he was banished from the country (1529), and turned towards Strassburg, where he was soon carried away by the Baptist opinions, becoming one of the community in 1530, and, after the old chiefs had fallen or been driven out, rising to a position of the highest prominence among them.

An eccentric and visionary enthusiast, he took up with Hans Hut's views on the millennium, which must now have found a still more favourable soil among the Brethren, as the persecu-

tion against them was still raging. In fact, if there had not
been some signs of a speedy deliverance, it would have been
difficult to remain steadfast in the midst of the cruelties of
the hunt for heretics. But the fiercer the persecution, the
stronger grew their faith in the promises which foretold the
approaching collapse of the existing state of society—that
most passionate desire of their hearts. Nothing more, however, was to be expected from the Turks.

Strassburg was looked upon as the heavenly Jerusalem by
Hofmann ; for it was confidently expected that power would
fall to the Baptists, in that place, within a very short time,
perhaps in the year 1533.

But Hofmann agreed so far with the Baptists' usual mode
of thinking, that he declared himself against all employment
of force. He relied upon the effect of his propaganda, which
was that God would bring about victory, and that all rebellion
was sinful.

At first Hofmann met with angry resistance in the community. Two different parties were formed, of which his
finally triumphed, perhaps more from his success in the
Netherlands than from the force of his arguments, or the
innermost needs of the Brothers.

He was too restless, however, to remain long in Strassburg.
In 1530 he went down the Rhine to promulgate his new
conviction in the Netherlands.

The Netherlands was the home of heretical communism
north of the Alps. There Beghardism had its origin ; there
" the Brothers of the Common Life " had worked, and educated
the people. But the rapid economic development of the
country which led to the creation of communism there, also
matured a strong government, the most dangerous enemy of
communism. At the beginning of the sixteenth century the
government was far more powerful and absolute than in the
neighbouring part of Germany.

The Burgundian House, and, after its extinction in 1477,
its successor, the House of Hapsburg, had united the seventeen provinces of the Netherlands into one whole, by the
most diverse means—through inheritance, by purchase, and
by conquest.

Moreover, in 1504, the Hapsburgs had also succeeded to the throne of Spain, in which country despotism had already made great progress. The Church especially was there reduced to almost total dependence upon the Crown. The Inquisition, which nowhere exercised such terrible power as in Spain, had become a blind tool of a despotism which crushed all intractable elements. Abroad the strength of the Spanish power was so great at that time that it ventured to take up the quarrel with France about Italy and the Papal rule. As kings of Spain, the Hapsburgs had even more reason for supporting Catholicism than they had in their capacity as rulers of Austria (then threatened by the Turks) and Emperors of Germany, whose power was undermined by the Evangelical princes, for the Catholic Church had become one of the most important, if not *the* most important of their instruments of power.

They had, therefore, every reason for being decidedly opposed to Protestantism ; but they could attack it with more energy in the Netherlands than in Germany. As Emperor of Germany, Charles V. united the Netherlands to the Spanish kingdom in 1516. Besides the highly efficient means of governmental power which the Netherlands offered him, he had at his command the forces of the Spanish throne with which he could crush all opposition in any of his dominions. Without outwardly touching the old forms of government, he took from them every vestige of political freedom. The despotism which assumed such terrible proportions under Philip II., and which later on could be put down only by a sanguinary war of nearly a hundred years' duration (1561–1648), and then in only a portion of the Netherlands, was initiated by Charles V., who, whenever it appeared necessary, relentlessly enforced his autocratic power.

The lower classes were kept down with an iron hand, and rendered powerless so long as there was no great conflict among the rulers themselves. This was the reason why the native land of heretical communism apparently remained an unfruitful soil for communistic propaganda during the first decade of the German Reformation. The mind of the people, however, was well prepared, and communistic tendencies were widespread before Hofmann appeared on the scene.

At the end of the fifteenth century "Waldensian" secret societies were reported to exist in Flanders and Brabant, and were called "Turlupins," or "Pifles," often also (and this is worthy of notice) "Tisserands" (weavers). "They were strict in their morals, charitable towards all men, and harboured no revengeful feelings. Many joined the Dutch Anabaptists, and added much to their strength."[1]

According to their own tradition, the Baptists had spread their propaganda to the Netherlands as early as the year 1534, and indeed it is known that three "Brothers" suffered martyrdom for the cause in Holland in 1527.

Hofmann's importance lay, not in his introduction of Anabaptism into the Netherlands, but in the courage he imparted to the members of the sect to propagate their doctrines. This courage flowed from his convincingly confident prophecy that the end of the existing order of society was at hand, and that the year 1533 would see the inauguration of the new state of things. The effect of his preaching was enhanced by the pestilence and famine which had been prevalent since 1529, as well as by the democratic movement in the adjacent provinces of Lower Germany, especially in Westphalia.

It is worthy of remark that the new sect (called Melchiorites, from Melchior Hofmann) could never obtain a firm footing in Flanders and Brabant, where economics and politics had reached an advanced stage of development, and where the executive power was strong and concentrated. The centre of the movement lay in the towns of the Northern provinces—in Holland, Zealand, and Friesland, which, though backward in politics and economics, had for that very reason preserved a large measure of municipal independence, and which, unlike Flanders and Brabant, were afterwards successful in freeing themselves from Spanish domination. Amsterdam became the seat of the leading community of Anabaptists.

[1] A. Brons, *Ursprung, Entwickelung und Schicksale der altevangelischen Taufgesinnten oder Mennoniten*, Harden, 1891, p. 57.

The Melchiorites had hardly begun to be numerous, when they divided themselves into two parties. All of course believed in the imminent coming of the New Jerusalem, but the more practical among them were forced to admit that it would not come of itself, by means of a miracle, but that the proletariat must free itself. They maintained that they must fight their opponents with the same weapon which had been used in the subjugation of the people : that the *sword*, which the godless had drawn from its scabbard against God's people, should now be turned against the hearts of their tyrants.

So taught Jan Mathys, a baker of Haarlem, who was the first of the Melchiorites to counsel violent measures. "Jan Mathys was the first to demand and inaugurate the use of arms and force against the authorities," said Jan van Leyden to his judges ; and in an earlier confession, he tells of the dissension which had arisen between Mathys and Hofmann.[1]

The doctrines promulgated by Mathys were favoured in the Netherlands by the circumstance that class antagonisms were much more acute in that province than in Switzerland, the native land of the Baptist sect. In the Netherlands, hardly a single representative of the upper classes was to be found in the ranks of the order, the movement in that country being eminently proletarian in character, and among classes who had nothing to lose but their fetters ; a fact which must have increased both the strength of their resistance and their eagerness for it.

Mathys succeeded in firmly establishing himself in the community of Amsterdam, and also gained many adherents outside that community by the instrumentality of his messengers, the number of which increased with the growth of the Melchiorites. By far the most prominent among them was the before-mentioned Jan Bockelson of Leyden. His mother, who was a tradeswoman from the neighbourhood of Münster, had been servant to Bockel, mayor of Soevenhagen, to whom she bore a son—Jan. (1509).

[1] *Berichte der Augenzeugen über das Münsterische Wiedertäuferreich.* Edited by C. M. Cornelius, vol. ii. of *Geschichtsquellen des Bisthume Münster*, 1853, pp. 370, 399.

She subsequently married Bockel, after having bought her freedom. Jan learned the craft of tailoring in Leyden, but received a very scanty mental training. His extraordinary natural endowments, however, compensated for this. After studying Münzer's works, he took a lively interest in the stirring questions of his day, and was especially enthusiastic concerning communism. His mental horizon was broadened by extensive travels also. As a journeyman tailor, after going to Flanders, he visited England, where he remained four years. On his return home, he did not pursue his craft, but married the widow of a mariner, and set himself up in trade. Business took him to Lübeck and Lisbon ; but having no luck, or perhaps lacking the requisite business capacity, he became a bankrupt just at the time when the Baptist sect made its appearance in the Netherlands. With all the ardour of youth, he now embraced the doctrines with which he had always been in sympathy. Much as he had seen and experienced, he was not yet twenty-five years old when he was won over to the cause of Jan Mathys (November, 1533).

Handsome, vivacious, enthusiastic and of captivating eloquence, he soon made conquest of hearts. Enjoyment of life and of the beautiful was a conspicuous trait of his character, in striking contrast to the bulk of his associates, who favoured a gloomy puritanism ; in this respect he also completely differed from Thomas Münzer. From early youth he had manifested poetical talent, and Kerssenbroick informs us that " he had also written all sorts of plays, which, as was customary in that country, he produced on the stage before the whole people, to gain money." His proclivity and aptitude for theatrical affairs were afterwards displayed in Münster.

Kerssenbroick, however, has little cause for deriding him as a " tailor " and " theatre king." The masters whose devoted servant Kerssenbroick was, trembled for fear of the tailor and theatre king ; for to the characteristics just described, the dictator of Münster united an inflexible will and a penetrating acuteness, which made him an opponent to be dreaded.

Before Bockelson became a partisan of Mathys, the latter was at the head of the Melchiorites in the Netherlands, Hofmann having left in the beginning of the year 1533 to return to Strassburg, as the time for the commencement of the New Jersualem had arrived. Hofmann had prophesied that he should be taken prisoner and remain confined for half a year, but that then the Redeemer would come. The first part of the prophecy was soon fulfilled, as he was arrested in May. The Brothers were now on the tenterhooks of expectation, and looked forward with feverish impatience to the time when, at last, there should be an end to all sorrow and want.

The remainder of the prophecy lacked fulfilment. The year 1533 drew to its close, and all continued to be quiet in Strassburg. As a chief result of Hofmann's agitation, the Council was spurred on to energetic measures against the Baptists. All their wavering adherents fell away from the sect, and their cause from that moment continued to lose ground in the town.[1] Just at this time, however, an impetus was given to the enthusiasm of the Brothers, which made it blaze up once more; for "throughout the Netherland communities a report was spread that the Lord had rejected Strassburg on account of its unbelief, and had in its stead chosen Münster as the seat of the New Jerusalem" (Cornelius).

Let us now see what had meanwhile been transpiring in Münster.

VIII. *How Münster was won.*

As early as the year 1532, Baptist and other similar tendencies had become noticeable in Münster, and during the following year rapidly gained in definiteness, strength, and range.

The Town Council was divided in its policy; for the election of March 3, 1533, had introduced into its midst a number of decidedly democratic elements. One of the two Burgomasters, Hermann Tilbeck, a patrician by descent, but a good democrat in opinions, was a partisan of these, and he subsequently joined in bringing about the union between the

---

[1] Hofmann never regained his freedom. After long years of imprisonment, he died in a dungeon.

radical section of the burgess democracy and the Anabaptists.

The guilds were quite as disunited, vacillating, and uncertain as the Council, knowing that the Bishop and clergy were only watching for a favourable opportunity to regain their control of the town. A part of the body of the guild-burgesses, however, began to feel anxious concerning the poor population, whose aggressiveness was stayed by no consideration of privilege or possession, and would, therefore, make no exception of the property of the guilds. This body weighed and compared the respective dangers threatening them from the masses on one side and the aristocracy on the other. Those among the democrat burgesses who had most to fear from priestly and aristocratic domination, remained true to their alliance with the proletarian elements; others joined the Lutherans and even the Catholics of the town; while the majority of the guild faction oscillated unceasingly hither and thither, concerned alone in keeping the mastery out of the hands of any of the other parties.

This condition of affairs was highly favourable to the Baptists, as it prevented all decisive action against them on the part of the Town Council; and they were not slow in taking advantage of their opportunity. Their zeal for the cause left nothing to be desired, and their numbers were augmented not merely by the accession of proselytes from the town, but (and this is worthy of remark) by the influx of immigrants, at first from neighbouring districts, but afterwards from distant ones, and especially from the Netherlands. These immigrants came partly as refugees from persecution and partly because they were impelled by a desire for great deeds; for they were not only in less danger in Münster than elsewhere, but there was greater scope for their activity in aid of the good cause. They became of the highest importance to the development of affairs in Münster, as they belonged to the most courageous and energetic party, and gave an important moral and military support to the Baptists in the town. Gresbeck, who was an eye-witness of events, ascribes to them the leading part in the triumph of Anabaptism and in all the incidents which took place in the town under the communist *régime*. He invariably speaks of the strict Baptists in Münster as " the Dutch and Frieslanders."

The "party of order" (as we may briefly designate the opponents of the Baptists) dwindled away from day to day ; for a panic had seized the wealthy inhabitants, and every advance made by the democracy drove some of them away in flight.

The propertied classes now displayed a disposition to combine ; but each endeavoured to turn the agitation to its own profit alone, and in spite of their co-operation they never could overcome a certain mutual distrust ; for while each member of the league wanted to deceive his associates, he also feared being deceived by them. Even when Münster had fallen into the hands of the Baptists, it was not easy to combine the propertied classes into a solid body.

As soon, however, as the beginnings of a "party of order" became visible, the more radical among the middle class democratic elements, under the leadership of Rothmann and Knipperdollinck, found it necessary to bind themselves more closely to the proletarian factions, and consequently went over to Anabaptism. On September 5, 1532, Rothmann, who had hitherto combated the doctrines of the Anabaptists, wrote to Busch : " I have had some trouble with the Anabaptists, who long since left us, threatening, however, to return with greater power. But ' if God be with us, who shall be against us ? ' "[1]

As early as May in the following year, Rothmann declared himself opposed to infant baptism.

The Town Council endeavoured to overcome the Baptists with " spiritual weapons." They induced Melancthon to write to Rothmann, in order to bring him back to the true faith. As this and similar letters bore no fruit, the Council ordered a disputation for August 7 and 8, 1533, which of course did not convert the Baptists, but rather encouraged them.

The Council now resorted to sharper measures. A number of municipal preachers had joined the Baptists. In

[1] Quoted by Kerssenbroick, vol. i. p. 183.

September the Council threatened them with dismissal if they refused to baptise infants : to which the pastors replied that they must obey God rather than man ; whereupon the Council endeavoured to carry out its menace. First of all, Rothmann was deprived of his office of preacher in the Lamberti Church ; but the attitude of the community was so threatening, that the Council installed him in another Church in October. The Baptists had thus gained their first victory.

In the beginning of November there was another trial of strength between the contending parties. The Council at that time made an attempt to combine all the different opponents of Anabaptism in united action. It invited the guildmasters and Catholic patricians to a conference on the best means to be adopted for gaining the mastery over the Baptist faction. At this conference it was agreed that an armed attack should be made on the following day.

In pursuance of this agreement the members of the party of order met under arms, and sought first of all to get possession of the Baptist preachers. Now, however, certain extreme reactionists (probably Catholics) demanded that all members of the Council in sympathy with the Baptists should be banished from the town, together with the preachers. Burgomaster Tilbeck was especially named. Not a word had been uttered to this effect on the preceding day, and the moderates among the party of order were so startled by the demand that they began to distrust their colleagues. In the meantime, the Baptists assembled and intrenched themselves in the Lamberti Churchyard. The following day the Council entered into negotiations with them, and the conflict which was to have ended in the dissolution of the Baptists, really terminated in a few insignificant concessions to them. Some of their preachers left the town ; but, though inhibited from preaching, Rothmann was allowed to remain. While open propagandism of Baptist doctrines was forbidden, the party of order had to submit to the retention of the leaders in the town. Thus the Anabaptists had successfully withstood a second and far more dangerous assault.

Kerssenbroick informs us that : " Although the compact

of November inhibited Rothmann from preaching, he did not cease to do so ; first of all secretly and by night, but afterwards, when his adherents grew in number, by day also, in the houses of some of the burgesses. The time of preaching was announced by musket-shot, and no one was admitted to the gathering who was not tainted with Anabaptism " (vol. i. p. 453).

The propaganda was carried on not only by these oral means, but also by printed pamphlets ; a printing-press being secretly set up in Rothmann's house, where it was afterwards discovered by the authorities.

Attempts at a practical realisation of communistic ideas were now initiated. The rich among the Brethren " laid all their wealth at Rothmann's feet, tore up and burned all written evidences of debt, and absolved their debtors from payment. And this was done not only by men, but by women as well, who at other times were wont to throw nothing away. Frau Brandsteinin, Knipperdollinck's mother-in-law, a very wealthy woman, was so moved by the spirit of God as to restore their bonds to her debtors, together with the interest already paid on them." [1]

Unselfish enthusiasm of this kind must have powerfully influenced the masses, and as a result the Baptists soon became so strong that they could openly defy their enemies. On the 8th of December the journey-smith, Johann Schröder, began to preach Baptist doctrines in public. On the 15th, he was arrested by order of the Council ; but the guild of smiths assembled, marched to the town hall, and extorted his release. Though Rothmann had been banished, he remained quiet and unmolested in the town. At the end of the year the preachers who had left in November returned, but were again exiled by the Council, January 15, 1534. They were led out by soldiers through one of the town gates, only to be brought back again through another by the Brethren, with whom the Council did not dare to interfere. As a matter of fact, the Baptists were already masters of the city.

[1] Kerssenbroick, vol. i. p. 455.

It is not surprising that the Brethren everywhere now admitted that Strassburg had been rejected by God, and that Münster was to be the seat of the New Sion. The centre of the movement was consequently transferred thither from Amsterdam. In the beginning of the year, Jan Mathys sent a series of messengers to Münster, among whom was Jan Bockelson, of Leyden, who arrived on January 13th. In February we find Mathys himself there.

Complete despair now seized the party of order. They saw only one possible means by which the swelling flood of communism could be checked; they threw themselves into the arms of the Bishop, and treacherously surrendered to him the freedom of the town.

The solemn compact by which Bishop Franz had guaranteed freedom of religious worship in Münster had, from the very first, been regarded by him as a mere scrap of paper, to be torn in pieces at the first favourable opportunity. The more democratic the town became, the more he longed to break the treaty. As early as December, 1533, he had begun to make preparations for taking the Münster democracy by surprise and annihilating it ; hence the treacherous proceeding of the party of order was most opportune for him.

" When, therefore," writes Gresbeck, " my gracious Lord of Münster saw that the Anabaptists in the town would neither listen to the Council nor plead for pardon of the Bishop, he came to an agreement with the Town Council, and some of the other burgesses who did not hold with the Anabaptist doctrines, that they should leave two gates to the town open for the Bishop ; namely, the gate of our Blessed Virgin and the gate of the Jewish quarter. Then were these gates opened for the Bishop, so that he brought into the town from 2,000 to 3,000 footmen, and a force of horsemen, and my gracious Lord of Munster became master of the city." [1]

This occurred on the 10th of February. The Bishop's forces, which had thus so treacherously fallen upon the town in the midst of peace, were joined by the " order loving

[1] *Berichte der Augenzeugen*, pp. 14, 15.

burgesses" who had been awaiting them and wore armour under their clothing. By previous arrangement they had hung wreaths of straw on their houses that they might be spared from the pillage of the town which it was expected would be carried out by the " defenders of property."

Success at first attended the conspirators, who laid hold of Knipperdollinck and a few other Anabaptists, and cast them into prison.

The Baptists, who had been taken completely by surprise, soon assembled, however, and showed that the spirit of the war-like party of Jan Mathys still lived in them. They gained the upper hand in the street combat which ensued ; the Bishop's troops fell back offering to come to terms, and " the footmen and horsemen were cleverly and skilfully driven out of the city" (Gresbeck). Their treachery had turned against the traitors themselves, and as a result the town, which had already virtually belonged to the Baptists, now fell into their military power, captured, not in aggressive riot, but in self-defence.

The fight of February had two results. From that time war was waged between the town and the Bishop. On the 28th of the month, Franz and his troops moved into Telgt, to begin the siege, and on the same day the legally-prescribed election of magistrates took place in Münster, which, without any alteration in the electoral views, ended in the complete triumph of the Baptist party. Knipperdollinck and Kippenbroick (a cloth-maker who had repeatedly distinguished himself in the Baptist cause) became Burgomasters. "The leaders of the movement were consequently raised by legal methods to the highest power, and the chief town of Westphalia lay at the feet of the new prophets " (Keller).

IX. *The New Jerusalem.*

(a) *Our Sources of Information.*—According to the representation usually given in the accounts of historians, the seizure of Münster was followed by frenzied orgies of debauchery and bloodthirstiness. "When the city fell into their hands," writes Bishop Franz, in an official report, "they overthrew all godly and Christian law and justice, all rules of Church, and secular government and policy, and substituted a *bestial manner of life*." This is the way in which these events have generally been depicted from the time of the Münster "commune" down to the present day.

A recent writer, the anonymous author of *Schlaraffia politica*,[1] tells us with awe : " Münster became the theatre of the lowest *debauchery* and bloody *butchery* . . . A power was thus established which carried into practice communism and polygamy ; a government in which spiritual insolence and fleshly concupiscence, *bloodthirsty barbarism* and *base epicurianism*, were associated with pious renunciation and self-sacrifice. The infamies of which the women of Münster were victims, the Nero-like debaucheries and barbarities of Jan van Leyden and his colleagues, are the historical illustration " of the aim of modern socialism. Nevertheless our writer thinks that in the socialist society of the future " the Saturnalia of Münster will doubtless be surpassed " (pp. 68, 70).

This is the key-note of nearly all representations of the Münster commune. The closing sentence of the above quoted passage discloses one of the reasons why middle-class historians have found it difficult to deal impartially with the Anabaptist communism. It bore for them too close a resemblance to modern socialism.

Another obstacle to impartiality respecting that order is presented by the character of our sources of information. The historians were too easily convinced of the truth of everything told by witnesses of the Anabaptist rule. Yet it is precisely here that the greatest caution is necessary in the use made of the evidence.

From the 10th of February, the day of the decisive Baptist victory, Münster was a beleaguered town, cut off from the outer world. After it was recaptured by the besieging forces, almost the whole population was massacred. No defender of the Baptist cause· escaped a

---

[1] *Schlaraffia politica, Geschichte der Dichtungen vom Besten Staat.* Leipzig, 1892.

bloody grave, who was in a position to give a literary account of the events of the siege. All the descriptions proceed from the enemies of the Anabaptists.

There are three main sources of information. Immediately after the fall of Münster a work appeared entitled : *Wahr haftige historie, wie das Evangelium zu Münster angefangen und darnach, durch die Widdertauffe verstort widder aufgehört hat*, &c. *Beschrieben durch Henricum Dorpium Monasterie-meem*, 1536. (" A True History of the Introduction of the Gospel into Münster, and its subsequent Destruction by the Anabaptists," &c. ; "written by Henry Dorpius of Münster.") In his treatise on the " Sources of the History of the Münster Insurrection," forming the introduction of his *Berichten der Augenzeugen* (" Accounts of Eye-witnesses "), Cornelius thus characterises the work : " It is a Wittenbergian *partisan production*, printed in Wittenberg, and with a preface by Luther's chief coadjutor and delegate for South Germany, Johann Bugenhagen . . . The object of the book is to compass the complete moral defeat of his opponents, and by this means advance the interests of his party " (pp. 16, 17). Even the title contains a falsehood. Cornelius points out that even if the author were named Dorpius, he was not a resident of Münster, although " the book makes it appear that he had himself been in Münster, and had personally experienced that which was, in fact, only reported to him " (pp. 11, 12). Hence he was a swindler, whose " book is not to be regarded as an accurate and unprejudiced account of the whole course of events." [1]

Kerssenbroick's work on the Münster Anabaptist *régime*, of which the Latin original is still in manuscript, is of far greater importance. When it was about to be printed in 1573, its publication was prohibited by the Münster Town

---

[1] The Protestant Hase endeavours to free Dorpius from the reproaches of Cornelius, but, in our opinion, unsuccessfully. (*Heilige und Propheten*. Leipzig, 1892, vol. ii. p. 291, *sqq*.) In other respects, Hase's account and the often quoted work by Keller are relatively the best which have appeared from the middle-class side. The classical work by Cornelius on the Münster rebellion was unfortunately not completed, but breaks off just at the capture of the town by the Baptists.

Council. It has been preserved in transcriptions only, but a translation appeared in 1771, of which we have availed ourselves. Born in 1520, Kerssenbroick went to the Cathedral school of Münster from 1534 until the Anabaptist victory, and was rector of the same school from 1550 to 1575. In the latter capacity he wrote his history, which has an importance on account of the numerous public documents given in it, but which, while uncritical and careless as regards the sources of information, is, in addition, full of party spirit. The following passage is enough to show this. Kerssenbroick affirms that he has not written for fame, but "to serve my country and posterity, so that the brilliant deeds may not be forgotten, which were done to the destruction of the most barbarous and infamous heresy, by the most Reverend Count and Lord in Christ Frantz—that righteous Bishop of the Münster Church, and branch of the ancient Waldeck stem. I furthermore give this history to the world, that all righteous people may avoid and detest the abominable and infamous madness of the Anabaptists." His purpose, therefore, is not to give an objective representation, but to glorify the Bishop and to vilify the Anabaptists. Hence everything is extolled which redounds to the credit of the hero, while, where possible, silence is maintained on all that might cast a slur upon him. On the other hand, the author eagerly seeks for the most pitiable gossip unfavourable to the Anabaptists, and, without examination or verification, inserts it in his work, even exaggerating it when he can.

Let us give an example. He tells us: "Just about this time" (the beginning of February) "the prophet Jan Mathys, who was an extremely sensual man, secretly called together the Anabaptists of both sexes by night in Knipperdollinck's rather spacious house. When they had assembled the prophet stood in the centre of the room before a copper candlestick fastened to the floor, in which three candles were burning, instructing the surrounding crowd, and by his prophetic spirit fanned into full flame the fire smouldering in the hearts of many. He then explained the first chapter of the first Book of Moses, and when he had read the words of the twenty-eighth verse, ' Be fruitful and multiply and replenish the earth,' the lights were blown out. What infamies were then practised may be inferred from the fact that on one occasion the prophet was found lying in a most indecent attitude in the lap of a maiden. They called this assembling together the ' Fiery Baptism.' *This is no fiction ;* for though mention was made of the Fiery Baptism here and there in the town, no one knew what was meant until a certain woman was induced to investigate the matter by a bribe from my landlord, Wesseling. After learning the Anabaptist sign this woman gained admission to the above-mentioned house, saw everything, and related it to us afterwards " (i. p. 504). Our trustworthy rector considered this sufficient ground for his assurance that his account of the Fiery Baptism is "no fiction "! Let us deliberate a moment. For the sake of a gratuity some woman relates any tale she likes to the landlord of the house in which Kerssenbroick lived when a youth of fourteen ; a generation later he writes it down from memory, and asks us on this single unsubstantiated piece of evidence to attribute the most unbridled licentiousness to the Anabaptists : scientific historians, too, scrupulously reproduce this woman's gossip—if it be not something worse—because in this way communism is to be " scientifically " annihilated !

The fact, to which we shall again allude, that in a particular work the Münster Anabaptists pronounce all such accusations " shameless and scandalous lies " does not seem to have been noticed by any one ; and quite as little that Kerssenbroick himself in other passages gives prominence to the puritanism of the sect.

" After he had gone over to the Baptists, Rothmann's morals became quite changed, because he had taken upon himself to propagate Anabaptist doctrines, and consequently displayed greater holiness and fear of God than formerly. He renounced all feastings and all sensual intercourse with the other sex ; in a word, all that could cast on him a suspicion of frivolousness. . . . In order, however, to make his teachings tally with his morals and to arouse the people to deeds of charity, he proclaimed in all his sermons that men should use their possessions in common and render each other service," &c. (p. 429).

This is exactly the picture of the typical Anabaptist and heretical communist in general with whom we have already become acquainted. At all events this description is accurate ; but how is it to be reconciled with the accounts given us of orgies ?

Kerssenbroick seems to have been particularly impressed by the gossip of the anonymous woman, as he expressly relies upon it to prove that he is relating " no fiction " ; and this is one of the few instances in which he finds it necessary to tell whence he obtained his knowledge. He generally gives none of the sources, so that these may have been of an even more lamentable kind !

By far the most important of the sources of information regarding the Anabaptist government is Gresbeck's narrative, already cited.[1] A joiner by trade, Gresbeck returned in February, 1534, to his native town, Münster, which he had left in 1530. He remained until the 23rd of May, 1535, and was consequently in a position to disclose the most eventful occurrences there, from personal observation ; but he wrote, perhaps eight or nine years after the end of the Anabaptist *régime*, entirely from memory and without any collateral aid. Hence he frequently confuses events. Moreover, the clearness of his memory was dimmed by one serious circumstance ; for Gresbeck was the man who betrayed Münster and brought the Bishop's forces into the town. He naturally hated his former associates, whom he had betrayed, more than they were hated by their open enemies. He almost invariably speaks of them as " miscreants " and rogues. This is the way with renegades and traitors. Quite as naturally he tries to distort facts, so as to make it appear that he had by merest accident come to Münster—when all the world was

---

[1] *Summarische ertzelungk und bericht der Wiederdope und wat sich binnen der stat Münster in Westphalen zugetragen in jair*, MDXXXV. Cornelius was the first to recognise the importance of this work, which is preserved in several hand copies. He reproduced it in the already quoted *Berichte der Augenzeugen über das Münsterische Wiedertäuferreich*, of which it forms the most prominent part.

full of the news that the town was in the hands of the Anabaptists—and joined them under the influence of fear alone! [1]
Hence he paints the picture of the reign of terror in the
coarsest tones possible, and by this means succeeds not only
in appearing blameless for his treachery, but in giving it the
aspect of a highly meritorious deed.

These are the chief sources of our knowledge concerning
the Münster episode. Although they should be used only
with the greatest circumspection, they have fallen into the
hands of historians who from the outset accepted as proved
the statement which these authorities wished to prove, viz.,
that communism of necessity engenders wildness and atrocity.
It is not surprising that under this method of writing history
the reign of the Anabaptists presents itself as a frenzy not
only of hideousness and vulgarity, but of inane and aimless
vulgarity and hideousness.

Nevertheless even these sources make it possible to comprehend the Anabaptist *régime* in Münster, provided they are
critically examined and compared with the scanty remains of
other contemporaneous testimony ; and if a view is kept both
of the generic character of heretical communism and of the
peculiar conditions prevalent in the town at that time.

(b) *The Reign of Terror.*—It is of the first importance to
remember that a state of war existed in Münster from the
day the Bishop surprised it on February 10th. A war
must be a remarkably insignificant affair, else how comes
it that historians who are acute enough to discover the most
trivial circumstance of possible moment to the often puerile
actions of a *monarch* almost invariably forget to take
account of the state of war, when they concern themselves
with the actions of a democratic and even communistic
commonwealth fighting for its life ? We refer in proof
of this to any of the traditional descriptions of the uprisings of the Paris Commune in 1871, or of the Reign of
Terror during the great French Revolution.

---

[1] In a letter written by him during the siege he admits that his
master's mother warned him against going to Münster, telling him that
he would assuredly allow himself to be baptized (*Berichte der Augenzeugen*, p. 323).

Precisely the same thing has happened with regard to the Anabaptists in Münster. If, however, we would understand them, we must not measure them by the standard of a condition of peace, but of a state of siege ; and indeed a *siege of peculiar severity*. They could not appeal to the customary laws of war ; they were precluded from making an honourable capitulation ; they had only the choice between victory and a most agonising death.

Together with this peculiar situation favourable to violent deeds, regard must be had to the characteristics of the century, which was one of the most, if not *the* most, bloodthirsty in history. The Anabaptists gained ample knowledge of this from personal experience. They—the most peaceable of all men—were hunted down like wild beasts, and handed over as victims to the most atrocious cruelties. It is not surprising that among this suffering people a party should have finally arisen who became wearied with sheepish patience and counselled violent resistance. The only cause for wonder is that this spirit was so long in developing itself and that it never affected more than a portion of the persecuted community.

A series of fortuitous circumstances had now placed a fortified town in the hands of this maltreated sect. Already, however, complete destruction threatened them from without. Let us see how they acted under these circumstances.

Janssen tells us (with a proper show of indignation) that ' On February 27th the Reign of Terror began with the proclamation of a decree that all the inhabitants must either receive the new baptism or leave the town." He then quotes the Bishop of Münster, who in a certain document grows wrathful over the fact that the " pious citizens " were driven in poverty from the city ; and affirms that " in no land, even of infidels, or Turks, or heathens, had such unheard-of and inhuman barbarities taken place." [1]

So great is the rage of the Catholic historian that he quite forgets to mention that the tender-hearted Bishop was at that time laying siege to Münster, nay, that on the 13th of January he had already issued an edict commanding his

[1] Janssen, *Geschichte des deutschen Volkes*, iii. p. 30.

officials to treat all "disobedient and rebellious" persons
conformably to the Imperial decree, that is, to slay them.
Moreover, this edict was rigorously carried out. Kerssenbroick exultantly tells us that "in order satisfactorily to
execute the Imperial decree and the ordinances of Justice
the Anabaptists remaining in various localities in the diocese
were severely punished, for at that time five women and one
man belonging to Wollbeck were thrown into the water and
drowned ; in Bewergern four women were drowned and two
men burnt. Many of those whom Rothmann had secretly
baptized were also punished, as they deserved, by being put
to death" (i. p. 517). Janssen says not a word concerning all
this, and in this respect affords us a specimen of traditional
representation. Of course Janssen is also silent about the
conspiracy entered into with the Bishop by the opponents of
the Anabaptists within the town to open the gates on the
10th of February for the passage of the Bishop's troops.
After the siege had begun the traitors were not executed, in
conformity with the laws of war and the good Bishop's
example, but were invited *to leave the town !* And this,
forsooth, is called the "reign of terror"! Was there ever
more pitiable cant?

In the course of the siege a rigorous government became
necessary within the city, and a series of executions took
place. If the cases adduced by Kerssenbroick and Gresbeck
are examined they will be found in every instance to relate
to offences against the safety of the town ; such as treacherous
communication with the enemy, offences against discipline
and attempts to desert, or to discourage the populace. Without doubt an execution is a cruel deed, but no more cruel
than war. The Baptists had not sought this war ; it was
forced upon them, for on all occasions they earnestly asseve-
rated their love of peace." [1]

A "reign of terror" existed not only in Münster, but also

---

[1] In a pamphlet issued to the besieging mercenaries they proclaim :
" Hear ye, young men and elders, who have encamped yourselves
against our city, as we wish not only to *live in peace with every one,* but
also to *prove by our acts our brotherly love in Christ for all men,* ye must
take heed how ye shall answer before pious persons—not to speak of

in the domain of the Bishop; and the comparison between the two does not redound to the credit of the latter.

The Bishop was the aggressor, the Baptists the defenders; the Bishop slew for his own gain; the Baptists slew that they might not be themselves slain. They fought for their lives. While the Bishop delighted in inflicting cruel modes of death upon the Baptists (especially drowning and burning) the condemned in Münster were not tortured, as there existed only *two* modes of execution, viz., beheading and shooting, and no less offensive form of capital punishment has been advanced in even the humane nineteenth century.

It has been regarded as evidence of a peculiarly strong spirit of bloodthirstiness that the heads of the town, 'King" Jan van Leyden, and his lieutenant, Knipperdollinck, carried out the executions with their own hands. This betrays a gross misconception of the feeling and the thought of that period. If the great lords, who at that time generally decided matters of life and death, did not themselves execute the condemned, it was not from humane sentiments, but because the loathsome and filthy work of the executioner's calling seemed too base for them. The executioner, whose trade was the handling of corpses, was everywhere looked upon as the most despicable of men, with whom all intercourse was anxiously avoided. If, then, the leaders of the movement in Münster undertook the office of executioner, they thus performed an act of unexampled self-abasement—an act which, far from evidencing a cruel disposition, merely exhibited a high feeling of *equality*.

That this is "no fiction" (to use Kerssenbroick's expression) is borne witness to by that worthy man himself, whom we can trust on this point. "Just at this time," he writes, "the prophet and man of God, Jan Bockelson, for the terror of evil-doers, handed over the sword to Knipperdollinck, whom, before the assembled multitude, he dubbed the 'bearer of the Sword'; *for as all the high were to be laid low*, and Knipperdollinck had hitherto been burgomaster and head of

God—for having laid violent siege to us and murdered us, against all written and signed treaties of peace, and without proper declaration. of war. The whole pamphlet is reproduced by Kerssenbroick, ii. p. 9.

the city, it was now the will of the father that Knipperdol-linck should fill the office of public executioner, *so ill esteemed by mankind*" (i. p. 545).

It is impossible to speak more plainly. The carrying out of executions with his own hands by Knipperdollinck, sprang from the same principle that caused him and the "Queen" to wait upon the multitude at the public meals.[1]

Where then, after all, is the unheard of Nero-like cruelty of the Anabaptists? Upon close inspection it vanishes like vapour. Far from being exceptionally cruel, they show themselves to have been unusually lenient for their time, and in view of their peculiar situation. Their cruelty lay in not patiently allowing themselves to be slaughtered—an unpardonable crime of course! Shooting *them* was a service of love, as Luther said; every shot on *their part* was an iniquitous brutality!

The charge of tyranny is closely related to that of cruelty. It is said that Münster shows us whither the freedom and equality of communism lead.

We have seen that the Baptists at Münster acquired their mastery by strictly legal means, the Council being composed of adherents to their cause. But for the very reason that the election was legal, it took place within the limits prescribed by the ancient electoral law, which restricted the franchise by a rule of eligibility; resident burgesses alone being represented in the Council. There was no representation of the proletarians or of the immigrants, who were about equal in number to the remaining population capable of bearing arms, and who bore their full share of the burdens of the conflict. On the other hand, the civil government was established for a time of peace, and was unequal to the demands set up by the siege.

A state of siege has always led to the temporary suspension of civil rights and privileges, and to the transference to the

---

[1] We have found no authentic evidence of the horrible story related by Kerssenbroick, that Jan van Leyden beheaded one of his wives; those remaining afterwards dancing round the corpse. It probably belonged to the same category as the "Fiery Baptism" spoken of by Jan Mathys.

military authority of an unlimited power over the life and property of the people ; so much so indeed that the words "state of siege" imply the setting aside of freedom and ordinary judicial methods. Communism has, unfortunately, not yet discovered the miraculous elixir which shall make this necessary consequence of a state of siege superfluous. Neither could it prevent the siege of Münster leading to a military dictatorship.

Besides conducting the very formless Church service, the preachers in the town gave their attention to questions of legislation and government. It was through their influence that a popular assembly was instituted apart from the Town Council, composed of members from the different parishes, in the election of which the non-guild portion of the population had votes as well as the burgesses. After the death of Mathys the preachers also proposed the formation of a "Committee of Public Safety," the members of which were appointed by them, subject to the approval of the community.

Gresbeck tells us that "the prophets and preachers wanted to abolish all government in the town of Münster. Prophets and preachers, Dutchmen and Frieslanders—the villains !— who were the true Anabaptists, wanted to be the only rulers. To this end they decreed that twelve from among the wisest elders, who were to be good Christians, should govern the people and take precedence of them ; and that these twelve elders should have power in the city. They thus supplanted the burgomasters and council (whom they had installed) as well as all guilds and aldermen, so that these were no longer to have any authority" (p. 35). Kerssenbroick expressly mentions among the elders three foreign brethren, of whom one was a Frieslander, the patrician Hermann Tilbeck, who was a member of the old Council, and indeed one of the two burgomasters of 1533, and who had from the outset sympathised with the Baptists.

As none of the community had received a classical education, but, like all heretical communists and democrats, based their order on the Old Testament, they did not call the members of the committee senators, or directors, or dictators, but "the elders of the twelve tribes of Israel." These were endowed with unrestricted power in judicial, legislative, and administrative affairs.

As a consequence of the state of siege, however, the supreme power fell into the hands of the commandants of the fortress, of whom the first was the prophet Jan Mathys. After he had fallen, fighting most bravely, in the sortie of April 5th, Jan van Leyden took his place, and, as the result shows, filled it satisfactorily.

In his capacity of commander-in-chief of the military forces, he became the autocratic ruler of the town. On the 31st of August, after a heavy cannonade, a severe attack was made upon the city, which was repulsed. After this success, Rothmann and the twelve elders, in the presence of the community, handed over their authority to Jan van Leyden, at the instance of the goldsmith and prophet Dusentschen, and with the consent of the most prominent Baptists (Knipperdollinck and Tilbeck, together with Henry and Bernt Krechtinck—two brothers who had immigrated in February). In so doing they only publicly recognised the state of affairs already existing.[1]

That the Baptists found no more suitable name for their municipal chief than " King of Israel," was due to their one-sided Biblical training, already noticed. Pious minds should least of all see evil in this ; and loyal historians should be especially sympathetic with those communists who make to themselves a king. These writers will in vain seek for the smallest trace of monarchial tendencies among Anabaptists while living in a state of peace (*e.g.*, the Moravians).

Like a good general, Jan van Leyden concerned himself not only about the sufficiency of military equipment and the drill of his troops, but also about the good psychological training of the people. In order to counteract the depressing inactivity and anxiety of the siege he endeavoured to keep them

---

[1] According to Kerssenbroick, of course, the whole Anabaptist government was arbitrarily framed by Jan, merely that he might become its ruler. " Jan Bockelson, of Leyden, had long striven for such things. For that reason he also repudiated and contemned all authority, and, to the same end, ordered that all citizens should share possessions in common, at the same time seizing them for himself," &c. (ii. p. 47).

employed and to amuse them.   The first object was attained
by work upon the entrenchments and the razing of superfluous
churches and old buildings.   We are told by Kerssenbroick—
not, of course, without his customary suspicion, " In order,
however, that the inhabitants of the town might have no time
for thinking of an insurrection against the king, they" (the
chiefs of the city) "unceasingly burdened the people with
labour ; and that they might also not grow too petulant gave
them only bread and salt to eat.[1]   As at that time" (January
15, 1535) "there were no new entrenchments to build nor
old ones to repair, the people were set to work razing the
churches, and old huts, and other low houses in the orchards,
and to digging up all the walls.   To that end they began on
January the 21st to remove the upper roof from the church ;
whereas previously their whole time had been occupied in
work on the fortifications" (ii. p. 142).

Jan, however, made provision for amusement as well as for
work.   Together with military and gymnastic exercises he
arranged public meals, games, and dances, festal processions,
and theatrical representations.   In these matters his joyous,
artistic nature stood him in good stead.   His appearance and
actions at these popular entertainments, especially in the
processions, may well appear theatrical to the modern spectator ; and we know, indeed, that he was at home on the
stage, and understood scenic effects.   Jan should not, however, be viewed with modern eyes.

Festal shows seem somewhat theatrical to us because we
get our ideas of them from the theatre only, whereas three
hundred or four hundred years ago they were a common
feature of social life.   Church, sovereigns, and nobility then
vied with each other in pompous display.   The Anabaptists,
like all other heretical communists, repudiated this splendour,
as it could be maintained only by spoliation.   They not only
wore the very simplest clothes, but in Moravia even refused
to make sumptuous clothing for others.[2]   In Münster, how-

[1] Thus out of the simple fact that provisions were short in the
beleaguered town, our objective historian contrives to twist a halter for
the Anabaptist leaders.

[2] A Moravian Baptist states : "Concerning the making of clothes, we

ever, abnormal conditions prevailed in this as in other respects. The sumptuousness of attire displayed by Jan and his people was not kept up by the spoliation of labourers. This "tailor-like," "theatrical" splendour had existed previously. "The Counsellor of the King (Jan van Leyden)," says Gresbeck, "had obtained possession of the garments formerly belonging to the wealthy persons who had been driven from the town" (p. 89, with which compare 136, where the former owners of the clothes are spoken of as burgesses and young noblemen). Kerssenbroick moreover informs us : "They seized and appropriated gold and silver whether it belonged to the town or to the burgesses, as well as the holy embroidered silken purples and all other ornaments employed in divine worship. They also appropriated everything else belonging either to the town or the burgesses, and even slew those who resisted and would no longer suffer and endure such robbery. Thus did they deck and adorn themselves for their own gratification, regardless of the fact that the means for this had been obtained by others through hard toil" (ii. p. 58).

Hence the pomp displayed by the Anabaptists was habitual in Münster; those who displayed it had alone changed.

The study of the Apocalypse must also have encouraged the development of pomp among the Münster Baptists. In that Book the New Jerusalem is depicted as being full of gold and precious stones; "And the kings of the earth do bring their glory and honour into it" (Rev. xxi. 24). It was imperative therefore in Münster to prove that the town was truly the long yearned-for New Jerusalem.

Imagination should not picture the splendour of Münster as being so excessive as is generally represented. Were the descriptions by Gresbeck to be believed, Jan and his soldiers must have carried about an incredible quantity of gold and

---

ought to and will serve our neighbour with all zeal in his necessity, to the praise of God and to the end that our diligence may be known ; but that which conduces to pride and arrogance only, such as sloped, bordered, and fringed work, we will make for no one, in order that our consciences may be kept undefiled " (Loserth, *Der Kommunismus der Mährischen Wiedertäufer*, p. 126).

silver. Whoever takes these descriptions literally will, on close inspection, be quite as much disappointed as were the Bishop's soldiers, whose mouths had been made to water by similar stories of booty. There was, for instance, a renegade from the Baptists, who related that " the king had a great treasure of gold, silver and money." Five or six tons of gold awaited them in the town! When, however, Münster had been taken, they found barely half a ton ; and it availed them nothing that they tortured Jan and his treasurer, and beheaded the soldier who told the silly tale ; they got none the more.

There could be no question of the treasure having been buried ; for the town had been captured by a night surprise, and the besieged had found barely time to seize their weapons, much less to bury treasure.

The theatrical representations carried out by Jan's orders are characteristic. One of them is described by Gresbeck. It is a didactic play : " As the common folk found great pleasure in anything that whiled away the time, the king caused them to be assembled in the cathedral. Men and women all obeyed the summons (with the exception of those who had to keep watch on the walls) in order to see the great show, and the wonderful thing that was to take place. The king had caused a stage with curtains to be erected in the choir where the High Altar stands, and so placed that it could be seen by every one ; and on this stage was performed the play of ' The rich man and Lazarus.' They began the piece and played it through, holding speech with each other. When the rich man had finished speaking to Lazarus, three fifers stood at the foot of the stage and played a three-part piece on German fifes. Then the rich man began once more to speak, and again the fifers played. Thus the play went on to the end. Then the devil came to fetch the rich man, body and soul, and dragged him away behind the curtains. There was great laughter in the cathedral when the people saw the great show " (p. 168).

The other popular entertainments, of which Gresbeck writes, were as harmless as this one. He is malicious and crabbed enough in regard to this cheerful scene, but makes no mention of licentiousness or even frivolity.

The most wicked of the " orgies," described by him, is the following:—" After the election by the people of the twelve gate-commanders, called dukes, the king held a feast, to which he invited all his dukes and counsellors, and the counsellors and handmaids of the queen, and all the highest servants of the king. . . . After having assembled, they behaved as if they were to remain at the head of the Government for their lives long. When the banquet was ended, they paid court to each other and danced, *each with his own wife*. The king banqueted with the dukes, and they all ate, drank, and were merry" (p. 184).

This is reproduced by Keller, with the words: " The king assembled at his residence all the dukes, counsellors, stadt-holders, and holders of office, with their wives, at a great feast, and caroused with them in great splendour and superabundance."[1]

In this way is history written! There is not one word about " carousal, splendour, and superabundance " in the whole account!

It appears from the context that it was not Gresbeck's purpose to call attention to the carousal, but to stigmatise the fact that the king and his retinue had enough to eat and drink, while the populace were starving; for he continues: " The common folk fled from the city through hunger, and a part began to die of starvation."

This is Gresbeck's most heinous charge against Jan van Leyden; not that he indulged in wild orgies, but that he withheld the necessary means of subsistence from the hungering population, while he himself had plenty to eat.

Gresbeck was not a personal spectator of these scenes, for he belonged neither to the king's *entourage*, nor to the officers of the army, nor to the Government officials. He, therefore, speaks of the above-mentioned " banquet " as of Jan's private luxury in general, only from hearsay. That many in the town grew discontented as the rations got lower and lower is extremely probable, and it is equally probable that they gave utterance to their discontent in evil reports about their commanders; but it is remarkable that the farther removed persons were from the " king," the more positive they

[1] *Geschichte der Wiedertäufer*, p. 237.

became in their assertions respecting his luxury in the midst of misery.

For example, Justinian von Holzhausen, a Burgomaster of Frankfort, who was in the camp before Münster, wrote to his father, June 8, 1535 : "The cows in the town [1] are eaten by the king and his people unknown to the public. *We wonder that the king's deception has not been discovered.*" [2] How then did the Burgomaster come to discover it in the camp outside the town ?

Gresbeck betrays himself on one occasion by his reference to the fact that Jan shared in the universal want : "Most of the women, therefore, had fled the town through great hunger. The king had fifteen wives, to whom, with the exception of the queen, he gave leave of absence, telling them that each should go to her friends, and that *all were to obtain food wherever they could.*" [3] Gresbeck relates this immediately after his account of the "great banquet." He had not acquired the art of writing history "systematically."

(c) *Communism.*—Community of goods was the basis of the whole Baptist movement. For its sake the great fight was waged at Münster. It was not, however, the chief factor in determining the character of the Münster Baptist government, that factor being the siege. The town was a great war-camp; the demands of war took precedence of all other matters, and sentiments of freedom and equality were active only in so far as they were compatible with military dictatorship.

Hardly had the city fallen into the hands of the Baptists on February 10th, when they sent letters in all directions, inviting comrades holding similar views to come to Münster. In one of these missives, still preserved, it says : "Here shall all wants be satisfied. The poorest amongst us, who were formerly treated like beggars, now go as sumptuously attired as the highest and most prominent with you or with us. Hence the poor are, through God's mercy, become as rich as the Burgomasters, or the wealthiest in the town."

[1] He writes on May 29th that the town still had 200 cows.

[2] *Berichte der Augenzeugen*, p. 354.

[3] This passage alone confutes the dreadful story before alluded to, of the beheading of one of his wives by the king. If he assembled them to their full number, and gave them permission to leave, he could not previously have murdered one of them.

This communism, however, stopped short in its beginning.

Historians are fond of assuming that all private proprietorship was abolished in Münster. Private property in gold, silver, and money was alone completely abolished. The prophets, preachers, and Council (the twelve elders had not yet been inaugurated) "came to an agreement, and decreed that all possessions should be in common ; each one should bring forward his money, gold and silver, and this was finally done" (Gresbeck, p. 32). This money served to defray the expenses of intercourse between the town and outer world, and especially the sending out of agitators, as well as proselytising among the mercenaries.

The single household, however, remained in existence, and private proprietorship, in articles of consumption and production, was abolished only to the extent demanded by the exigencies of the war.

That rights of inheritance were not abrogated is shown by the following regulations of the elders, recorded by Kerssenbroick (ii. p. 80) : " If any one should, by God's dispensation, be shot, or in other way fall to sleep in the Lord, no one shall dare to take away his property for himself, be it in arms, clothes, or other things ; but it shall be brought to the Sword Bearer, Knipperdollinck, who shall spread it before the elders, so that, by their instrumentality, it may be adjudged to the rightful heirs."

Even a portion of the war-booty might become private property. The fourteenth of the twenty-four articles submitted by Jan van Leyden to the people (January 2, 1535), directed that : " If booty be captured from the enemy, no one shall keep it for himself, or dispose of it after his own caprice ; but, as is fit, he shall notify the authorities in the matter. If they give him a part of it, he may, without injustice, use it for his own needs."

The next article says : " Under penalty of the last judgment, no Christian is to trade with his brother, or buy anything from him for money ; nor shall any one act deceitfully or fraudulently in exchange and barter."

After the abolition of money, exchange and barter became inevitable, if private proprietorship in articles of production and consumption was to be preserved. How little this right had been abrogated is shown by the following incident, which occurred after the raising of Jan to the kingship, and is narrated by Gresbeck (p. 144): "Then came Knipperdollinck to a shopkeeper, *who still carried on his trade.* Knipperdollinck said to him : 'Thou wouldst be in truth holy, yet art not willing to give up thy shop. There thou sittest, and ponderest how thou canst get profit from it. Thy shop is thy God. Thou must yield it up if thou wouldst be holy." From this it appears that shopkeeping was not deemed honourable ; but the "government of terror" was far from resorting to violent measures to make it impossible to keep a shop.

It is true that we find common repasts in Münster ; but these were in part occasional festal assemblages of the populace, and in part a war regulation. " Before every gate there was a house belonging to the community, in which every one took his meals who kept watch at the gate, or worked on the walls, or in the trenches. A sermon was preached every morning in these houses, the management of the food being undertaken by the deacons, each of whom had his own gate.

" Each parish had its community house, for which a manager was appointed whose duty it was to cook and take care of the house. At noon a young man stood up and read aloud a chapter from the Old Testament or the Prophets. After they had eaten they sang a German Psalm, then rose and went back to their watch " (Gresbeck, pp. 34, 35).

Not only men, but women shared in these meals ; for women also took an active part in the defence. The picture of these " bacchanalia," drawn by Gresbeck, is completed by the regulation prescribed by the elders and given by Kerssen-broick (ii. p. 5): " That a due regard to order may be had in the management of eating and drinking, not only shall those who serve the meals be mindful of their duty, and give the Brothers what they have hitherto received, but the Brothers and Sisters are always to sit apart at the tables assigned to them, preserving fit modesty and asking for no other food than that which shall have been provided." According to Kerssenbroick, not a word was spoken at table, attention being given to the reader.

All this reminds us more of a meeting of pietists than of libertines ; but it accords with the general character of heretical communism.

The expenses of these common meals were thrown upon the Catholic Church and the emigrants from the town, the provisions being taken from the monasteries and deserted houses.

Three deacons were appointed for each parish (by whom chosen Gresbeck unfortunately does not tell us, but probably by the populace), whose duty it was to look after the poor. Christian communism has never gone beyond that limit in communities which retained the system of single households. " The deacons," Gresbeck informs us, " sought out the poor in their respective districts and supplied all needs. They made a good show in Münster of allowing no one to want for anything.

" These deacons went into every house and made a written memorandum of what it contained in the way of food, grain, or meat. When all had been recorded, the householder had no further control over the provisions" (p. 34). This regulation was not an outcome of communism, but a war measure, always absolutely necessary in a beleaguered town where the military authorities must know the quantity of provisions available. This very regulation presupposes the existence of a single household. Only afterwards, and under the pressure of necessity, was it ordered that all superfluous clothing should be delivered up as well as the stores of provisions. This measure did not, however, do away with the single household ; for the deacons had to give to each family its share in the common store, of bread as well as of meat, so long as these lasted. " They killed a number of horses, and had the meat carried to the house to which the people went for their provisions. The deacon first asked how many persons there were in each house, and then served out the meat accordingly, writing down what had been given, so as to prevent any one from being served twice" (Gresbeck, p. 174).

Moreover, such land as necessity compelled them to cultivate was not held in common, but was allotted among the households. " The king appointed four administrators of land,

who went over all the farms, and allotted from them one or
two pieces of land to every household, according to the
number of its inmates.   These allotments were planted with
cabbages, turnips, roots, beans, and peas.   The owner of a
large farm was not allowed to use more of it than had been
allotted to him by the land administrators.   They had even
proposed to move all hedges and fences from the farms inside
the town area, so that these might be in common " (Gresbeck,
pp. 175, 176).   This last measure, however, was not carried
out.   The regulation that all house doors should be left open
day and night was probably of a moral rather than an
economic nature, and designed to increase the feeling of
brotherhood.

The preservation of the single household was closely
allied with the maintenance of the disciplinary power of
the house-master over the members of the household.   In the
Middle Ages a family consisted of more persons than the
married couple with their children.   The large households
of that period demanded a staff of servants, and hence, in
Münster, we find the authority of the husband over the wife
combined with that of the master over the servants.   In one
of the edicts of the elders, the third clause treats of " the
dominion of the husband and the subjection of the wife " ;
while the fourth deals with " the obedience of house-servants
to the house-masters, and the duties of house-masters to their
servants " (Kerssenbroick, ii. 1).   The common meals were
participated in by " each Brother and his wife, together with
his house servants " (Gresbeck, p. 106).

There was no abolition of the distinction between master
and journeyman, nor of production in single petty shops,
so closely bound up at that time with the single household.
In an already quoted edict of the elders, certain craftsmen were designated to work for the town and populace.
This should not be regarded as a socialistic organisation of
labour, but as a regulation engendered by the exigences of
war ; *i.e.*, the specified craftsmen were exempt from guard
duty (Kerssenbroick, p. 221).   The edict says : " No one
shall carry on the trade of fishing except the master fisher-
men, Christia Kerckring and Hermann Redecker, together

with their men, who, moreover, when necessary, shall not refuse fish to the sick and women with child. . . . Hermann Tornate and Johann Redecker, with their six journeymen, shall make shoes for the New House of Israel. . . . Johann Coesfeld and his journeymen shall make iron keys " (Kerssenbroick, ii. p. 6).

Hence historians are by no means accurate in asserting that "a far reaching community of goods " was inaugurated in Münster.[1] That it did not arrive at that stage may be explained in the same way as the small activity in social affairs of the Paris Commune of 1871. It was an inevitable consequence of the siege, which left its evil trail at every step and laid claim to every thought and act. A time of war has never yet proved itself to be the suitable moment for the inauguration of a fundamentally new order of society.

In so far as the introduction of a new state of things was concerned, the Anabaptists were as unsuccessful in ecclesiastical matters as they had been in those relating to economics. Keller wonders at this. " It was to be expected," he says, " that their activity would begin with the promulgation of a new Church discipline, or with a regulation concerning the form of divine worship, or similar affairs ; yet not only was there a lack of all necessary provision for these things at the inception of their government, but, so far as we know, no regulation of Church ritual was ever made " (*Geschichte der Wiedertäufer*, p. 202). This does not seem so surprising to us. We ascribe this circumstance in part to the war, but in part also to the indifference to the form of divine worship shown by the Anabaptists, quite as much as by the Bohemian Brethren and the disciples of Münzer.

The predilection for the Old Testament shown on every occasion by the Baptists is quite in harmony with the universal spirit of heretical communism, as is also their contempt for erudition, evidenced by their burning of all books

---

[1] Lamprecht, *Deutsche Geschichte*, vol. i. p. 356. Lamprecht contrives to delineate the " grotesquely abominable conditions" in Münster without in the least connecting them with the state of siege, this being afterwards mentioned in two lines as an insignificant trifle, having no effect on the internal life of the town.

(with the exception of the Bible) and all letters found in the town.   Moreover, they confirmed the rule that disdain for learning among the committee went hand in hand with care for popular education.   In spite of the siege, they established five or six new schools "where children, youths, and maidens were made to learn German Psalms, and read and write.   All their instruction appertained to Baptism, and was given in the manner of the sect" (Gresbeck, p. 47).

Mysticism is once more met with among the Münster Baptists, *e.g.*, the belief of some few enthusiastic Brothers in direct intercourse with God, and in revelations and prophecies. In regard to Knipperdollinck, Jan Mathys, Bockelson, and other prophets of the New Jerusalem, many features of morbid ecstasy are recounted which, although in many cases distorted and exaggerated, are probably not wholly without foundation.

However great may have been the resemblance of their conduct in these matters to that of their peaceable forerunners in Moravia, they were (if we may trust their Chronicles) completely dissimilar in one respect, viz., their *dissoluteness*.   We have already had frequent occasion to touch on this point, but will now examine it more closely.

(d) *Polygamy.*—Modern sentiment is generally offended by the austerity and puritanism of the Anabaptists, but it has had no reason to complain of their dissoluteness. If these characteristics were prominent among peaceable Baptists, it may, at the outset, be anticipated that they were not weakened by the exigencies of a siege demanding, before all things, the strictest discipline.   Closer inspection confirms this, and we should not allow ourselves to be misled by the accounts of the popular entertainments already mentioned.

That good behaviour and discipline were zealously preserved, is proved by some of the twenty-eight articles of January 22, 1525, in which among others we read:—

"6. No one who fights under the standard of Justice should defile himself with the infamous and hateful vice of drunkenness, with disgraceful shamelessness, with fornication and adultery, or with gambling—a vice which betrays a greed for gold and often engenders dissension and hatred ; for such sins shall not go unpunished among the people of God."

" 16. No Christian " (*i.e.*, no Anabaptist) "shall be admitted from one society or community into another, unless he shall have previously shown that he is blameless, and has not been guilty of any crime ; if, however, the contrary is discovered he shall be punished without forbearance."

" 20. No Christian shall resist a heathen " (*i.e.*, a non-Anabaptist) "authority who has not yet heard the Word of God, nor been instructed therein ; nor shall he do the said authority any injury, provided it forces no one into disbelief and ungodliness. On the other hand, the Babylonish tyranny of priests and monks and all their partisans and adherents, who darken the justice of God with their violence and injustice, shall be crushed in every possible way."

" 21. If, after the commission of a crime, a heathen shall fly to the community to escape punishment, he shall not be admitted by Christians, but so much the more certainly be punished, provided it is proved that he has acted directly against God's command, as it is not to be permitted that a community of Christians should be a refuge for the doers of infamous deeds and crimes " (ii. pp. 133–137).

As lovers of peace, they exhorted to obedience where it was possible, and carefully guarded themselves from association with common criminals. Drunkenness, gaming, and every kind of illicit sexual intercourse were severely punished.

A striking example of the strict discipline maintained in Münster is given by Gresbeck : " On the 28th of June, 1534, it so happened that ten or twenty soldiers were seated in a house in the town, where they had a drinking-bout and had become merry. They were frolicsome, as soldiers are wont to be, and consequently the landlord and his wife would draw no more for them; whereupon the soldiers said, ' Landlady, if you will not draw, then we will,' and upbraided her. Upon this the landlord and his wife went before the twelve elders, and accused the soldiers of having been violent in their house, and of having chidden the landlady. The twelve elders immediately had the soldiers arrested and thrown into prison. The next day a congregation was convened in the Cathedral yard and the soldiers were brought before it. Then the chancellor, Heinrich Krechting—the rascal!—proclaimed what was said to have been done by the soldiers, who immediately sued for pardon. At last the door of mercy was a little opened ; some received pardon, but six had to die " (p. 36).

This case of severe discipline is adduced by Keller as a proof of "the criminal character of their proceedings." Yet only two pages further on he is forced to praise this discipline, whose stern punishments so operated that drunkenness was hardly ever seen among the Baptists, while in the Bishop's camp it raged to such an extent that it caused many military operations undertaken by the besieged forces to be successful.

We will cite only one more passage from Gresbeck's work illustrative of the spirit prevalent among the Baptists : " Now the Anabaptists often used to sally out for a skirmish with the soldiers; at such times they held themselves as boldly as if they had done twenty years' service, and moreover did everything with sagacity, dexterity, and calmness. For the prophets, preachers, and head men of the town sharply forbade any one daring to drink himself full, so that they always retained their senses, were never drunk, and were invariably calm. When, therefore, they sallied out they acted with wisdom and skill " (p. 50).

It is this that constitutes the "brutal dissoluteness," and "wildness," delineated by an eye-witness who was least of all given to palliation.

But how is it with regard to unchastity—polygamy? On this point at least, it is possible to speak of brutal dissoluteness?

We have now reached the most difficult and obscure phase in the history of the Münster Anabaptists. Polygamy is so opposed to the generic character of that sect (*e.g.*, the Moravians, and indeed to heretical communism in general) that we were at first inclined to assume the existence of a misapprehension, based upon a confusion of terms. There is, in fact, no more difficult task for an observer than that of correctly and impartially estimating the features of an unusual relation between the sexes. Nowhere does the extraordinary produce such repulsion and repugnance as in sexual matters. To this prejudice is chiefly due the fact that only within the last generation has it been possible to conduct a scientific and unprejudiced investigation into the sexual relations of the folk of primitive times and among modern savages and uncivilised races.

Those who know what nonsense has been proclaimed to the world by missionaries concerning the intercourse between the sexes in the South Sea Islands, might well surmise that the assumption of the prevalence of " polygamy " in Münster was based upon a confusion of that term with a sort of community of wives similar to that existing among the Adamites—a form of sexual intercourse associated, as we know, with many kinds of communism in the means of consumption. This surmise, however, is untenable, as there never was any talk of a community of wives in Münster.

The edict with which the twelve elders inaugurated their government, imposed the *death penalty* on *adultery* and the *seduction of a maiden.* At about the same time the Münster community must have published their written defence entitled : *Bekentones des Globens und lebens der gemein Christe zu Münster* ("Confession of Faith and Life of the Community of Christians at Münster"). [1] In the chapter *On Marriage* (pp. 457 *sqq.*) it says: " In respect of that with which we are charged, and the malevolent lies by which many good-hearted persons are led to suspect that we live in illicit wedlock, together with numerous fabricated and slanderous accusations unnecessary to repeat, we wish herewith to set forth our judgment and usage concerning the holy state of matrimony. . . .

" Marriage we say—and we hold by the Scriptures—is a

---

[1] Reproduced in *Berichte der Augenzeugen*, pp. 445-464. Concerning the probable date of this document, compare V. W. Bouterwek, *Zur Literatur und Geschichte der Wiedertäufer.* Bonn, 1864, p. 37.

union and an obligation between man and woman in the Lord . . .

"God in the beginning created man; 'male and female created He them,' and joined the two in holy matrimony, so that the two souls were to be one flesh. For this reason no man may sunder such a union. . . .

"Marriage is an image of Christ and His holy bride, *i.e.*, the congregation of His believers. As Christ and His congregation care for each other and hold to each other, so those who are married in the Lord and joined together by God, should care for and hold to each other. While then it so stands with the married state, we make a distinction between it and the marriage of heathens and disbelievers, which is sinful and unclean, and is not marriage in the sight of God, but only harlotry and adultery. . . .

"For as is plainly seen, they marry only for the sake of friendship and kinship, or for money and possessions, or for the flesh and adornment. Nay, they seldom or never rightly consider what true marriage is, or how one should be married; much less do they see to it that they are truly married and keep their vows. . . .

"Since then marriage is a glorious and honourable state, no one should be frivolous respecting it, but enter into it with pure and true heart, so that nothing but God's honour and will be sought for, as, thanks and praise be to God, is the custom with us, and shall be spread abroad to the glory of God.

"We hear that many other evil things are imputed to us: that we have our women common to all in a platonic way, or after the manner of the Nikolaitans" (Adamites), "together with sundry other vile accusations, as if we made no distinction in matters of blood-relationship. But this is a shameless lie, as are all other abusive and wicked things published with intentional deceit respecting us.[1] We know

---

[1] Master Gresbeck found it necessary to spread these miserable lies (p. 80); it did not trouble the worthy gentleman that he thereby contradicted his other deductions regarding the married state in Münster. They seemed suitable for compromising his opponents, and that was his chief purpose.

that Christ said : ' Ye have heard that it was said by them
of old times, Thou shalt not commit adultery ; but I say
unto you, That whosoever looketh on a woman to lust after
her, hath committed adultery with her already in his heart.'
Were such a one to be found among us—which God forbid—
we should in no wise suffer him, but excommunicate him,
and deliver him unto Satan for the destruction of the flesh."

We see that the " sensuality " (called " Neronic " by a
modern German author) declares even flirting with a maiden
to be sinful.   The opinions prevalent in Münster are in complete harmony with the austerity in sexual matters which
characterised the majority of other Anabaptists.   Jan van
Leyden ratified these views on January 2, 1535, in his
Twenty-eight Articles already mentioned, by providing for
the punishment of adultery and harlotry (the latter word
implying not only prostitution, but every illicit intercourse
between the sexes).   Moreover, this was at a period when
polygamy had already been introduced.

How, then, is the apparent inconsistency to be accounted
for ?   The usual explanation, based upon the assumed innate
sensuality and immoderation of communists, is very convenient, but it has one defect—it has no certain foundation.
The explanation rests wholly and solely on the thing to be
explained.   Everything else contradicts it, for we have seen
that abstinence and discretion were conspicuous characteristics
of the Anabaptists.

Neither can the solution be found in the character of
Baptist communism ; on the contrary, it makes the matter
more inexplicable.   There remains nothing but to seek for
the elucidation in the peculiar relations between the sexes in
Münster during the siege.   Moreover, these relations were of
such a strikingly singular kind, that it would have required an
incredible degree of obduracy or a great lack of good intention
to prevent their being recognised.

We must remember the large emigration from Münster of
aristocratic and middle-class citizens.   The *men* went, but
they left their women and female servants behind.   There
was thus an excess of women over men, which, from the
figures given by Gresbeck, must have been enormous.   He

writes of an evening meal on Mount Sion: "Men, old persons, and youths were there to the number of *two thousand*. The number of men in Münster capable of bearing arms was never greater than fifteen hundred. The women in the town, old and young, numbered eight or nine thousand, more or less—I cannot be exact about the children who could and could not walk, they were perhaps one thousand or twelve hundred." [1]

The situation was further complicated by the fact that quite half the men were unmarried ; such being the case with the majority of the numerous immigrants, and of course with the soldiers who came as prisoners or deserters, and joined the sect.

In face of the strictness of the Baptist in sexual matters, these conditions must, in the course of the siege, have become insupportable for the majority of the marriageable population, cut off as they were from the outer world. The very strictness which threatened all illicit sexual intercourse with severe punishment, finally made a revolution in the relations between the sexes unavoidable.

The very persons who cannot show enough indignation over the polygamy of Münster look upon prostitution as a self-evident necessity. This vice was of course prevalent under the reign of "respectability." In the Thirty-six Articles formulated by the Münster insurrectionists in 1525 (compare p. 265), the eighteenth required that: "All lewd women and the concubines of the priests shall be distinguished from virtuous women by certain marks."

---

[1] P. 107. The Baptist Werner Scheiffurth von Merode, who was made prisoner in a sortie, gave a smaller number in his judicial examination on December 11, 1534 : "The men, women, and children in the town number approximately between eight thousand and nine thousand, of whom about fourteen hundred are able to bear arms" (*Berichte der Augenzeugen*). This number of men available for the defence nearly agrees with that named by Gresbeck, and the estimate of the total adult male population is probably correct, as he gives it with great preciseness. They had evidently been counted. If to this we add one thousand children, the number of marriageable women must still have been from five thousand to six thousand, and therefore twice or thrice as great as the number of men.

These " lascivious debauchees " put an end to prostitution. Prostitution and communism are two reciprocally incompatible conditions. The various forms of communism are compatible with the most diverse kinds of sexual intercourse, but not with one kind—venal love. Where there is no production of commodities for sale, where nothing is bought or sold, the body of woman, like the power to work, ceases to be saleable ware. Incomplete as was the communism of Münster, no maiden of that town was forced to sell herself during the reign of Anabaptism. The wenches who from habit would gladly have obtained the gains of the trade they carried on under the old society, found no buyers in Münster, where no private person possessed money. Such women were forced to seek their pay among their old customers in the camp of the " defenders of morality and order," *i.e.*, among the soldiers, the reputable burgesses, and the secular and spiritual aristocracy.

The natural working of communism was, in addition, favoured by the sexual austerity of the Baptists. Is it conceivable that prostitution should not have existed among the thousand and more unmarried men and several thousand husbandless women living together for months in a town which, according to modern ideas, was of small size? It was inevitable that adultery and illicit sexual intercourse should make their appearance. The severest penalties must have been powerless to prevent it. There was only one means by which the destructive sexual confusion could be remedied, viz., a new regulation of the condition of marriage. In July, the fifth month of the siege, and after long opposition, the elders and preachers set about the work.

The task was a difficult one, nay almost impossible; for it concerned the making of marriage-laws in harmony both with the austere morality of the Anabaptists in matrimonial matters, and the unique sexual conditions existing in Münster. It was quite in conformity with this difficulty, that the new marriage law did not appear in the form of a unified and completely elaborate statute, but in numerous regulations, partly supplementing and partly abrogating each other. The Anabaptists never got beyond the *search* for a suitable form of marriage, and indeed could not do so under the abnormal conditions of their existence.

Gresbeck follows their uncertain gropings after a marriage law, but his account is so confused and so full of contradictions and absurdities, that it is difficult to get a clear picture from it. [1] It enables, us however, to distinguish two features of this search. One consists in the effort to make marriage a free union. First of all it was necessary to pronounce all marriages invalid which had been contracted before the adoption of the Anabaptist faith; otherwise a new marriage union would have been impossible for the wives of the burgesses who had emigrated. This decree of invalidity came the more easily from the Anabaptists, since although they declared marriage to be an indissoluble union, they held "heathen" marriage to be no true marriage, just as infant' baptism was said to be no true baptism. Hence they now required a renewal of vows on the part of those who had been married before joining them.

The second feature shows itself in the attempt to bring all the women into the married state; at the outset, however, not in a corporeal, but in an economic state.

In order to understand the "polygamy" of Münster, it must be borne in mind that the single household was never abolished. As a result of the emigration of burgesses, it came about that there were many households which contained no man, and indeed some in which there was no mistress, but only maids. In a beleaguered city holding so many unmarried soldiers, this state of things must have entailed numerous disadvantages; hence it was ordered that no woman should be without male protection and also male guardianship. For as the Münster Anabaptists did not do away with the system of single households, they were quite as little advocates of the emancipation of woman as

---

[1] Kerssenbroick's account is absolutely idiotic. He relates that a soldier had surprised Jan van Leyden as the latter was creeping to one of Knipperdollinck's maids. To save himself from falling into bad odour, Jan thereupon persuaded Rothmann and the other preachers ("who were not less given over to lasciviousness and lewdness"), to introduce simply—polygamy!

emancipation of the flesh. The third clause of the already quoted edict of the elders, which treats of "the sovereignty of the man and the subjection of the woman," says, "Husbands love your wives. Let wives be subject to their husbands, as to their lords. And let the wife fear the husband."[1]

In this connection Rothmann expresses himself very drastically in his *Restitution*—a pamphlet which appeared in October, 1534.[2] "The husband is therefore to accept the sovereignty over his wife with manful feeling, and to keep his marriage undefiled. In most places wives have the mastery, and lead their husbands as bears are led. . . . It is highly needful that wives, who almost everywhere now wear the breeches, should humble themselves in right and becoming obedience; for it is agreeable to God that every one should keep in his place—the husband under Christ, and the wife under the husband."

The women who are without masters were now ordered to attach themselves to households in which there were men; not as drudges or servants, but as *companions of the wives*.

This regulation was not based upon actual conditions— they were not so materialistic in those days—but upon Biblical precedent. There was, however, but one example in Scripture which in any way suited their case, viz., the polygamy of the ancient Jews, more especially of the patriarchs; and they appealed to this with the greater confidence as the patriarchs had undoubtedly been highly pious men, whom God had honoured with personal visits, or with visits from His angels. That which had been done by these prototypes of Christianity could not possibly be sinful. Moreover, the Baptists could rely upon the most prominent evangelical lights of the Church for support to this mode of thinking. On August 27, 1521, Melancthon had advised the King of England to take a second wife

---

[1] Kerssenbroick, ii. p. 1.

[2] *Eyne Restitution edde Eyne wedderstellinge rechter unde gesunde Christliche leer, gelanens unde lenens uth Gades genaden durch de gemeynte tho Münster, an der Dach gegenen . . .* Münster, 1534. A long extract from this work, with many quotations, is given by Bouterwek in his *Literatur und Geschichte der Wiedertäufer*, pp. 15-34.

in addition to his first, and had declared that "polygamy was not forbidden by Godly law." [1]

The true character of Münster "polygamy" has been much obscured by its religious dress. It has, moreover, been made no clearer by the pile of odium, slanders, and distortions heaped upon it by antagonistic chroniclers; while the unfair interpolations of partisan accounts have completely concealed almost every trace of the true nature of this regulation. Fortunately, however, the chroniclers were too shortsighted to remove every vestige of the truth. A few statements which they have handed down to us suffice to show that the aim of the Baptists in introducing "polygamy" was the uniting of several women in one household, but not in one marriage-bed; though it is not to be denied that the latter condition was favoured by the former.

It is highly important to point out the fact that *every* woman was obliged to seek a man; not only those who were suitable for sexual intercourse, but the old and those who had not yet reached the age of puberty. [2]

This is not the only point in support of our views. Another is the following communication by Kerssenbroick, " In the beginning of October the wife of one Butendick was

[1] Even after the introduction of polygamy into Münster had caused such scandal, and been everywhere condemned, Luther and Melancthon declared to Landgrave Philip of Hesse that : " What the Mosaic law permitted is not forbidden in the Gospel." He might, therefore, be tranquil with regard to polygamy. (See also numerous similar quotations by Keller, *Die Reformation*, p. 454 *sqq.*) It was, therefore, not polygamy itself which so enraged pious persons against the Baptists, but their impertinence in transforming it from a privilege of rulers to a common right.

[2] Gresbeck is of the opinion that the last measure had for its aim the forcing of young maidens into sexual intercourse. It is not impossible that some heads of households (perhaps rough soldiers) abused their position. Even Kerssenbroick said no more than this. Similar things may happen elsewhere. That, however, the *aim* of the regulation was the ravishing of *young children*, we must have more than a Gresbeck to make us believe ; for however valuable many of his statements are when they deal with facts, he can only adduce odious and unsupported gossip respecting the motives and aims of the Baptists. We hold that those eminent gentlemen who levy maiden-tribute in our modern Babylons are incapable of demanding the enforcement of this brutality by law.

publicly accused by her lord and husband. The cause was that she resisted him, and insulted him with many slanderous and abusive words, saying that he lived with the rest of his women and fellow-sisters not in a spiritual but in a fleshly manner, and often had carnal intercourse with them." She was found guilty and sentenced to death, but pardoned after having asked forgiveness of her husband (p. 80).

Hence a distinction was made between a lawful wife and the sisters of the community living with her. Not all female members of a household were the lawful wives of the head of the house, although they were designated as his wives.

Meanwhile, it is presumable that, with the prevalence of such intimate life in common, the same state of things arose which is not absent elsewhere, viz., that the husband sometimes remained unsatisfied with his lawful wife alone, which was the reproach brought against Butendick by his wife. This was made more probable by the austerity of the Baptists, which, under certain circumstances, prohibited sexual intercourse even between husband and wife, *e.g.*, when she was barren or pregnant, on the ground that sexual intercourse was not to serve for the gratification of sinful lust, but solely for the perpetuation of the human race.[1] Hence, in certain cases, a man was allowed to make natural wives of those women who had been commended to his protection, in addition to his first wife. Thus Rothmann says in his *Restitution*, " If a man should be so richly blessed of God as to impregnate *one* wife and, in consequence of God's commands, should not wish to abuse such a blessing, then, on necessity, he shall be free to take to himself several fertile wives ; for to know a woman out of wedlock is adultery and harlotry."

It is, however, always possible to distinguish clearly between this sexual polygamy and that which was of an economic character. In the former the man chose the women ; in

---

[1] Rothmann says in his *Restitution:* " That a man neither should nor ought to know a woman who is pregnant or barren can be proved, in the first place, by the fact that God commanded mankind to increase and multiply ; and for that end alone should husband and wife employ the blessing of God, and not for lust."

the latter the women chose the man whom they wished to acknowledge as their protector and master. The former kind was, under certain conditions, allowed ; and, in the state of things described, impossible wholly to prevent. The law-givers of Münster contented themselves with the effort to keep it in the paths of regulated marriage. The polygamy, on the contrary, which was for a long time prescribed by law, was economic; that is, the union of several women under the protection and guardianship of one man. The Münster marriage-law imposed on women the obligations of the latter kind of polygamy, but not those of the former. Moreover, this compulsion soon ceased, as is proved by the Twenty-eight Articles promulgated by Jan van Leyden. We will give those which treat of marriage, as they are highly characteristic of the spirit of the Münster marriage law :—

" 24. No one shall be forced to marry ; since marriage is a voluntary compact, entered into more from a natural instinct and the bonds of love than through mere words and outward ceremonies.

" 25. If, however, any one is afflicted with epilepsy, venereal disease, or other complaints, he shall not marry unless he previously makes known his malady to the person whom he wishes to marry.

" 26. No one who is not a virgin shall give herself out to be such, and deceive and entrap her fellow-brothers. More-over, such deceit shall be severely punished.

" 27. Every unmarried woman, or those who have not their regular husbands, shall be authorised to choose a guardian or protector from the congregation of Christ."

The final clause contains a prophecy, " The voice of the living God has instructed me that this is a command of the All Highest : The men shall demand a confession of faith, as well from their legal wives as from those whom they are charged to guard and protect ; not that which is commonly recited—' I believe in God the Father,' but a confession of faith of the marriage-union in the New Kingdom—why and to what purpose they were baptised. They shall show and disclose all this to their husbands " (ii. pp. 138, 139).

This is the last form of the marriage-law among the Münster

Anabaptists. It completely agrees with the sober and rational simplicity which we have learnt was their distinguishing characteristic; and the most dexterous and unscrupulous annihilator of socialism will find it a hard task to produce therefrom a trace of unbridled licentiousness.

These Articles of January 2nd contain an important amelioration of the marriage-law introduced on July 23rd of the previous year. By the latter, every woman had the obligation imposed on her of seeking a protector and master, whose household she was compelled to join. This regulation seems to have had manifold disadvantageous consequences, as it was abrogated in the autumn of the same year, and those women who wished to do so were allowed to leave the "lords" to whom they had attached themselves. From the obligation resting upon women there grew up a right which they were free to exercise.

Whatever mental picture one may make of this "polygamy," it should in no case be that of an Oriental harem. The latter implies the complete enslavement of the woman. There was no question of such a thing in Münster; indeed, it was the women who had free choice of their husbands, protectors, and guardians. How little they were oppressed by the new regulations may be seen from the circumstance that the majority of them were numbered among the most enthusiastic combatants for the New Kingdom.

Some, of course, were discontented. Not every one had remained in the town through conviction; and the new marriage law, which engendered such an abnormal state of things, was in too sharp contradiction to deeply-rooted sentiments. Moreover, the new regulation could not set aside existing complications without now and then creating fresh ones. Nevertheless, we very rarely hear of any resistance on the part of the women,[1] while we very often hear

---

[1] How well some historians contrive to exaggerate this resistance may be seen from the following example. Keller writes in his *Geschichte der Wiedertäufer*, p. 211: "It is certain that many women, married and unmarried, showed the greatest repugnance to the new regulation. It is related that one of them chose a voluntary death to escape from the infamy to which it was proposed to subject her." What is actually related? Gresbeck writes: "On one occasion a

of the enthusiasm with which they embraced the new order of things.

An example of this is afforded by the Mollenheck insurrection. This is represented as an uprising of the moral portion of the citizens against polygamy. "Though the complete community of wives was not introduced," says Bezold, "the command of the prophets, that no woman should be without a husband, led to the institution of a kind of polygamy which was not much better. The feelings of the native-born Brothers revolted against these horrors; but their attempt at insurrection was frustrated in blood, and the distribution (!) of the women (who formed by far the larger part of the population) among the male minority—the 'lords'—was proceeded with" (*Geschichte der deutschen Reformation*, p. 710).

What are the facts? Mollenheck, a former guild president, "gathered round him a part of the burgesses, pious inhabitants and soldiers," not merely to do away with the new marriage law, but "that every one might receive back his property, the Burgomasters and Council be reinstated in their control of the town, and things in general be as they were previously" (Gresbeck, p. 73). The deserters from the besieging army were in the vanguard of this movement, which, ostensibly in defence of chastity, was in reality a counter-revolution. Success attended the first efforts of the insurrectionists, who even went so far as to make prisoners of Jan van Leyden and Knipperdollinck. Gresbeck further says that if they had immediately opened

woman was found lying in the water, drowned and floating on the surface of the water in her clothes. The common people did not know how she came to that pass; whether the prophets and preachers had caused her to be drowned, or if she had done so of her own will. The people of the town were of the opinion that she had drowned herself, because she was grieved by the marriage regulations. I am not able to write more concerning the true cause of her misfortune" (pp. 64, 65).

Hence it was "related" simply that a drowned woman was found in Münster. Whether it was a case of crime or suicide (or a mere accident, in regard to which possibility Gresbeck is strangely silent), is totally unknown. From this, forsooth, a tale of murder is concocted; and this *single* story of murder serves as proof that *many* women "showed the greatest repugnance to the new regulations!"

one of the gates, the Bishop's forces would have obtained possession of the city ; but the revolutionists were thinking of plunder only. "They were more anxious to get hold of booty than to capture a gate. They had their sleeves full of money, and sat the whole night drinking wine until they were drunk. This was the cause of their defeat by the Frieslanders and Dutchmen."

The saddest feature of the overthrow of this counter-revolution is the circumstance that while the soldiers ventured their lives for "chastity and morality" in drunkenness and pillage, those whose cause they were espousing—the "down-trodden women"—fought most resolutely against them in defence of "rape and incest." When the rebels barricaded themselves in the town-hall, it was women who brought heavy guns to the market to blow in the doors.

Kerssenbroick and Gresbeck give numerous proofs of the enthusiasm and joyfulness with which women fought on the walls when an assault had to be repulsed. Moreover, they were ready to take part in the sorties. On one occasion Jan van Leyden made preparations for a sortie in force to assist the relieving army which he expected from the Netherlands, and called for volunteers for the hopeless undertaking from the women as well as the men. "The next day those women who wished to take part in the sortie assembled in good order three hundred strong in the Cathedral yard armed with various weapons, one having a halberd, another a pike, and so forth. As the king did not wish to take all, he had them mustered and selected fifty-one, a written list being made of their names.

"The next day all women who wished to remain in the town, were ordered to assemble in the Cathedral yard. These also came with their weapons, and marched about in good order, like soldiers." After being divided into as many sections as there are gates to the town, each section, together with a body of men, was detailed to guard a gate. They thereupon marched off singing the Marseillaise of the German Reformation, the Psalm : *Eine fest Burg ist unser Gott* ("A tower of strength is our God") (p. 128).

This was the way in which the women of Munster defended themselves against the "infamies heaped upon them."

Enough has been said respecting the "woman question" in Münster. There is still much to clear up, many lacunæ still to be filled ; but what has been given is, we think, sufficient to make the new regulation of sexual matters in Münster quite comprehensible, and to show that in spite of its imperfection, its simplicity, and even its crudity, it had much that was in sympathy with modern sentiment. The defenders of the society of to-day have least cause of any to grow irate over the "shameless licentiousness" of the Münster Anabaptists ; those defenders of a society which has for one of its supports the most shameless and debauching form of sexual intercourse, viz., the taking advantage of the poverty and ignorance of young girls, for the noble purpose of debasing them to passive instruments for the gratification of men, and to a condition in which they are helplessly abandoned to every form of lust. But for this high-minded regulation, where would be the prosperity of a great number of our industries, and where the virtue and modesty of our middle-class maidens ?

The picture by middle-class historians of the sexual licentiousness of Münster is in reality a picture of the present time. It is a true portrayal of what takes place day by day in every modern civilised town ; and the last exhibition of wisdom in our society is—the regulation of these "Saturnalia" by law !

X. *The Fall of Münster.*

Our investigation into the character of the Münster "commune" has grown wider in its range and more polemical than was originally intended, or than quite suits the plan of this work ; but no little labour is required to remove the mountain of falsehood which rests on the true picture of the Anabaptists of that town. It is impossible to preserve scientific equanimity when one sees how an originally quiet and peaceable people are systematically stigmatised as a band of bloodthirsty and lascivious villains, simply because on one occasion, under the oppression of constant maltreatment and danger, they did not passively submit to destruction, but rose in energetic resistance, and not only suffered but fought for their convictions, opposing fierce attack by fierce defence, and exhibiting much military heroism!

After the treacherous surprise of February 10th had been repulsed, Bishop Franz undertook the siege with a light heart, for he felt sure of soon making an end of the crowded mob of starving vagabonds, as he regarded the mass of Anabaptists. He had at his disposal several thousand veteran troops under experienced generals, and before Whitsuntide had assembled about 8,000 men.[1] But the Baptists, though inferior in numbers (they were never more than 1,500 strong) and without military experience, had an advantage over their opponents not only in the strength of their fortifications, but in discipline, spirit of self-sacrifice, and enthusiasm.

Examples of the state of discipline in the Bishop's camp have already been given. Drunkenness proved especially prejudicial to all their military operations, as was shown by the first assault on the town.

The first bombardment began May 21, 1534, and lasted five days. On the 25th the besiegers attempted to storm the town; but some of their soldiers, being drunk, advanced prematurely, and were driven back, throwing those behind them into disorder. In spite of this the rear-guard reached the walls with their scaling ladders, only to meet with such powerful resistance that they fell back in confusion and retreated to their camp.

Shortly afterwards the besieged forces made a sortie against an outpost, surprised the soldiers while they were gambling and drinking, drove them off, spiked the guns, and attacked the main body of the army (which had hurried to the scene) so vigorously that it did not dare to pursue them, but allowed them to return unmolested to the town.

The besieging army fared no better at the second storming, which took place on August the 31st, after a violent cannonade lasting three days. It led to a furious battle and ended in the complete defeat of the attacking force, whose loss was

[1] Jörg Schenck's account (*Berichte der Augenzeugen*, p. 260).

enormous, amounting to forty-eight in officers of rank
alone.[1]

From that day the besiegers abandoned all hope of taking
the town by assault, and limited their operations to maintaining a blockade, for the purpose of starving it into a
surrender.

Yet in the end *the entire German Empire* was engaged in
the war against this one town.

At the outset the different enemies of Anabaptism showed
an unwillingness to come to an agreement. It soon became
clear, however, that the forces of the Bishop alone were
insufficient for the capture of Münster. Franz, therefore,
sought allies among both Catholics and Evangelicals; but
each member of the league being eager to get the better of
the others, the fight over the bear's skin seriously retarded the
fight against the still living bear. Meanwhile, in spite of all
intrigues, the number of the besiegers and the strength of
their military equipment continued to increase, through the
instrumentality of diplomatic adjustments and the decrees of
Congresses and Diets, until finally the German Reichstag
met at Worms, April 4, 1535, and conferred the dignity of
an Imperial affair on the siege of Münster by levying a tax
for carrying it on. In addition to this, the burgomasters of
Frankfort and Nurenberg were despatched to the besieged,
with orders to summon them to surrender in the name of
the Empire. All idea of surrender, however, was repudiated.

Yet the position of the town was already hopeless. From
the outset the Münster Baptists must have known that, in
face of the embittered enmity of the propertied classes
throughout the whole Empire, their insurrection could be
maintained only by ceasing to be local and spreading to other

[1] In a folk-song of that period a soldier who was present is made to
sing :

> " Die Landsknect waren in grossen Noth,
> Da blieben wohl dreitausend todt
> Zu Münster unter den Mauern."

> (" The soldiers were all in dire need,
> A good three thousand lay there dead,
> Under the walls of Münster.")

parts of the nation. Their prospects in this respect were by no means unfavourable, for they had numerous adherents in all the towns of North Germany ; in fact, in Lübeck the reins of government were in the hands of a party friendly to their cause. Messengers were sent out in all directions, and endeavours made to operate on the outer world by means of circulars and pamphlets. We have already quoted from one written by Rothmann, which is worthy of special mention. It was entitled, *Restitition oder Wiederherstellung der rechten und gesunden chrislichen lehre, Glaubens und Lebens* (" The Restitution or Restoration of True and Sound Christian Doctrine, Belief, and Life "), and appeared in October, 1534, as a vindication of the Baptist tenets and institutions. It advocated the use of the sword against the "godless," and in defence of communism and polygamy. The pamphlet was smuggled out of the town and distributed so freely that within a short time a second edition became necessary.

In December a tract appeared entitled, *Das Buchlein von der Rache* ("A Tract on Vengeance").[1] Vengeance, it says, is at hand ; it will be accomplished on those who have hitherto been in power, and when it is accomplished, the New Heaven and the New Earth will appear to the people of God. The pamphlet ends with a summons to revolt : " Now, beloved brethren, the time for vengeance is come to us ; God has raised up the promised David, armed for vengeance and the punishment of Babylon and its people. You have heard how it shall come to pass ; what a rich reward awaits us, and how gloriously we shall be crowned if we only fight bravely and manfully, and know that whether God grants us life or death, we cannot be lost. Wherefore, beloved brethren, arm yourselves for the fight, not only with the humble weapons of the apostles, for suffering, but also with the glorious armour of David, for vengeance ; and with God's might and help destroy the Babylonian power and all that godless

---

[1] *Eyn gantz troeftlick bericht van der Wrake unde straffe des Babilonis-chen gruwels, an alle ware Israeliten unde Bundgenoten Christi, her unde dar vorstroyet, durch de gemeinte Christi tho Münster.* Reproduced in its entirety and in the original tongue by Boutenwek, in his *Zur Literatur und Geschichte der Wiedertäufer*, pp. 66–80.

estate. . . . All wisdom, plans, skill, and methods must be employed to grieve the godless enemy of God and strengthen the standard of the Almighty.   For consider what they have done to you !   But this can you again do to them ; yea, with what measure they meted, shall it be measured to them again; and, what is more, shall be poured into the same cup.   Take heed that you make no sin of that which is not sinful.   Now, beloved brethren, make diligent speed to hold to the cause with zeal, and hasten, as many as possible, to come under the banner of God.   May God, the Lord of the army hosts, who hath decreed this from the beginning of the world and pro-claimed it by His prophets, arm you and all His Israel as pleaseth Him, for His praise and for the increasing of His Kingdom.   Amen." When this stirring appeal was issued, all the insurrectionary movements in German towns had already been suppressed.   Since the occurrences at Münster, the municipal authorities had been particularly cautious, and had succeeded in either opportunely checking all Baptist uprisings, or in putting them down by violent measures, *e.g.*, in Warendorf, Sveft, Osnabrück, Minden, Wesel, Cologne, &c.   In May, 1534, however, war broke out between the Lübeck democracy and Denmark, making it thenceforth impossible for that town to lend more than moral aid to the Münster struggle.   Moreover, this war soon took a turn highly unfavourable to the ancient Hanseatic city, whose ultimate overthrow led to the downfall of democracy and to Wullenweber's ruin.

At the end of the year 1534 the Münster Baptists had no further expectation of help from Germany.   One hope still remained, viz., assistance from the Netherlands, from which country the Münster insurrection had already derived so much of its strength.

When Münster had fallen into the hands of the Baptists the movement had become powerful in the Netherlands, especially in Amsterdam, which, after Münster, was looked upon as the metropolis of the sect.   It had a foothold also in other towns of Holland and Friesland.   "In April it was estimated that two-thirds of the population of Monnikendam were adherents of Jan Mathys, and a like state of things existed everywhere in the environs of the capital of the Netherlands."[1] They were also strong in Oberyssel, and particularly so in the town of Deventer, where in fact the Burgomasters joined them.

On the 6th of February, 1534, Erasmus Schetus wrote from Amsterdam to Erasmus of Rotterdam : " In these provinces, and above all in Holland, we are made extremely anxious by the Anabaptist conflagration ; for it is mounting up like flames. There is hardly a spot or town where the torch of the insurrection does not secretly glow."[2]

These revolutionary masses, however, were not like the Brothers in Münster, confronted by a powerless executive, and a mingling of princely and municipal authorities, but by a strong central government, which at once summoned all the means at its command to crush the impending revolt. It is impossible to give the long list of executions which then ensued ; the same cruel things repeat themselves *ad nauseam.* But in spite of all these, the Government did not succeed in preventing the formation of armed bodies, whose plan was to proceed to Vollenhove (mostly by water) with a view to marching to the relief of Münster.

On March 22nd thirty vessels, with armed Baptists on board, arrived at Vollenhove from Amsterdam. These were followed on the 25th by twenty-one others carrying three thousand men, many partisans going at the same time in vehicles or on foot. The Netherland authorities, however, who had got wind of the affair, attacked and dispersed each of these bodies separately.

In this way the attempt at relief was frustrated at the outset. But the great victories of the besieged at Münster on May 25th and August 31st revived the Baptist agitation in the Netherlands, which was also fanned by emissaries from the beleaguered city. Jan van Leyden proposed a bold plan for relieving the scarcity of provisions which had begun to make itself felt in the winter of 1534–35. The associates in the Netherlands were to rise ; he would cut his way through the

[1] Cornelius, *Münsterischer Aufruhr,* p. 234.
[2] *Berichte der Augenzeugen,* p. 315.

besieging army with a part of his men, join the relieving
forces, spread the insurrection, and thus set Münster free.
We have seen that he called on volunteers for this hopeless
undertaking. He exercised his troops for this purpose, and
had a special fort constructed, made of army waggons, to be
used in the sortie.

But the scheme ended in failure. One of Jan's envoys,
the "apostle" Johann Gräss, a whilom schoolmaster, turned
traitor. Despatched for the purpose of assembling the
Brethren outside the town and leading them to Deventer,
whence they were to push on to Münster, he left the latter
place on New Year's Day, 1535, only, however, to go straight
to Bishop Franz, divulge the plan, and betray the names of
the most prominent associates in the Lower Rhine country, as
well as their places of meeting. Thus the attempt to raise
the siege was nipped in the bud.

Once more Jan van Leyden endeavoured to carry out the
plan. On this occasion the ardently longed-for relief was to
come on Easter Day. Keller, who has accurately followed
up these movements, informs us that : " It is related that
the Baptists proposed having four banners raised at a time
previously agreed upon ; one at Eschenbruch, near the river
Maas in the Julich district; one in Holland and Woterland ;
the third between Masstricht, Aachen, and the district of
Limburg, and the fourth near Gröningen in Friesland.
Until the stipulated time had arrived the brothers were to
busy themselves in obtaining weapons and money, and as
soon as the command was given, each was to betake himself
to the nearest banner, for the purpose of assisting in the
relief of Münster.

"This plan was, in part, actually carried out. The very
next Easter Day, March 28th, the so-called Olden Monastery,
between Sneek and Bolswarben, in West Friesland, was occupied by the Baptists, and fortified. It was a strong position,
with fourfold walls and ditches.

"When the Imperial governor received information of this
he at once marched against the place, hoping by a sudden
attack to recapture it ; but he saw himself forced to a regular
siege, and had to bring up heavy artillery.

" After having increased his forces by enrolling every third man in the town and country, he began the bombardment on the 1st of April, and immediately afterwards stormed the works. Four times did he have to lead his soldiers under fire. The first two attacks were repulsed, but at the third and fourth he succeeded in occupying a few of the advanced positions. Some of the outworks, however, together with the church, remained in the possession of the defenders, thus compelling the besiegers to renew the bombardment on April 7th. When breaches had been made at five points the place was stormed at about three o'clock in the afternoon, and after a severe fight finally taken. Eight hundred or nine hundred lay dead about the walls."

The greater part of another force, which went to Deventer by water, was destroyed by Duke von Geldern ; but Keller was unable to discover any information with regard to the other places in which uprisings were planned.

Once again, however, a dangerous insurrection broke out in Amsterdam, whither the Münster Baptists had despatched " one of their best officers," Johann von Geel, who succeeded in reaching his destination, and in exciting a revolt.

" The insurrection broke out at about eight o'clock in the evening of May 11th. Five hundred armed Baptists seized the town-hall, slew one of the Burgomasters who fell into their hands, and put the position into a state of defence."

" The rebels, however, were by no means strong enough to surprise the whole of the large town without further trouble. Moreover, the outbreak seems to have taken place before all the conspirators had assembled, as a few days later some fresh allies appeared before the walls. At all events, after his first success, Johann von Geel found himself confronted by a resistance which it is possible he may not have anticipated. The main body of citizens took up arms with one accord, and a sanguinary fight ensued, which lasted through the whole night, and ended in the complete overthrow of the Baptists. The hatred of the victors displayed itself in the most horrible barbarities. Johann von Campen, for example, whom Jan van Leyden had installed as Bishop among the Baptists, had his tongue torn out and his hand cut off. While in this maimed condition a tin mitre, bearing the escutcheon of the town, was placed on his head in mockery; after which he was led to the pillory. Not till then was he beheaded."[1] The hearts of the other prisoners were torn from their living bodies and thrown in their faces. Nevertheless, what a brutal horde were—*the Anabaptists !*

The overthrow of the Amsterdam insurrection signified the downfall of the only portion of the war-party of Anabaptists outside of Münster who were capable of action, and destroyed the last hope of the besieged for help from without.

Starvation was already rife among the defenders of Münster. " At first they ate horses, head and feet as well, together with the liver and lungs. They ate cats, dogs, mice, rats, slugs, fish, frogs, and grass, while moss was their bread. Salt, as long as they had any, was their fat. They also ate the hides of oxen, and even shoes, after they had been soaked. . . . One after another the children and aged died of starvation " (Gresbeck, pp. 189, 190).

When the famine had become insupportable, Jan issued a proclamation to the effect that all those who no longer took part in the defence, and wished to leave the town, should give notice thereof at the town-hall. Every one was at liberty to leave the city within four days. Not a few took advantage of this permission—women, children, aged persons, and even some who were able to bear arms. A part of those who went out were slain by the Bishop's soldiers, and the others thrown into prison. The young women were seized by the soldiery, who carried on *polyandry* with them—this seeming to be the best means of relieving those miserable creatures from the infamies with which they had been burdened by the *polygamy* of the Baptists.

Those who remained in the town were for the most part resolved to hold out till the last gasp, that when all should be lost they might be buried under the ruins of burning Münster. Their pitiable condition was known in the Bishop's camp. They had very little powder left. " They have ceased to fire; their doom is certain. According to the accounts given to us by prisoners their stock of powder is reduced to

[1] Keller, *Geschichte der Wiedertäufer*, pp. 276, 279.

a ton and a half." Thus wrote the already-mentioned Burgomaster of Frankfort, Justinian von Holzhausen, from the camp before Münster, May 29th. [1] On May 24th Jan mustered " all the folk in the town who could bear arms, amounting, as we are informed by prisoners, to about two hundred men. The others, women, children and men, were lying ill, or going about sick, many of them on crutches. They were all swollen and weak, and dared not go far outside the gates, as they could not run away from our soldiers." [2]

Yet, so much were the forces of Jan van Leyden feared that the besiegers did not dare to storm the town openly, so long as the defenders felt themselves possessed of a vestige of strength to resist. The Bishop's forces remembered too well that they had already lost six thousand men in their fights with the little body of Baptists (Holzhausen, *op. cit.* p. 343). Hence the Frankfort Burgomaster could again write, to his father on the 8th of July : " As far as I can judge of affairs before Münster, I fear that unless we are aided by treachery the town will not be captured this summer ; for the ' king,' his ' dukes,' and foul adherents, have obstinately set themselves to so managing the rascally business, that they may die and rot with the whole town " (*op. cit.*, pp. 353, 354).

When Holzhausen wrote the above letter, the traitor whom he hoped for had already been found—the man Gresbeck, so well known to us. He deserted the town on May 23rd, and, on being taken prisoner, offered to conduct the besiegers to a part of the walls where there was no danger. The Baptists were in fact no longer able to guard the whole line of fortifications. Gresbeck's information was confirmed by Hans Eck von der Langenstraten, a soldier who had previously deserted from the Bishop's camp to the Baptists, but had returned when things began to go badly with them. In spite of this it was long before the cautious besiegers ventured on the surprise. After all had been most carefully prepared, and under cover of a severe thunderstorm, they set about the task on June 25th.

Under Gresbeck's guidance, the vanguard of the soldiers, about two hundred strong, succeeded in scaling the wall in

[1] *Berichte der Augenzeugen*, p. 343. [2] Holzhausen, *op. cit.*, p. 343.

the vicinity of the Gate of the Cross. The nearest guards were killed and the gate opened. Five or six hundred of the Bishop's forces rushed in, and to all appearances Münster was won.[1] Once again, however, was their wild thirst for booty to prove dangerous to the "defenders of the rights of property."

Drunk with victory, those who had forced their way in, rushed forward to plunder, leaving the gate unguarded. In the meantime the nearest watch of the Baptists had hastened to the scene of action, and before the main body of soldiers could force their way in, had recaptured the gate, thus cutting off the soldiers in the town from those outside. Instead of attacking with the latter and coming to the rescue, the commander of the Bishop's forces, Count Wirich von Dhann, when he saw the gate once more in the hands of the Baptists, gave the order to retreat. Derisive laughter and flights of arrows followed him from the defenders on the walls—men and women. Meantime the Baptists had risen throughout the town. Far from joyously casting off the yoke of the reign of terror, all who could hold a weapon, threw themselves in furious onset against the soldiers who had penetrated to the town ; so that, instead of the two hundred whom they had expected to meet, the Bishop's forces found themselves confronted by eight hundred armed antagonists.[2] The intruders were reduced to great straits, and at three in the morning held a parley with Jan van Leyden. A few of the soldiers, however, had succeeded in cutting their way to an unoccupied part of the walls, and when morning dawned attracted the attention of their comrades outside the walls. The main body now advanced to the attack, and scaled the weakly guarded walls. "Thus

---

[1] Compare General Wirich's report to the Duke of Cleve, July 29th. (*Berichte der Augenzeugen*, p. 359.)

[2] Holzhausen, in a communication through the town of Frankfort, July 1st, *op. cit.*, p. 366. On one occasion, Keller remarks : "It is impossible to note without astonishment how a few immigrant rascals succeeded in reducing the entire native population more and more to a condition of slavery" (*Wiedertäufer*, p. 103). Still more astounding is the fury with which those who were "freed" from the reign of terror fell upon their "deliverers."

the town was taken by the grace of God alone, and not by the skill of the soldiers " (Holzhausen, *op. cit.*, p. 366).

A frightful street fight ensued. Where they could the Baptists barricaded themselves, and at eight in the morning the pick of their forces, two hundred strong, occupied the market which had previously been put in a state of defence. A council of war of the Bishop's generals decided that to drive the Baptists from their last position was a hazardous, and, in any event, a too costly undertaking. Freedom and safe conduct were consequently promised to the besieged on condition of laying down their arms.

Driven to bay, and with no further hope left to them, the Baptists accepted the conditions. Hardly had they given up their arms and left their barricades when they were massacred. One infamous deed more or less was a matter of no consequence to the princely banditti.

On the day of the capture four hundred and fifty Baptists were slain, the following days being given up to the slaughter of the unfortunates who were found hidden in the houses.[1]

A vigorous part had been taken in the fight by the women, of whom the larger number were also massacred. Those who survived were brought before the Bishop, who told them that he would grant them pardon if they would renounce Anabaptism. As few accepted this offer (the rest continuing firm and obstinate in their undertaking) " the most prominent among them were executed, and the others driven out of the town. Many of these are said to have gone to England." [2]

The greater number of the leaders had fallen, among whom were Tilbeck and Kippenbroick, and probably Rothmann. Only a few, like Heinrich Krechtinck, managed to escape. His brother Bernt, as well as Knipperdollinck and Jan van Leyden, fell into the hands of the victors, and were kept for purposes of a delightful spectacle. In accordance with the custom of the times of accusing those who were most dreaded with cowardice, Kerssenbroick relates that Jan acted the poltroon and ran away. Neither before or after the

---

[1] Sigmund von Beineburgk's report to Philip of Hesse, July 7th, *op. cit.*, p. 368.

[2] Gresbeck, p. 213, and Beineburgk, *op. cit.*, p. 368.

capture of the town does his conduct betray cowardice.   It would indeed have been hardly possible to assert with certainty anything regarding the behaviour of individuals during the night's fight in the streets.   When the Bishop had entered the town he summoned Jan to his presence. " Then my most reverend lord said, ' Art thou a King? ' The king replied, ' Art thou a Bishop ? ' "   This answer does not savour of cowardice.

The treatment experienced by the prisoners was the one usually dealt out to the defenders of the exploited classes at that time—and of other times.

Iron collars were forged for Jan, Knipperdollinck, and Krechtinck, who were afterwards dragged about the country. It seems as if their torments were never to cease.   Not until January 22, 1536, were they executed at Münster in the presence of the whole populace, the Bishop also being a witness of the edifying spectacle.   " The first act of the executioners was to bind the victims to the stake by their iron collars.   Seizing white-hot pincers they then proceeded to pinch the king in all parts of the body in such a manner that flames blazed out from every part which was touched by the pincers, until nearly all who were standing in the market-place were sickened by the stench which arose.   The same punishment was meted out to the others, who, however, endured their tortures with greater impatience and irritability than the king, and made known their anguish in plaints and screams.   Terrified at the sight of the horrible torture, Knipperdollinck hung himself by the iron collar, trying by this means to cut his throat and hasten his death ; but when the executioners became aware of this they raised him up once more, forced his jaws wide asunder, put a rope between his teeth, and bound him so firmly to the stake that he could neither sit nor break his neck, nor (since his throat was quite wide open), choke himself.   When they had been tortured long enough, and while they were still living, their tongues were pulled out from their throats with red-hot pincers, and a dagger driven home to their hearts."   It is well known that the corpses were put into iron cages and hung in the Lamberti Church.   " The pincers with which they were tortured are still to be seen in the market-place on a bolt of the town-hall, where they were hung to serve as an example and terror to all rebels and enemies to the authorities." [1]

A modern historian has the effrontery to call this the "merited punishment for their misdeeds" (Keller, *Wiedertäufer*, p. 280). We challenge the noble masters of " German Science" to point out a single instance in which, during the terrors of the siege, the uneducated, rough proletarians of Münster practised on their enemies a hundredth part of the bloodcurdling cruelties which the right reverend Bishop, in perfect tranquillity of mind, had prepared and carried out before his own eyes six months after his victory! Yet these gentlemen, who cannot too highly extol their own transcendent ethics, exult over the triumph of the priestly bloodhound, while they drag his victims through the mire as infamous criminals.

* * * * *

Anabaptism, the proletarian cause, nay, the collective democracy in the German Empire, lay helpless in the dust; and outside of Germany also the fighting party of the Baptist order had lost all support.

At the Congress of Bockholt in 1536 a rupture occurred between the Netherland Baptists. The war party began from that moment to disappear; but the peaceable and millennarian section maintained itself some time longer. Its leader was Davis Joris, who was born in Brugge, in the beginning of the sixteenth century, and brought up at Delft. The Obbenites (so named from Obbe Phillips), who completely acquiesced in the existing order of things, now became the most important party among the Anabaptists. They taught that no other condition of the world than the existing one was to be looked for, and that mankind must adapt themselves to it.

Menno Simons subsequently became the head of this party, whose adherents were named after him, Mennonites. Born in Witmarsum, a Friesland village near Franecker, he became a Catholic priest, but united himself to the Baptists in 1531, and in 1533 was already a partisan of the submissive section

---

[1] Kerssenbroick, p. 212. We may give complete credence to this account.

and an opponent of Jan Mathys. While his brother, who belonged to the war party, joined the force which set forth from West Friesland to the relief of Münster on Easter Day, 1535, and fell, fighting bravely, Menno did not hesitate to stab his grievously afflicted Münster associates in the back, by initiating an agitation against them.

After the fall of Münster his faction became the most prominent of all the Baptist divisions.

Menno's end, like that of Joris, is indicative of the character which the Baptist order was thenceforth to assume.

These two leaders had to pass through many persecutions ; but both died respected and in easy circumstances.

Joris had saved up a snug sum, and, in order to enjoy it in peace, this prophet of the latter day emigrated to Bâle in 1544, and settled there under the *alias* of Johann of Brugge. Not until after his death was his true name discovered, when his body was burnt by order of the Bâle Council.

Menno Simons died soon afterwards in 1559. The last years of his life were passed at Oldesloe in Holstein, on the estate of a nobleman who, while in war service in the Netherlands, had learnt to know the Baptists as a very harmless and industrious people, and had offered them an asylum on his property, to his own great advantage.

But the Netherlands themselves were soon to become the refuge for persecuted Baptists. The casting off of the Hapsburg yoke brought freedom of belief to the country about the mouths of the Rhine, and a higher form of tolerance came into vogue there at almost the same time that it disappeared in Bohemia and Moravia, where, though crude and incomplete, it had existed since the Hussite Wars. After the close of the sixteenth century the Mennonites were tolerated in the Dutch Republic, until, in 1626, their freedom of belief was officially confirmed. Like the Herrnhuters, who were the successors of the Bohemian Brethren, they have maintained themselves till the present day ; but for a long time have formed nothing more than a small, well-to-do middle-class community, of no importance, either to the proletarian struggle for emancipation, or to the development of socialistic ideas.

From the Netherlands, which in the times of the Beghards were already in close intercourse with England, Baptist ideas spread to the latter country. In the last part of the reign of Henry VIII., more especially, there were many edicts issued against the Anabaptists, and in 1525 and the following years a great number were executed, of whom a large proportion were Dutch. But the Governments of Henry VIII. and Elizabeth were too strong to allow Anabaptism to publish itself otherwise than by martyrdoms. It was different with the wars of the seventeenth century, which even brought Anabaptist ideas into the foreground. The close of one century, however, had altered those ideas in many points; and great as may be the apparent resemblance between the Anabaptists and the democratic and socialistic section of the party of independence, their views are essentially different.

As a real, effective force in public life, Christian communism came to an end in the sixteenth century. That century saw the birth of a new system of production, the modern State and the modern proletariat; and it saw also the birth of modern socialism.

A new era was dawning for mankind.